Dynamic Korea and Rhythmic Form

Katherine In-Young Lee

DYNAMIC KOREA
AND RHYTHMIC FORM

Wesleyan University Press   Middletown, Connecticut

Wesleyan University Press
Middletown CT 06459
www.wesleyan.edu/wespress
© 2018 Katherine In-Young Lee
All rights reserved
Manufactured in the United States of America
Designed by Mindy Basinger Hill
Typeset in Minion Pro

This publication was supported by the
Academy of Korean Studies Grant (AKS-2018-P13).

We gratefully acknowledge the support of the AMS 75 PAYS
Endowment of the American Musicological Society, funded
in part by the National Endowment for the Humanities
and the Andrew W. Mellon Foundation.

Library of Congress Cataloging-in-Publication Data
available upon request

Hardcover ISBN: 978-0-8195-7705-4
Paperback ISBN: 978-0-8195-7706-1
Ebook ISBN: 978-0-8195-7707-8

5 4 3 2 1

TO MY PARENTS

CONTENTS

Acknowledgments ix

Notes on Translation and Romanization xv

Introduction 1

ONE Space and the Big Bang 11

TWO The Dynamics of Rhythmic Form 32

THREE Dynamic Korea and Samul Nori 61

FOUR Global Encounters with Samul Nori 80

FIVE Transnational Samul Nori and the Politics of Place 108

Epilogue 132

APPENDIX ONE English Translation of Pinari Text 139

APPENDIX TWO SamulNori: "Tradition Meets the Present" 147

Notes 157

Bibliography 169

Index 183

ACKNOWLEDGMENTS

Since the theme of "encounters" figures prominently in this book, it seems only apropos to recount some of my own encounters with the many friends, mentors, and advocates who have nurtured this project over the past decade. I first express, from a deep reservoir of gratitude, my auspicious fortune to work with and learn from Kay Kaufman Shelemay—my dissertation adviser and mentor for life. I can say with certainty that this book would not have materialized without the expert advice, feedback, and cheerleading provided by Kay—doled out strategically and knowingly at key moments since our first encounter in Cambridge, Massachusetts. I am also indebted to Richard K. Wolf and Ingrid T. Monson, my other committee members, for their intellectual support and friendship throughout the years.

I give special thanks to Deborah Wong—whom I have always admired—for reaching out to me and asking about my research when I was a new assistant professor at UC Davis. That encounter led to a new circle of connections at Wesleyan University Press. I am grateful to Suzanna Tamminen and the Music/Culture Series editors for taking a chance on a first book. The staff at Wesleyan University Press has been a pleasure to work with. My sincere thanks to Glenn E. Novak for superb copy editing, and also to Marla Zubel for her help in the early stages of the publication process. The two reviewers of the manuscript took immense care to provide me with invaluable feedback. This book has improved as a result of their critiques and suggestions.

The SamulNori Hanullim community in Korea—an extended family of personalities who have proven to be brilliantly talented, endearing, challenging, and avuncular—are next. As Suzanna Samstag once explained to me, "Once you become a member of the SamulNori family, you gain membership for life." I have often felt this to be true, especially in the moments when I have been sheltered and fed. I have received more than I could ever reciprocate. I am indebted to Kim Duk Soo Sŏnsaengnim for allowing me to tag along, hang out, and be included in events that ranged from the ordinary to the spectacular. Suzanna Samstag, one of SamulNori's most influential yet hitherto unrecognized figures, has been a role model and a stalwart supporter since the early 2000s. I am also eternally grateful to SamulNori's former managing director, Joo Jay-youn, with whom I worked closely in 2003. During my fieldwork period, Mr. Joo arranged for me to meet with SamulNori's original members Lee Kwang Soo and Choi Jong Sil, and Konggan Sarang's first presenter, Kang Joon-hyuk [Kang Chunhyŏk]. Staff members and former coworkers at SamulNori Hanullim (both past and present) also deserve special mention: Lyeum Joon-suk, Chung Hee-young, Han Kwang-hee, Lee Sekyung, Kim Dong-won, and Yeo SangBum. Members of the Samul GwangDae team — Jang Hyun-jin, Shin Chan-Sun, Park An-ji, and Kim Han-bok — have been exceptionally supportive throughout the years. I would also like to give thanks to other members of the extended SamulNori community who have offered their hospitality and warmth to me: Kang Minsok, Hong Yunki, Lee Dongju, Lim Pyŏnggo (of the Puyŏ SamulNori School), Lim Seung Duck, Kim Ju-hee, Kim Hee-jung, Lee Kyoung-phil, Ryo Hommura and Emi Kobayashi at Planet Arts, Charles Hong, Mun Kwang-in, Min Kyoung-ah, Hyun Seung-hun, Kim So Ra, and all members of the SamulNori Hanullim troupe who visited Harvard University in 2011 and UC Davis in 2014. I am grateful to have first met saxophonist Wolfgang Puschnig, bassist Jamaaladeen Tacuma, and Linda Sharrock (vocalist) — longtime collaborators with SamulNori — during my tenure as a SamulNori Hanullim staff member in 2003. I thank Wolfgang especially for being a kindred spirit and for offering me a place to stay in Vienna in 2011 and 2015.

To the SamulNorians around the world, may you continue to drum! Vincent Mangado and Dominique Jambert, Matthieu Rauchvarger, Hendrikje Lange, Suzanne Nketia, Nathalie Baumann, Violette Nys, Kenichi Yanaka, Mayumi Abe, Yuki Goto, Stephen Wunrow and Martha Vickery, Han Yong Wunrow, Sam Sangho Kim, Sarah Lee, Nik Nadeau, Lia Bengtson, Shirley Sailors, Viry Sánchez, Wendy Rodríguez, Ariadna Ramírez, Itto Cario Martínez, Alik Son, Inga Sin, Nastia Alexuyk, Bo-sung Kim, Myung-hyun Park, Hyo Jin Shin, Han Song Hiltmann, and Na-Rhee Scherfling: I look forward to many future encounters. To those of you who were kind enough to grant interviews or host me in your countries, I bow my head deeply. Your passion for *samul nori* is at the heart of this story. I hope that I have accurately conveyed some of that passion in this book.

In 2012, I moved cross-country to California and began a new life at UC Davis. I also gained a family. Henry Spiller has been a wonderful colleague, mentor, friend, and kindred spirit. Thank you, Henry, for reading drafts and for supporting me intellectually and emotionally during the past five years. I am so fortunate to have you in my life. The Music Department is a special place, and one that I will miss dearly in my departure for UCLA. I would like to acknowledge Beth Levy, Laurie San Martin, Sam Nichols, Chris Reynolds, Anna Maria Busse Berger, Carol Hess, Jessie Ann Owens, Kurt Rohde, Pablo Ortiz, Mika Pelo, D. Kern Holoman, Ross Bauer, Jeffrey Thomas, Amelia Triest, Christian Baldini, Matilda Hofman, and Chris Froh for their collegiality and warmth. The staff at the UC Davis Department of Music also supported my frequent endeavors to bring artists and scholars to campus: Josh Paterson, Phil Daley, Stephen Bingen, Joy Li, Courtney Kievernagel, and Karen Nofziger. Thanks especially to Stephen Bingen for providing excellent advice on sound-related matters and for a stimulating discussion on "dynamics" from an audio engineer's point of view. To all the graduate students at UC Davis: I have learned so much from our conversations. Thank you. And a very special hello to all my former students of the Korean Percussion Ensemble at UC Davis. Andrew Park enthusiastically took my ensemble for nearly three years, and went above and beyond the call of duty by leading voluntary review sessions for students in the class.

I was blessed to encounter Seeta Chaganti, Meaghan O'Keefe, Carey Seal, and Catherine Mike Chin at UC Davis. Our weekly dinners and conversations nourished me in more ways than you will ever know. You must all come visit me in Los Angeles. I am particularly indebted to Seeta Chaganti for generously sharing her brilliant and daring work on medieval poetic form with me. My sole colleague in Korean Studies at UC Davis, Kyu Hyun Kim, has also been very supportive.

It is only through the generous financial and administrative support from various institutions that I have been able to see this long-term project to fruition. The Blakemore Foundation made it possible for me to focus exclusively on language study for eighteen months, early on in my academic journey. Funding for both archival and ethnographic research has come from the following sources: the Harvard Music Department, the Korea Institute at Harvard, the Steve S. Kang Young Artists and Scholars Fund, the Institute of International Education (Fulbright), the Social Science Research Council, UC Davis, the Association for Asian Studies, the Mahindra Humanities Center at Harvard, and the Andrew W. Mellon Foundation. Archival work was conducted at UCLA, UC

Berkeley, Seoul National University Archives, the Korea Democracy Foundation, and the Harvard-Yenching Library. A faculty research fellowship from the UC Davis Humanities Institute gave me one quarter off from teaching to begin the hard intellectual work on this manuscript. And a generous Hellman Fellowship allowed me to travel to Europe in the summer of 2015 to meet several people connected to samul nori in Berlin, Brussels, Paris, and Vienna. I had the good fortune to work with and befriend a number of administrators and staff through these various affiliations. I credit them here: Griffith Way and Cathy Scheibner of the Blakemore Foundation, Susan Laurence and Myong Chandra of the Korea Institute, Steven Biel, Mary Halpenny-Killip, and Sarah Razor of the Mahindra Humanities Center at Harvard, Mary Dunn (American Academy of Arts and Sciences), Molly McCarthy and David Biale (Davis Humanities Institute), Shim Jai Ok and the staff at Fulbright Korea, and Nicole Restrick Levit of the Social Science Research Council.

I was fortunate to present drafts of chapters and papers at the following institutions: UC Berkeley, Stanford University, the University of Chicago, Columbia University, and Harvard University. In 2011, I participated in the SSRC Korean Studies Dissertation Workshop, where I received valuable comments from fellow participants and mentors Suk-Young Kim, Jun Yoo, Seung-sook Moon, and the ever-luminous Nancy Abelmann. An earlier draft of chapter 3—presented at the "Rising Stars of Korean Studies" Junior Faculty Mentoring Workshop at USC—benefited greatly from incisive feedback given by Joshua Pilzer and Nojin Kwak. I am grateful for Lee Yong-shik's thoughtful and expert critique of chapter 2. A slightly revised version of chapter 3 is based on an article published by the *Journal of Korean Studies*.

On the thread of intellectual communities and affiliations, my cohort during graduate school has been a source of tremendous inspiration and support. I entered the doctoral program at Harvard University in 2005 with my sole colleague in ethnomusicology—Corinna Campbell—and two historical musicologists, Ryan Raul Bañagale and Anna Zayaruznaya. Our many conversations in formal and informal settings have yielded important insights, friendship, and inside jokes. I have also been enriched by my friendships with many other Music Department colleagues: Sheryl Kaskowitz, Marc Gidal, Jean-François Charles, Andrea Bohlman, Mike Heller, Meredith Schweig, Glenda Goodman, Emily Abrams Ansari, Wenqi Kai Tang, Nathalie Kirschstein, Alexandra Monchick, Peter McMurray, and Will Cheng. Faculty members have also offered abiding support. I owe a great deal to Anne Shreffler for encouraging my incipient research project on "drumming and protest" during her Music and Politics Seminar. I am also thankful for the opportunity to have studied with Suzannah Clark, Thomas Kelly, and Carol Oja. I would be remiss not to include the staff at the Harvard Music Department, who function as an all-star team, helping to ensure the humor and well-being of the department. Thanks to Nancy Shafman, Kaye Denny, Charles Stillman, Jean Moncrieff, Lesley Bannatyne, Karen Rynne, Mary Gerbi, Eva Kim, and Fernando Viesca for shepherding the graduate students along their academic journeys. The staff at Harvard's Loeb Music Library also deserves a special acknowledgment. I cannot think of a more knowledgeable or professional crew: Andrew Wilson, Kerry Masteller, Sarah Adams, Liza Vick (now at the University of Pennsylvania), and the incomparable Virginia Danielson (now at NYU–Abu Dhabi).

I am not able to give due justice to the many mentors and friends who have helped me in some shape or form with this manuscript. I am beholden to my *halmŏni*, the late Lee Kwang-kyu, Lee Yong-sik, Marié Abe, Choi Haeree, Kim Eunhee, Lee Soobeen, Shin Mikyung and the Happynist samul nori team, the Won family at the Kumhyŏn Kugakwŏn, Michael Sprunger, Franklin Rausch, Olga Fedorenko, Jenny Wang Medina, Eleana Kim, Marcie Middlebrooks, Nicholas Harkness, Jimmy Jung, Robert Garfias, Michael Seth Orland, Tim Haggerty and Mack Liu, Andrew Thompson, Tanya Lee, Anna Schultz, Ling-ju Lai, Elena Tsai, Aimee Lee, Steph Rue, Charlie Kim, Matthew Sussman, Kate Davidson Harkness, Kevin Mora and Amy Lee, Terttu Uibopuu, Tommy Tran, Julia Kim, Jeongin Lee, Andrew Park (UC Davis), Gary Rector, the late Brian Barry, Jacques-Yves Le Docte, Nikki Guarino, Ro Jaemyeong (Korean Classical Music Record Museum), Chŏng Yusuk and her family, and my relatives from San Diego: Michelle, Ben, and Lorraine Chu. Thanks to Julius Gyu Cheon Hwang, who went along with my idea and produced the calligraphic artwork that appears in chapter 2. The talented graphic designer Benjamin Shaykin produced the artwork and design that grace this cover. And Derek Harkness provided unparalleled technical support when my computer began to fail me just before my final manuscript was due. To my fellow travelers in Korean music studies—Donna Kwon, Hilary Finchum-Sung, Roald Maliangkay, Jocelyn Clark, Nathan Hesselink, CedarBough T. Saeji, Joshua Pilzer, Heather Willoughby, Chan Park, Andy Sutton, and Chae Hyun Kyung—may we continue to converse, drink, and sing, and find reasons to meet in Insa-dong! I extend my gratitude to Dr. Byoung Sug Kim and Dr. Ji-Yeon Yuh for granting me permission to include their collaborative translation of SamulNori Hanullim's "Pinari" text in this manuscript.

The translation is an impressive feat, and a resource that I am sure many samul nori ensembles will benefit from in the future.

My close circle of friends that I first met in Seoul continue to provide me with sustenance, shelter, laughs, and inspiration. You are my family. Thank you to Kim Stoker, Su-Yoon Ko, Krys Lee, Tammy Chu, Sora Kim-Russell, Linda Kwon, Mihee Nathalie Lemoine, and Andrew Park. My Tokyo homestay parents—Yukiko and Shigeo Katsuoka—welcomed a stranger into their home and gained an adoptive daughter. I can never repay you for your generosity and kindness. And to Sindhu Revuluri: this book is a testament to your faith in me and this project.

Lastly, I reserve my deepest gratitude for my parents. It was only after I had lived in South Korea as an adult that I became aware of their courage and the sacrifices made in order to chart a new path as immigrants in America. They have been my strongest advocates, and for that, I am immeasurably blessed.

On a final note, my father, John Jonghyo Lee, has been a silent partner in this project from the beginning of my graduate studies. When my Korean language skills faltered, when I needed assistance with tracking down resources, or when I was overwhelmed with life's challenges, he has always been there for me. In many ways, he has learned much more about samul nori and Korean music than he ever could have imagined. I also believe that he is the only retired research engineer who can now sing the entire "Pinari" if prompted. In the eleventh hour he provided additional Chinese-language support on the "Pinari" (Sino-Korean version of the text) that appears in appendix 1. It joys me to know that his countless hours of research are now inscribed in this manuscript.

NOTES ON TRANSLATION AND ROMANIZATION

Korean words are rendered according to the McCune-Reischauer system of romanization. Two terms that figure prominently in this work—samul nori and SamulNori—will refer to the genre and the name of the quartet, respectively. Since copyright issues and cases of mistaken identity have plagued the SamulNori percussion quartet from its inception, I have made a conscious decision to respect these orthographic preferences (over samullori and Samulnori), in addition to adopting the quartet's English rendering of names such as those of SamulNori Hanullim's artistic director, Kim Duk Soo [Kim Tŏksu / 김덕수], and managing director Joo Jay-youn [Chu Chaeyŏn / 주재연]. In these cases, I generally provide the McCune-Reischauer spelling in brackets at their first appearance in the text. Other more standard exceptions to the McCune-Reischauer system include a decision to retain the more familiar romanization of historical figures and place names, such as Park Chung Hee [Pak Chŏnghŭi / 박정희] and Seoul [Sŏul / 서울], as well as the names of Korean authors who publish predominantly in English. Korean names are written with the family name preceding the given name. In the bibliography, author's names appear with the romanizations used in the original publications. When necessary, I include the McCune-Reischauer rendering in brackets for clarity.

The names of specific SamulNori compositions, such as "Yŏngnam nongak" and "Pinari," will appear in quotations. Terms such as *kil kunak* and *pan kil kunak* (italicized and in lowercase) will refer to the name of particular rhythmic patterns. Korean and Japanese terms generally appear in italics on first appearance in the text. For clarity, some less commonly used Korean terms appear in italics on first appearance in a chapter.

Unless otherwise noted, all translations (Korean to English; Japanese to English) are my own.

Dynamic Korea and Rhythmic Form

INTRODUCTION

Hip-hop. Gamelan. *Taiko*. *Samul nori*. These are just a handful of musical genres that have become truly global in the past century. Not only are these musics enjoyed by diverse audiences; they are regularly performed in locales that may have little or no connection to the genre's country of origin. While cross-cultural musical interaction is neither novel nor surprising, the widespread transmission of these genres to musical communities around the world beginning in the late twentieth century is nonetheless remarkable. This phenomenon has often been explained by some of globalization's grandest narratives—Westernization, neoliberalism, and the widespread diffusion of media technologies.

But what makes one form of music go global and another one stay relatively put? And what compels people with limited musical training to actually learn how to perform music that may be culturally distant from them? Lastly, what are some of the mechanisms that facilitate the pedagogical transmission of a musical practice, across cultural and national boundaries? *Dynamic Korea* explores these questions through the lens of a South Korean percussion genre called *samul nori*. First created in Seoul in 1978, samul nori (which translates simply into "four things play") is a neo-traditional musical repertory that features the use of four different percussion instruments. Since the 1980s, the drum-and-gong-based genre has been performed on many international stages by professional ensembles. It also holds the distinction of having been transmitted to amateur musical communities around the world. Samul nori is performed by musical groups in Korean diasporic communities and also in places where a connection to Korea is limited or unexpected, such as Mexico City and Basel, Switzerland. Like other expressive forms that have "gone global," samul nori has been uneven in its charted movement, with certain pathways tread more frequently than others because of proximity (Seoul to Osaka, Japan), ethnic ties (Los Angeles and

Berlin), or idiosyncratic reasons (Paris). But even despite this asymmetry, samul nori is undeniably a genre that has traveled far and wide. It is actively practiced outside the country of its origin.

With its transmission abroad and regular appearances on international stages, samul nori is regarded as an important sonic and cultural symbol of South Korea. The prolific scholar of Korean music Keith Howard proclaimed that by 1994 samul nori "was firmly established as an icon of Korean identity and was arguably the most popular genre of traditional music both at home and abroad" (2006, 2). Samul nori, in fact, precedes the trendier "K-pop" genre as one of South Korea's successful musical exports. One could argue that it was the first ripple in what would later become known as the Korean Wave.[1] And although it is rooted in much older musical traditions that date back to a unified Korean peninsula, samul nori is a genre of music that is a quintessentially South Korean creation.

Dynamic Korea is animated by the question of how samul nori became a global music genre. In this book, I argue that samul nori's rhythmic form has served as a critical site for cross-cultural musical encounters and its global journeys. This rhythm-based form has helped to draw in international fans with little prior knowledge of traditional Korean music or even of South Korea. Additionally, it has aided enthusiasts on their path to the actual learning and performance of Korean percussion music. In some extraordinary cases, it has served as a gateway for even more rigorous explorations of traditional Korean music and transformational life experiences.

There are, of course, other factors that have contributed to the outward spread of samul nori to far-flung destinations. This book will consider some of those other factors, such as state support, circulation of recordings, the world music industry, and the development of musical notation. But it will invest more time reflecting on the dynamics of rhythmic form in relation to global samul nori. Born out of a collaborative musical experiment in the late 1970s, samul nori as a case study provides us with a special opportunity to witness the creation and development of a musical genre. Soon after its creation, the nascent samul nori genre began to be performed outside South Korea—first by way of international tours by the legendary SamulNori quartet, and then through imitation by amateur and semiprofessional percussion ensembles. Samul nori's journey of globalization allows us to examine how rhythm-based forms can travel swiftly across boundaries. This rhythmic form, I posit, has been the key to its mobility. At first blush, framing this study in terms of musical form may seem unfashionable or even anachronistic. Why *form*, of all things? Let me explain.

MUSICAL GLOBALIZATION

Many important studies of global musics have shed light on the political, economic, institutional, or ideological issues that undergird music's globalization. Scholars aptly turned their attention to the politically fraught issues that were imbricated with global music circulations, such as the Western music industry's appropriation and exploitation of non-Western musical traditions in the creation of "world beat" or the "world music" genre (to name just a few, Feld 1988, 2000; Meintjes 1990; Garofalo 1993; Erlmann 1999). Along with this critique came critical Marxist and postcolonial readings of the production, circulation, and consumption of sonic and cultural difference in global markets (Taylor 1997; Erlmann 1996).

Second, a significant number of scholars have also gravitated toward the "global-local" relational analytic in their work. To that end, dozens of studies of global music genres such as hip-hop, reggae, taiko, *bhangra*, and gamelan have explored diverse processes of localization, hybridization, and diaspora formation, often through a political lens.[2] Third, the question of cross-cultural "exotic" appeal has also been considered from multiple perspectives. Michelle Bigenho (2012) examined Japan's courtship with Andean music, and recent ethnographies of American converts to Balkan music and Javanese gamelan identify a shared fascination with the distant sounds of non-Western music (Laušević 2007; Spiller 2015).

When viewed as a whole, these common approaches to the study of globalization and music demonstrate that nonmusical considerations dominate analysis. Yet this seems peculiar. And a missed opportunity. Ethnomusicologist Martin Stokes has questioned how and why it is that "particular musical forms, styles, processes, sounds, rhythms, and metrical practices traverse national cultural boundaries" (2004, 65). And what is it about certain musics that compels people—who may have little or no connection to the genre's origin—not just to listen to but also learn *to perform* such genres? Do some genres have a more user-friendly entry point than others? Like Stokes, I believe that there are indeed musical (as well as political, social, and economic) reasons as to why particular cultural practices circulate (Stokes 2004, 68).

Although many studies of global musics consider how music has traveled via structures of Western imperialism, the widespread diffusion of media technologies, and resistance movements, very few have actually engaged in trying to understand the *musical* reasons as to why certain musical practices move with apparent ease. The exceptions include Ingrid Monson's study of "riffs" (defined as short, repeated segments of sound, deployed singly, in call-and-response, in layers, as melody, accompaniment, and bass line) and her exploration of how these "pervade African-American musics and various world popular musics, especially those of the African diaspora" (1999, 31). Monson is interested in how riffs, repetition, and their composite grooves circulate within and between cultures, and how these musical devices can tell us something about musical circulation.[3] Timothy Taylor's work on global pop and world music markets, and music and globalization—while posing provocative questions about the larger political and economic structures that shape the circulation of music—also attends to the ways in which musical form and style can reveal social and political transformations (1997). And Jocelyne Guilbault's multi-sited and multifaceted study of the popular music genre known as *zouk* chronicles (partly through musical analysis) how this genre developed and spread throughout the Caribbean (1993).

Like these examples, this book also emphasizes a music-centered analysis. I contend that a genre's global reach often has much to do with the kinetic appeal of the music itself and its ability to connect with people. I take the term "dynamic"—a word that is often used to describe samul nori—and develop this as an analytic to assert the accessibility and portability of rhythm-based forms in global circulation. Anthropological work on circulation as a cultural process provides a framework for me to interrogate an aesthetic form as it travels, performs, and transforms across boundaries (Lee and LiPuma 2002, 2004; Novak 2013). As Benjamin Lee and Edward LiPuma suggest, "circulation" should be viewed not simply as processes that transmit meanings, but as constitutive, performative acts in themselves (2002, 192). By thinking of circulation as a site for cultural analysis, I am able to examine some of the reasons for samul nori's ability to travel or circulate—from the particularities of its rhythm-based form to how it is taught to individuals around the world.[4]

THINKING ABOUT FORM

In her recent publication *Forms*, literary theorist Caroline Levine revives a debate on formalist analysis and issues a call to expand our understandings of form and to think of form's functions in broader social contexts (2015). Levine builds on the concept of affordance theory that was adapted for design studies by Donald Norman (1988, 2013). An *affordance* refers to a relationship between the properties of an object and a person; this relationship affords or furnishes an opportunity for a certain kind of action to be performed by the person. Psychologist James J. Gibson first coined the term in 1977, and later expanded on his theory of affordances in *The Ecological Approach to Visual Perception* (1979). Gibson's original formulation of affordance considered the relationship between the environment and animals: "The affordances of the environment are what it offers the animal, what it provides or furnishes, either for good or ill. . . . It implies the complementarity of the animal and the environment" (1979, 127). Gibson moves from describing ecological niches and terrestrial surfaces to objects such as "sheets, sticks, fibers, containers, clothing, and tools" that afford manipulation. The focus on objects (and the affordances provided to humans) eventually became a point of interest and departure for Donald Norman, who then applied the ideas to design theory. With a background in electrical engineering and cognitive psychology, Norman refined his usage of affordance to the potential uses or actions latent in materials or designs.[5] A chair is for support, and affords sitting. Glass affords transparency, and a doorknob affords turning, pushing, and pulling (2013, 10–13). Norman also took care to explain that an affordance is not an inherent property of an object, but rather a *relationship* between the qualities of an object and the abilities of the agent or user that is interacting with the object (11). This distinction is key.

Levine applies affordance theory to form—and uses the tools of formalist study to investigate how forms (broadly construed) organize not only art, but also society. She is interested in "both the particular constraints and possibilities that different forms afford, and the fact that those patterns and arrangements carry their affordances with them as they move across time and space" (2015, 6). Levine investigates the specific ways that four major forms—wholes, rhythms, hierarchies, and networks—have structured culture, politics, and scholarly knowledge across periods, and she proposes new ways of linking formalism to historicism and literature to politics. For rhythm, Levine takes an expansive view. One example looks at the cycles of time that are essential to the endurance of institutions. Patterns of repetition and recurrence—which are used to impose order on courses, curricula, conferences, and scholarships—suggest to Levine that institutions preserve forms. These repetitive rhythms afford stability, which is essential to the work of institutional organizations. While I find Levine's reappraisal of forms a compelling one, Levine's reading of "rhythm" is unsatisfying to me—namely because she does not address a more literal, or rather a more granular understanding of rhythm. In this book, I take up Levine's proposition by engaging in a *musical* analysis of rhythm in tandem with long-term, multi-sited ethnography. By doing so, I consider the affordances of samul nori's rhythmic form in its global journeys and encounters.

When thinking about form in relation to *music*, there are a few things to consider—especially for readers unfamiliar with Western music theory and musicology.[6] First, some definitions. The *Oxford Dictionary of Music* defines musical form as the "constructive or organizing element" in compositions (Whithall 2001). Next, based on the specific repertoire of Haydn, Mozart, and Beethoven, music theorist William E. Caplin introduced form as a "hierarchical arrangement of discrete, perceptually significant time spans, what has been termed the *grouping structure* of the work" (1998, 9). And more broadly, theorist and composer Wallace Berry described form in music as "the sum of those qualities in a piece of music that bind together its parts and animate the whole" ([1966] 1986, xiii).

Teaching musical form is often a part of the musicologist's and music theorist's stock-in-trade. Instructors of a Western music history or a "Form and Analysis" collegiate course will introduce basic musical forms such as ternary, rondo, sonata, theme and variations, and strophic. In fact, learning to identify musical forms may be one of the first sets of musicological skills that nonmusicians (or non-music majors) will take away from a Western music survey course. Forms can be useful pedagogical tools; they provide students with concise models to understand how certain musical works are organized.

Yet, formal analysis in music can also be fraught. As musicologist Mark Evan Bonds reminds us, musical form is merely an abstraction. Forms are reductive schemas; they "function as a priori ideal types to which a given work can be compared" (Bonds 2010, 265). The study of musical form, as music educator Edward Brookhart put it, has often been approached from the standpoint of deriving "conventional, static structural patterns" from the works of the "great" composers of Western music (1964, 91). Graying musical textbooks present patterns or models that have become reified and endowed with a fixity that students may view in uncritical terms. Thus, the practice of formal analysis in music—excavating form as object—concomitantly raises thorny issues surrounding the value that is arbitrarily placed on formal exemplars, the hierarchies in Western art music, and the implication that Western music is superior to other kinds of musical traditions from around the world.

But other questions soon follow. What is the standard upon which an "ideal form" is based? And when a musical composition deviates from an idealized form, how should we evaluate the work? Lastly, how might we reconcile the practice of locating "objects"—detached and disembodied—with a more productive and humanistic formal analysis? While it is not my intention to resolve these questions in this manuscript, this book intervenes in traditional music formalist studies with its unequivocal commitment to ethnography—thus offering a variation on an old music-analytical theme: form and ethnographic analysis.

AN ETHNOGRAPHY OF SAMUL NORI

In *Dynamic Korea*, I am concerned with the ways in which musical forms serve as entry points for the intercultural appreciation and acquisition of musical genres. The rhythm-based form of samul nori serves as this book's primary focus. In particular, I pay ethnographic attention to people with little or no formal training in music. These nonmusicians, whom I will often refer to as enthusiasts, begin a process of learning how to play music outside that of their own culture. Whereas linguistic, harmonic, or modal forms require various degrees of cultural translation and training, a rhythm-based form, I maintain, offers a point of entry that privileges the sonic and the somatic. It is this rhythmic form that guides amateur enthusiasts on their transformative path from musical appreciation (or zealous fandom in some cases) to active musical performance of samul nori.

This monograph is far from the only study of the SamulNori quartet or, to a lesser extent, the samul nori genre. Prior studies have highlighted the quartet's rise to popularity, the complex relationship to "tradition," the politics of innovation, and canon formation (e.g., Hesselink 2012; Howard 2006, 2015; Kim Hŏnsŏn 1995; Park, Shingil 2000). Yet conspicuously absent in this literature is multi-sited ethnographic research of samul nori and a consideration of its global journeys. By presenting this ethnographic, multi-sited study of samul nori alongside formal analysis, *Dynamic Korea* endeavors to join a larger conversation on global music genres and contribute a theorization on the power and portability of rhythmic forms in circulation.

The foundations for this project began over a decade ago. In 2003, I worked as the overseas coordinator for Kim Duk Soo's SamulNori Hanullim—one of the premier samul nori ensembles in South Korea. Kim Duk Soo [Kim Tŏksu], as we will learn in chapter 1, was one of the founding members of the SamulNori quartet, which gave rise to the samul nori genre. In addition to working on numerous performances and festivals in South Korea, I served as tour manager for SamulNori Hanullim's three-week tour of Denmark (Copenhagen, Randers, Skive) in August 2003, and I assisted in the planning of the 2004 U.S. tour. I translated program notes, handled correspondence with presenters in Europe, Asia, and the United States, and interpreted at various public events. Much of what I have learned about the samul nori genre and its global iterations has come directly from my own experiences as a former staff member of the ensemble, interacting with many members of the SamulNori community as well as international samul nori enthusiasts. During field research in South Korea (August 2008–November 2009), I utilized this existing network to conduct over thirty interviews with founding members of the SamulNori quartet, former managing directors, and members of the SamulNori Hanullim troupe. I also became acquainted with several amateur samul nori ensembles that participated in the World SamulNori Festival and Competition in South Korea in October 2008. At the festival, I volunteered as a coordinator and translator for over one hundred participants from eleven countries. I was able to interview several leaders of the ensembles, as well as visit some of the groups in their respective countries (e.g., Mexico, United States, France, Belgium, and Japan) in the years following (Lee, Katherine In-Young 2017). I continue to consult for and assist SamulNori Hanullim. I have written essays on SamulNori for concert programs, and I also helped to arrange lectures and master classes with Kim Duk Soo and SamulNori Hanullim at Harvard University and at UC Davis (November 2011 and March 2014, respectively).

CHAPTER SUMMARIES

Chapter 1 tells the story of the early reception of the SamulNori quartet and the development of the samul nori genre. Unlike other genres of traditional Korean music, samul nori has a specific place and point of origin that can be traced back to the Space Theater (Konggan Sarang) in Seoul in 1978. The genre began as a musical experiment when four musicians decided to recontextualize and "stage" the rhythmic cycles derived from *p'ungmul*—an older genre of rural band percussion music and dance that was part of the social fabric of life when Korea was a preindustrialized, agrarian society. The success of the experimental collaboration eventually led to requests for performances within and outside South Korea. Beginning in the early 1980s, SamulNori toured extensively on the world music circuit in North America, Europe, and Japan. Within the span of a few years, the repertory and performance style of the quartet became so popular that its specific brand of percussion music inspired the classification of a new genre of music in South Korea—a genre that took the quartet's name.

Chapter 1 brings focus to the quartet's spirit of experimentation and the process of musical arranging that develops into a repertory. Drawing on interviews that I have conducted with members of the SamulNori community as well as a substantial archive of published materials, I show how the unexpectedly enthusiastic reception of SamulNori and samul nori was connected to the Space Theater and the Konggan Project.

Chapter 2 reflects on one of the most popular samul nori compositions that is learned by amateur enthusiasts around the world. I provide an analysis of the formal properties of "Yŏngnam nongak," which is an arrangement of rhythmic patterns drawn from the p'ungmul regional variant that comes from southeastern Korea. Although it is an introductory-level piece, it features many of the formal elements that are common to other samul nori pieces—a modular formal structure, a general progression from complex rhythmic cycles to ones more simplified and compressed, and significant contrasts between tempi, volume, and levels of energy exerted in performance. Based on recordings of the piece made by the SamulNori quartet, notation that was published by SamulNori Hanullim, and audiovisual materials, I analyze how the rhythm-based form in "Yŏngnam nongak" exhibits these aforementioned properties. In this chapter, I develop the term "dynamic" as an analytic to think through the ways in which the rhythmic form in samul nori compositions features a series of contrasting yet balancing forces. These built-in moments of dramatic change draw in listeners on a sonic level and also assist in the learning of a sequence of different rhythmic cycles. This chapter asserts that samul nori's rhythmic form is a dynamic musical form. As such, it has elicited a response that has moved well beyond its original local context.

Chapter 3 considers how samul nori's global circulation was also supported by the South Korean government. As the SamulNori quartet began to tour regularly in Europe and the United States, the state took note. The quartet was invited to perform at high-profile events such as the 1988 Summer Olympics in Seoul and the Taejŏn Expo '93. When amateur samul nori ensembles formed outside South Korea, the South Korean government financially backed certain efforts by SamulNori and SamulNori Hanullim to develop pedagogical materials and to lead percussion workshops overseas. Prior to the Korean Wave and K-pop, samul nori was South Korea's first successful musical export.

Chapter 3 centers on the state's cultivation of samul nori as a sonic symbol of South Korea. I employ South Korea's first nation-branding campaign as a case study to view the ways in which the music of samul nori was linked with the "Dynamic Korea" brand and how the state trumpeted its own dynamic image as a modern, economically viable nation-state.

Chapter 4 draws extensively on ethnographic interviews conducted with individuals from around the world who have engaged with samul nori in some depth. I analyze the individual moments of listening to and experiencing samul nori for the first time. In these "encounter narratives," I chronicle the ways in which the music had a profound impact on its listeners. For some individuals such as Suzanna Samstag (the first managing director of the SamulNori quartet), this experience led to a major life change. For others, the experience led to a desire to learn how to perform samul nori, even without the presence of an instructor. In the case of the latter, pieces such as "Yŏngnam nongak" were accessible through notational booklets, recordings, audiovisual materials, and YouTube videos. Chapter 4 includes profiles of encounters that resulted in the formation of four different samul nori ensembles—Shinparam (United States); Swissamul (Switzerland); Canto del Cielo (Mexico City); and Sinawi (Japan). The chapter also sets the stage for chapter 5, by introducing some of the groups who participated in the 2008 World SamulNori Festival and Competition in South Korea.

The thirtieth anniversary of the founding of the SamulNori quartet was marked in 2008. Many events were planned to celebrate the occasion, including the hosting of the World SamulNori Festival. The festival (and competition) was the largest that was ever organized by SamulNori Hanullim, and featured more than seventy participating samul nori ensembles and over one hundred participants from nine different countries. Based on close ethnographic observation and research, chapter 5 examines the cultural politics that emerged when international samul nori enthusiasts converged at the same time and place, on the native terrain where the samul nori genre was conceived. I focus on the opening ceremony of the festival, where a performance of "Yŏngnam nongak" by all international participants was designed to highlight samul nori's successful transmission outside South Korea. This collective performance of animated drumming in synchrony is contrasted with the production of the "International Pinari." As the sole textual piece developed by the SamulNori quartet, the *pinari* narrates a cross-section of Korea's history, geography, culture, and a composite of spiritual beliefs. Unlike "Yŏngnam nongak," the pinari is seldom performed by international samul nori ensembles. In this chapter I show how a vernacular text-based form and a rhythm-based form are strategically deployed in the festival's opening ceremony, unleashing a set of complex cultural politics. I examine how the organizer's promotion of the internationalization of samul nori is put into tension with a nationalistic desire to accentuate the uniqueness of South Korea. Chapter 5 speaks to the success but also to the limits of samul nori's story of globalization.

I conclude with ruminations on rhythmic forms in global circulation and future possibilities for music researchers.

ONE

Space and the Big Bang

> In actuality, *Konggan* [Space] did not embark only to explain Korea to the Koreans; it was its ceaseless wish, too, to explain Korea to other countries.
>
> *Alain Delissen, 2001*[1]

> SamulNori became SamulNori Hanullim, Inc. (Hanullim means big bang) in 1993. This growth from a four-man performance ensemble into a company of thirty artists meant that SamulNori's new genre in traditional Korean arts, music, and dance over the last two decades had now also become a viable educational and research enterprise.
>
> *SamulNori Hanullim, n.d.*[2]

In 1993 the SamulNori quartet officially disbanded, ending their remarkable run. As many histories of the group narrate, the quartet began as a modest experiment in 1978 and developed unexpectedly into a global musical phenomenon. Few could have predicted this rise, or this spread. Within the span of fifteen years SamulNori claimed over thirty-five hundred performances. They were credited with catapulting their brand of music into South Korea's sonic landscape as the country's representative genre of *kugak* (literally, "national [Korean] music"). Their success on international stages spurred a reappraisal of the status of traditional Korean arts on a domestic front. And the music that the quartet performed was soon embraced and imitated by many fans both within and outside South Korea.

But as is sometimes the case with things that have a steep and sudden ascent, the ending can be abrupt. Typically glossed over in SamulNori narratives or confined to the domains of conversation and hearsay, such difficulties as internal strife, conflicting agendas, financial disputes, and burnout all factored into the dissolution of the SamulNori quartet. This did not lead to the demise of samul nori as a genre, however. To the contrary, it was during the 1990s that the genre of samul nori flourished. A growing base of fans became samul nori practitioners, owing in large part to pedagogical outreach efforts sponsored first by the quartet, and later by samul nori's most tireless and ambitious advocate, Kim Duk Soo.

Master of the hourglass *changgo* drum, Kim Duk Soo took up the reins and launched a reconfigured and expanded enterprise in 1993, calling it SamulNori Hanullim. Translated literally, *hanullim* means "grand reverberation"; Kim Duk Soo chose to render this in English as SamulNori "Big Bang." Broadening his artistic horizons, Kim presided as the director for an organization that featured a roster of samul nori quartet "teams," an educational division, and a managing staff.

The transformation from a stand-alone quartet to an artistic troupe capable of deploying separate teams to different events reflects the popularization of the percussion genre by the early 1990s. Not only was there an increased demand for samul nori performances, but there was also a younger generation of musicians who had essentially become adept (and even fanatic) at playing samul nori. The quartet attracted serious musicians and amateur enthusiasts—many of whom flocked to train with the quartet members at workshops or at the Sinch'on Live House Nanjang Studio.[3] Ethnomusicologist Nathan Hesselink describes the quartet's impact in even broader terms: "By the 1990s, SamulNori / samul nori in various incarnations had become a prominent fixture of the Korean musical landscape, seen on television broadcasts and in concert halls, disseminated on CD, VHS, and DVD recordings, studied in chapters of music history and appreciation textbooks, and taught at the primary, secondary, and collegiate levels throughout the peninsula" (2012, 3). Thus Kim's SamulNori "Big Bang" was a fitting appellation to describe the longer-lasting reverberations of the SamulNori quartet, while at the same time forecasting Kim's more ambitious agendas.

Beginning this story with the quartet's demise is an unconventional narrative move. But it strategically foregrounds SamulNori's popular reception—a reception that outlived the quartet's dissolution. It shifts the emphasis away from SamulNori the quartet to samul nori the global music genre. It also offers another way of thinking of SamulNori—not as a singular, all-star quartet that emerged fully formed overnight—but as part of an evolving musical collaboration and a cultural project. As many Korean music insiders already know, what is usually referred to as the first or "original SamulNori quartet" is actually a misnomer.

The quartet's membership was never truly fixed, as the "original" designation suggests. One of the founding members, Kim Yong-bae [Kim Yongbae], left the quartet in 1984 when he was recruited by the National Center for Korean Traditional Performing Arts (now known as the National Gugak Center) to establish its own in-house samul nori quartet. Kim was replaced by Kang Min-seok [Kang Minsŏk]. And Choi Jong Sil [Ch'oe Chongsil] departed the group in 1989 in order to pursue academic studies. Because of the fluid membership of the group—even from the first performances at the Space Theater—it is problematic to liberally use the term "original" (see Hesselink 2012, 56–57).[4] Viewing the quartet less as a fixed entity and more as a collaborative project that involved numerous individuals and membership changes over time will be instructive here.

Dynamic Korea hews closely to the book's animating question of how a musical genre goes global. While this chapter chronicles some of the early history of the SamulNori quartet, it does so for the purpose of bringing into relief the social and cultural environment that facilitated the quartet's emergence and development at a specific moment in South Korean history. And since early accounts of the SamulNori quartet already exist, I direct readers with interest in finer historical details to monographs in both Korean and English (Kim Hŏnsŏn 1988, [1991] 1994, 1995, 1998; Hesselink 2012; Howard 2015; SamulNori Hanullim t'ansaeng samsip chunyŏn kinyŏm saŏphoe 2009). I also base my analysis of samul nori's global journeys through two groups in particular: the SamulNori quartet and SamulNori Hanullim. The stories of professional samul nori groups such as Durae Pae SamulNori, Dulsori, and Samul Gwangdae—while important in the context of samul nori's globalization—are not featured here.[5]

In this chapter I begin with a description of the setting—the Seoul-based Konggan Sarang and the community of cultural activists who nurtured what I call the SamulNori project. This is followed by my examination of the ways in which the sounds of samul nori first captivated listeners. Through careful analysis of ethnographic interviews, oral histories, and the accounts of music critics and fans, I reveal the strands of the positive reception that eventually led to the outward spread of the genre and the South Korean government's promotion of this repertory of music as a dynamic symbol of South Korean culture.

FIGURE 1.1 Sign for the Space Theater (Konggan Sarang). Photograph by author.

SPACE THEATER: SETTING THE SCENE

Most histories of SamulNori begin by paying tribute to the Space Theater / Konggan Sarang Sogŭkchang ("Love of Space" Small Theater) located in northern Seoul (figure 1.1). This was the vaunted place where the percussion quartet first debuted in 1978. More precisely, it was a small theater tucked in the basement of a redbrick building that became the site of many important performances of traditional Korean music (figure 1.2). The building served as the headquarters for the Konggan (Space) Group and was designed by Kim Sugŭn (1931–1986), one of South Korea's most esteemed architects of the twentieth century.[6] Kim's Konggan Group oversaw distinct but connected ventures: an architectural firm; an influential monthly publication; an art gallery and café; and the Space Theater.[7]

Konggan—an arts, architecture, and culture periodical—frequently published Kim's thoughts on a wide range of topics.[8] Kim wrote essays on history, culture, and identity. He also reflected frequently on South Korea as a modernizing nation. Historian Alain Delissen's meticulous survey and analysis of the *Konggan* publications from 1960 to 1990 paint a portrait of Kim Sugŭn as an ardent cultural nationalist who was simultaneously invested in researching and reclaiming South Korea's "lost" history while also contributing to its modern infrastructure. As an architect, Kim chose to "pursue the bolder ambition of pulling architecture out of the then purely technical field of construction engineering for transformation into an art, socially legitimate, that would be both genuinely Korean (rooted in the past) and distinctively modern (opened onto the time of the world)" (Delissen 2001, 246). His commitment to the traditional culture of Korea's past was reflected in his patronage of the arts. As a "cultural activist" interested in giving voice and a venue to traditional Korean culture, Kim Sugŭn was instrumental in creating the artistic milieu that fostered the genesis of the SamulNori quartet.[9]

Kim appointed Kang Chunhyŏk [also written as Kang Joon-hyuk] as the artistic director of the Space Theater. Kang (1947–2014) had a background in Western classical music and earned a degree in aesthetics from Seoul National University.[10] He presided over a diverse range of programming; regular series included the Evening of Ballet, the Evening of Jazz, and traditional Korean dance.[11] Kang utilized Konggan Sarang's austere form to his advantage in planning an adventurous array of performances:

> It [Konggan] wasn't an example of a proscenium stage—there was no such operative concept. That's likely what people dubbed it, though, since it seemed [superficially] to meet some of the criteria. But there was really no place to call a "stage" as such, no seats. . . . You place seats in that open space, and that becomes the seated area, and the remaining area will become a stage. So to call it a conventional theater would really be a misnomer. I think the only way you could characterize Konggan would be to call it an experimental stage. (Kang Chunhyŏk interview, September 8, 2009)

Kim and Kang's "experimental stage"—also known as a black box theater—was a flexible space that could accommodate a variety of different configurations and performances. Dancers, chamber musicians, singers, actors, puppeteers, and even shamans performed at Konggan Sarang. In its heyday the Space Theater was at times an avant-garde venue in Seoul that brought together a coterie of like-minded individuals, interested in the folk and modern arts and cultural activism. It was also the first theater of its kind to regularly sponsor and promote traditional Korean music (kugak), inaugurating the monthly Evening of Traditional Music series in 1978. Many of South Korea's most famous and revered figures in traditional arts performed at the theater (including *p'ansori* artists Kim Sohŭi and Im Pang'ul,

Space and the Big Bang 15

FIGURE 1.2 Konggan Sarang's small theater (Sogŭkchang) in 2009. Photograph by author.

kayagŭm player Pak Kwihŭi, and dancer Yi Maebang).[12] This high-caliber presentation of Korean folk music was facilitated in large part by Kang's discriminating ear and Kim's personal interest in preserving and revitalizing Korean traditional arts and culture. A year prior to the opening of the Space Theater in April 1977, Kim Sugŭn elaborated on his vision for the experimental stage: "Beyond providing the place to nurture traditional arts, as a theater space, we aim to expand the possibilities and cultivate creative work. The small theater was built in a way so that its form could facilitate the creation of new [types of] theatrical plays. But besides theater, there are also plans to present the best quality chamber music, and to have monthly musical appreciation concerts of p'ansori."[13]

February 22–23, 1978, marked the first installment of the Evening of Traditional Music series at the Space Theater.[14] In this program a group of Korean folk music specialists who were part of the Minsogakhoe Sinawi (Folk Music Society "Sinawi") performed a selection of pieces.[15] At the end of the evening a new work was debuted. Four musicians—Kim Duk Soo, Kim Yong-bae [Kim Yongbae], Ch'oe T'aehyŏn, and Yi Chongdae—performed a percussion improvisation called "Uttari p'ungmul."[16] Taking the core percussion instruments used in an older genre of percussion music and dance known as p'ungmul, the quartet offered a sampling of rhythmic patterns drawn from regional p'ungmul variants of South Korea's Kyŏnggi and Ch'ungch'ŏng Provinces (sometimes referred to as the Uttari region).[17] Inside the Space Theater, the four men presented rural percussion music that was traditionally performed outdoors by a large number of farmers and villagers.

Kim Duk Soo and Kim Yong-bae were the bona fide percussionists of the group; Ch'oe had majored in *haegŭm* (two-string fiddle), and Yi specialized in wind instruments.[18] But as many folk musicians are proficient in more than one instrument, this difference in musical training did not hinder the performance. The reception of that first performance was unexpectedly enthusiastic, and it has since been inscribed with mythic import as the "birth of SamulNori" (samul nori *ŭi t'ansaeng*) by the South Korean media and in SamulNori's own press materials. Although the "original SamulNori quartet" with members Kim Duk Soo, Kim Yong-bae, Lee Kwang Soo [Yi Kwangsu], and Choi Jong Sil [Ch'oe Chongsil] did not actually convene on February 22, 1978, the seed of the samul nori genre sprouted at that first performance.

NOVEL YET FAMILIAR

A symposium organized by SamulNori Hanullim in 2006 brought together experts and scholars to examine SamulNori / samul nori's past, present, and future. Reflecting on SamulNori's "past," Kang Chunhyŏk discussed the reception and unforeseen impact of the first performance of "Uttari p'ungmul" at the Space Theater.[19]

> On that day, the audience heard *nongak* [literally, "farming music"] being performed in a seated position for the very first time.[20] The *karak* [rhythmic patterns] themselves were old since they were steeped in the world of nongak; rather it was the configuration of such rhythmic patterns that was new. If in the past, the people who came to see nongak were spectators, then on that day, these were the curiously inquisitive who came to see a musical performance—thus, an audience. In other words, it was the first performance of its kind where we were able to focus more on the auditory dimensions over the visual ones in our [p'ungmul] rhythms. It was a revelation to both the performers themselves and the audience alike that our rhythms were this diverse, charming, exciting and energetic. (Kang Joon-hyuk 2006, 11)

Space and the Big Bang **17**

Kang's testimony conveys the sense of wonder that audience members felt at hearing something that was at once both new and familiar. Although Koreans were well acquainted with the sounds of p'ungmul as part of Korea's folk heritage and agrarian past, the setting for the performance of "Uttari p'ungmul" at the Space Theater was a drastic change from p'ungmul's outdoor context. The quartet took music that was traditionally performed by local percussion bands (for hours at a time, by large groups of people) and streamlined it into a more concise form. This recontexualized performance of p'ungmul directed the audience's attention to p'ungmul's sonic features—in a way that had not been so isolated before. As we know now, the quartet and its arrangement of p'ungmul rhythms proved to be a big hit. And in many ways, the quartet's spirit of experimentation resonated with the Konggan Group's philosophy of being at the vanguard of innovation while maintaining a firm sense of tradition.[21]

Kim Duk Soo explained in his 2007 autobiography that the idea to perform the rhythms from p'ungmul in a new presentational format was not his own. Instead, he credits folklorist Sim Usŏng (b. 1934) as the one to suggest to Kim (and the other performers) to take the four primary percussion instruments from p'ungmul—one of each—and create a piece with them while playing in a seated position. Kim acknowledged that Sim's proposal was a great idea—recalling that he was "full of excitement and anticipation" at trying out this suggestion on that "unforgettable evening" (Kim Duk Soo 2007, 180–82).[22]

SIM USŎNG: FOLKLORIST AND ADVOCATE

Before moving on, it is necessary to pause and explain Sim Usŏng's central role in supporting the percussion quartet.[23] Although he has worn many hats, Sim is best regarded for his work as a researcher of the folk performing arts and culture of Korea. During the 1960s he began extensive research on the tradition of itinerant performing arts troupes known as *yurang tanch'e*, focusing in particular on the *namsadang* (itinerant troupes of male performers).[24] Sim was part of the first generation of South Korean folklorists to conduct ethnographic fieldwork with folk musicians. He also served as an advocate for the preservation of folk arts. Through his research on the namsadang, Sim met Kim Duk Soo, whose father (Kim Munhak) was a member of the 1960s Minsokkŭkhoe Namsadang (Folk Theater Association Namsadang) (Hesselink 2012, 32; Sim Usŏng [1974] 1994, 53).[25] Sim taught Korean music history and theory at the Seoul Arts High School and also served as the faculty adviser for the Minsogakhoe Sinawi ensemble—a group that he named and helped to form (Ch'oe T'aehyŏn 1991, 31–32; Hesselink 2012, 53). He later introduced Kim Yong-bae (a member of the Seoul-based namsadang troupe in the 1970s) to the folk arts society. It was Sim who was in fact the link between the Minsogakhoe Sinawi group and the Space Theater's Kang Chunhyŏk. From this connection arose the artistic roster at the Space Theater in its early years.

Sim is also generally credited with bestowing the quartet with the name Samul-Nori, which is translated into English as "four things play" or "the play of four objects." There are discrepancies in the written record and in oral testimonies as to precisely when and where the bestowal of the group's moniker occurred, however. In an interview that I conducted with Sim in 2009, Sim recounted that he was approached in haste one day by three members of the Minsogakhoe Sinawi—Yi Ch'ŏlchu, Ch'oe T'aehyŏn, and Kim Mukyŏng (Sim Usŏng interview, October 28, 2009). According to Sim, the meeting (which took place at the Seoul Arts High School) followed immediately on the heels of the quartet's second appearance at the Space Theater in late April 1978. By this time—just two months after the quartet's debut—the group's membership had changed. Ch'oe T'aehyŏn and Yi Chongdae were replaced by two brothers from the southern port city of Samch'ŏnp'o—Choi Jong Sil [Ch'oe Chongsil] and Ch'oe Chongsŏk.[26] With two expert percussionists now incorporated into the lineup, the quartet had created such a stir at the concerts that Sim was called on to swiftly coin a name for the group that still lacked one (figure 1.3). In an essay commissioned for SamulNori's thirtieth anniversary, Sim wrote about the pragmatic approach to the quartet's name: "Well, if only four people are performing, why not call it—'*sa mul*' [four objects]? And if you are performing with the *samul* [a term used to refer to the core set of p'ungmul instruments], why not say that you are 'playing' the samul?" (Sim Usŏng 2008, 16).[27]

A second, relatively unknown account by Ro Jaemyeong [No Chaemyŏng] (director of the Korean Classical Music Record Museum) points instead to an archived document—an invitation to a birthday celebration event for the theologian and human rights activist Ham Sŏk-hŏn—that lists "samul nori" on the program. No performers are mentioned, but the invitation appears to be the first documented reference to the samul nori genre that predates Sim's account. Since most Koreans would not have known what the term "samul nori" meant at the time, an explanation was provided in parentheses: "*kkwaenggwari, ching, puk,* and *changgo*" (Hŭngsadan 1978; see figure 1.4).[28] The event took place on March 18, 1978, at the Seoul office of the Hŭngsadang (Young Korean Academy) and

FIGURE 1.3 Sim Usŏng with members of the SamulNori quartet at the Space Theater. *Top row, left to right:* Sim Usŏng, Lee Kwang Soo, Kim Duk Soo, Choi Jong Sil. *Bottom row, left to right:* dancer Kim Myŏngsu, Space Theater's art director Kwŏn T'aesŏn, Kim Yong-bae. Photograph courtesy of Sim Usŏng.

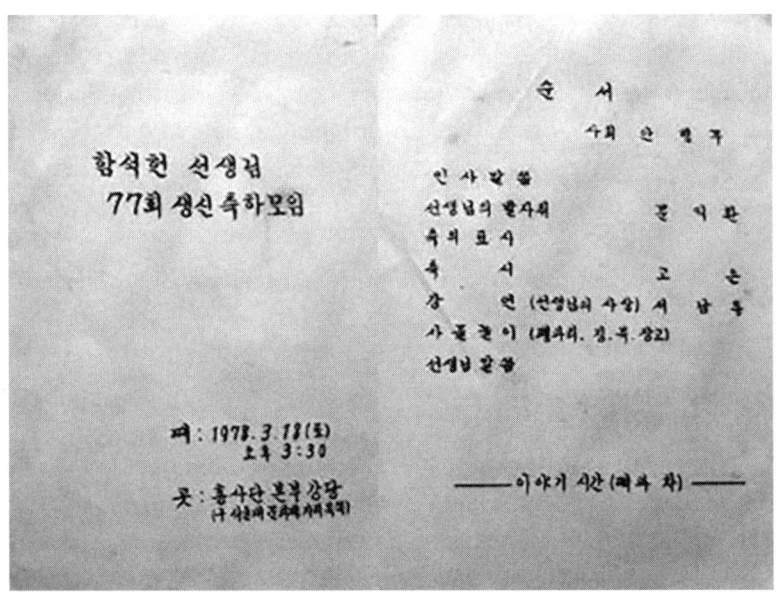

FIGURE 1.4 First documented reference to samul nori on a program, dated March 18, 1978. Photograph courtesy of the Korean Classical Music Record Museum (director Ro Jaemyeong).

appears to be the quartet's first documented "gig," following its successful debut a month earlier. Although conflicting versions of SamulNori's christening exist, the relevant point to draw out here is that the name of the quartet was in fact a neologism that took two ubiquitous terms and combined them, forging a new meaning. And with the conflicting latter account, the parenthetical explanation gives us the first clue of what would eventually serve as the core instrumentation for a new genre of music.

THE SAMUL NORI PROJECT

Meanwhile, the fledgling percussion quartet continued to evolve. At each consecutive appearance at the Space Theater, the quartet began to expand and develop its repertory in an organic manner. The rhythms of p'ungmul provided the musical grammar for SamulNori's experiments in reconfiguring their own "language"—a slick and streamlined, yet somewhat recognizable urban dialect of p'ungmul. Interestingly, these musical explorations were always informed by the sonic identifiers of *place*—each "piece" an interpretation or "rearrangement" of rhythmic patterns from the central, southeastern, and southwestern regions of p'ungmul performance. The members of the quartet became a de facto study group, learning and researching rhythmic patterns associated with a variety of local percussion bands throughout South Korea. For this reason, the quartet's incipient years can be viewed as part of the SamulNori "project," which I base in part on Alain Delissen's "Konggan Project."

Kim Sugŭn's Space Theater was the perfect incubator for this project, and influential figures such as Kang Chunhyŏk and Sim Usŏng served as trusted advisers. Similar to Kim, Kang, Sim, and the Minsogakhoe Sinawi, the quartet members (even while in flux) also shared a desire to rekindle Korea's dwindling folk arts. Founding member Kim Duk Soo reflected on this preservationist impulse in the context of South Korean history:

> After the division of North and South [in 1948], our country went from being an agricultural society to an industrialized one.[29] In this period of great change, our traditional culture changed drastically. When I was in elementary school, 70 percent of Korean citizens were farmers. The music that the farmers played was a natural and essential part of the life cycle; you heard the sound of the samul [four percussion instruments from p'ungmul] at feasts, festivals, ancestor worship rituals, and at funerals. But as we developed into an industrialized society,

aspects of our traditional lifestyles were modified or rendered obsolete. It is because of this tremendous change that we had to bring the instruments from the *madang* [traditional courtyard, village common, or large open ground] to the inside. And at the same time, we had the twofold objective to "bring back what was lost" and *"to show what is magnificent about our culture to others"* (Kim Duk Soo interview, October 27, 2002).[30]

In their efforts to preserve and promote Korean music genres that were threatened because of industrialization, changing economic structures, and shifting musical tastes, the members of the SamulNori project thus engaged in both formal and informal research on Korea's traditional arts. But in their representations of Korean percussion music, there was also a certain degree of latitude in updating or innovating "traditional" music for modern audiences. Seoul's urban audiences were not necessarily keen on sitting through hours-long performances of noisy and rustic p'ungmul. Nor could performance venues like the Space Theater even accommodate such large performing forces. One significant change made by the SamulNori quartet—which will be discussed at length in chapter 2—was the distillation and adaptation of elements drawn from the larger sphere of p'ungmul into a condensed presentational format.

While this recontextualized indoor setting of the samul instruments would vex p'ungmul purists later on, the principal motivation behind the SamulNori project ultimately echoed the *Konggan* ethos. This ethos was inscribed in the very pages of the *Konggan* periodical. Appearing on the title page of a volume in 1976 was a working version of *Konggan*'s mission statement. The statement—composed in English—underwent extensive revisions over time: "We will think over tradition and history of the arts and various questions on the environment. We will try to help each Korean to know better about his nation and himself. And we will report, record and study the situation in which he lives. We are going to go forth bravely with him to the better future that is desirable to all of us" (*Konggan* 1976, 103).

In 1989, *Konggan* had further revised its mission statement, framing its vision in more urgent and global terms. The Konggan Project was no longer relevant for just Koreans; it was also oriented toward the world.

> With foremost emphasis on the problems of our environment and on contemporary architecture and art, properly focused in a historical perspective, our evaluations of the past and present day Korea will enable us to understand her better and will forge a powerful vision of a better Korea for all of our readers.

What does Korea mean to us here and the rest of the world, or vice versa? In each of our fresh issues, our dear philosophical readers, we attempt and answer with all our emphasis on art, architecture and environment, for when nothing is contemplated about the past, present and future in those fields of human endeavor, life might even prove meaningless. (*Konggan* 1989, 266)

Delissen aptly describes Kim's Konggan Project as "Korean history without a historian," where the assembled team of writers and contributors "strove to elaborate Korean identity through aesthetics and aesthetics through history" (Delissen 2001, 243–44). Besides focusing on art and architecture, *Konggan* magazine devoted critical attention to traditional Korean music genres, and often featured detailed pictorial essays of village rituals or traditional dance genres. And while most articles were written in Korean, some titles would appear solely in English—with aims to reach a wider readership: "Instrumental Music for Dure [*ture*: a cooperative labor unit used in Korean farming] in Kosan, Taegu"; "Character of Korean Traditional Music"; and "The Stage of Korean Folk Drama—Ogwangdae nori." One entire issue from 1975 was devoted to the theme of preserving Korean traditional music (*Konggan* 1975, vol. 6). And very much in line with the *Konggan* mission, folklorist Sim Usŏng contributed essays on "Disappearing Heritage" (1971); "What Have We Done, and What Has to Be Done?" (1975); "What Is Gut [*kut*] (and What Has Been Studied over [*sic*] It)?" (1980). These examples shine a light on how *Konggan* presented research on (combined with concerns and hopes for) Korean folk music and culture to its readers. In a similar vein, the SamulNori project engaged in an intensive study of Korean rhythm. For the musicians, this was not so much a scholarly endeavor as it was one driven by a spirit of discovery.

KŎLLIPP'AE P'UNGMUL: A CASE STUDY

Here I present one compelling case for my framing of the SamulNori project. While other examples can be summoned, I highlight this one since it is curiously absent in other studies of SamulNori. Furthermore, it is directly linked to the Space Theater and underscores a key issue in the study and reception of SamulNori.

On September 29, 1980, the Space Theater gave the SamulNori quartet its own billing for the first time. Prior to this, the quartet had performed at the theater under the umbrella of the Minsogakhoe Sinawi (Folk Music "Sinawi"). This concert featured a new member—Lee Kwang Soo [Yi Kwangsu], who replaced the elder of the Choi [Ch'oe] brothers. Lee came from Yesan County in the southern part of Ch'ungch'ŏng Province, and was son to a father who was part of a professional itinerant performance troupe (Lee Kwang Soo 2009, 119–20). He met Kim Yong-bae through their membership in the Seoul-based namsadang troupe that Sim Usŏng had fostered in the 1970s.[31] Initially, Kim had approached Lee about the quartet in 1978, but it was not until 1980 that Lee officially joined the group.[32]

If SamulNori's premieres of "Uttari p'ungmul" (1978), "Samch'ŏnp'o 12-ch'a 36 karak" (1978), and "Honam udo karak" (1979) were inspired by the musical logic and the inflections of p'ungmul from those respective regions, then the 1980 "Kŏllipp'ae p'ungmul" program laid claim to the namsadang connections of its performers. The namsadang were itinerant troupes of male performers who traveled from village to village during Korea's middle to late Chosŏn dynasty (1392–1910).[33] In exchange for food, shelter, and money, the namsadang (translated literally as "male temple group") performed a variety of entertaining acts for locals: tightrope walking, masked dance drama, acrobatic tumbling, saucer spinning, puppet plays, and p'ungmul. By the middle of the twentieth century, the namsadang had diminished in significant numbers. These traveling groups faced resistance and found it increasingly difficult to sustain an itinerant lifestyle—especially within the context of the Japanese colonial period (1910–1945) and the Korean War (1950–1953).[34] In the 1960s, owing to the efforts of Sim Usŏng, a Seoul-based namsadang group was established.

Members of the 1980 SamulNori quartet lineup were no strangers to the namsadang culture. The fathers of Kim Duk Soo and Lee Kwang Soo belonged to namsadang troupes while supporting their families in Taejŏn and Yesan, respectively, and Kim Yong-bae and Lee Kwang Soo were the youngest members of the Seoul namsadang troupe. Later, SamulNori's promotional materials would accentuate this connection as lineage.[35]

The performance at Space Theater was the first time the quartet introduced the elements of dance and song—drawn in part from the namsadang repository—into their project's expanding orbit. As the quartet's newest member, Lee brought an expertise that added a welcome dimension to the group. A gifted singer, Lee took the lead with a narrative prayer song called "Pinari." The *pinari* was typically performed by the namsadang to mark their arrival at a village. A complex text, the chanted song seeks to clear the grounds of malevolent forces and beseeches the village's tutelary spirits to bless all inhabitants. The pinari is infused with religious sensibilities that nod to an older Korea's syncretic relationship with

FIGURE 1.5 "Kŏllipp'ae p'ungmul" program: the SamulNori quartet's first solo appearance at the Space Theater. Photograph courtesy of SamulNori Hanullim.

Buddhism, shamanism, and Confucianism. Lee explained in an interview that as a young child, he would often accompany his father, Yi Chomsŏk, to namsadang performances. With a special aptitude for words, he became familiar with the basic contours of the text in his youth (Lee Kwang Soo interview, February 20, 2009).[36] Lee's rendition of the pinari did not stray far from the version that was performed by the Seoul namsadang troupe, and was later passed on to younger musicians such as Park An-ji [Pak Anji] (Howard 2006, 16).

Space Theater's pamphlet for the concert included a rare image of SamulNori (figure 1.5). The musicians were photographed from a higher vantage point, circumambulating the iconic stone pagoda in the courtyard of the Konggan Group Building.[37] The aerial shot shows three tasseled hats (*sangmo*) captured in midspin, with white streamers creating arcs around the performers while they play their instruments. This image documents a moment when the SamulNori project embarked on a new direction. Previously, the quartet's performances at the Space Theater involved playing only while in a seated position—dubbed "*samul nori anjŭnban*" by Sim Usŏng. After September 1980, dance (and song) would find a natural place in SamulNori's diversifying portfolio. And the all-male quartet (now with its storied lineup) was able to draw on another rich reservoir—the namsadang—for its ongoing project.

Additionally, the program also marks the SamulNori project's turn toward embracing (and adapting) aspects of religiosity in its performances. Of the different types of itinerant or semi-itinerant performance troupes that traversed the Korean peninsula, the *kŏllipp'ae* maintained the strongest association with Buddhism and shamanism. According to Sim Usŏng's study of the namsadang, the kŏllipp'ae (fund-raising group) would travel and sojourn at Buddhist temples. In exchange for food from the monastic and lay communities, the troupe would perform acts like the pinari and the *tangsan kut*—a ritual drawn from shamanistic ceremonies that propitiates the village shrine's god. Because I discuss the pinari in chapter 5, Nathan Hesselink's English translation of Sim's analysis of the kŏllipp'ae is particularly instructive here:

> A typical group was composed of fifteen or so male members organized hierarchically under a top-ranking *hwaju* (leader). Their primary function was to perform household rituals for individual families on behalf of a local Buddhist temple. After a dramatic prelude or pre-show in which the troupe would perform percussion music and dance (*p'ungmul*), mask dance, and (depending on the skills of the members) bowl spinning, they would then engage in a series of propitiatory rituals for the deities of the living quarters, kitchen, and domestic well. Once the majority of the household rituals had been completed, the troupe would then conclude with a *sŏngju kut* (house god ritual). This performance of percussion and vocal music featured the recitation of a ritual offering (*pinari*); during and after this concluding ritual, grain and money were collected as payment. *Kŏllipp'ae* activity was absorbed into the local (rural) *p'ungmul* scene sometime during the Chosŏn period, and it continues to be an important component of student-based and community-led *p'ungmul* organizations in modern times. *The* namsadang *would take on many of the kŏllipp'ae's roles in the early twentieth century.*[38] (Hesselink 2012, 21–22)

At the September 1980 concert, the quartet performed eight elements stemming from the kŏllipp'ae. They appear in this order on the program: *mun kut* (ritual performed at a gate); tangsan kut (ritual performed at the village shrine); *chowang kut* (ritual for the kitchen god); *tŏju kut* (ritual for the house god); *umul kut* (ritual played at the village well); pinari; *mul soji* (ritual burning of paper); and *p'an kut* (an exuberant showcase of p'ungmul drumming and dance).[39] In an effort to evoke some spatial semblance of temple grounds, the quartet made strategic use of the Konggan Building's unique architectural features—features that were designed by Kim Sugŭn.

With Lee Kwang Soo taking the lead as the kkwaenggwari (small gong) player, the quartet performed the tangsan kut in front of the pagoda (*t'ap*) in the building's courtyard. The audience moved with the performers as they processed down the stairs to the Space Theater, located in the basement. As they entered the theater, Lee began the pinari, which then segued into the offering of the mul soji. The latter involves the burning of white *hanji* (traditional handmade paper), designed to appease the spirits. And despite the cramped quarters, the p'an kut—a danced number—was performed inside Konggan's experimental stage (i.e., black box theater). In an interview, Lee confessed that although there were minor details that were not perfectly executed, the concert on the whole was an enormous success (Lee Kwang Soo interview, February 20, 2009).[40] The concert also yielded an important development of the SamulNori project—the mun kut, pinari, and p'an kut began to be incorporated into the quartet's later performances. The combination of the mun kut / pinari and p'an kut became the bookends for what eventually became the standard ninety-minute SamulNori program: mun kut / pinari; *samdo sŏl changgo karak* (rhythms from three regions, played on changgo); *samdo nongak karak* (rhythms from three regions, played in samul nori formation); and p'an kut. In just a few years' time, the quartet would then regularly present this program at venues in the United States, Europe, and Japan (figure 1.6).

With a growing buzz over the quartet's performances, and the celebrated SamulNori cast now in place, the group began to take off both literally and metaphorically. In the midst of travel to various theaters in and around Seoul, the group continued to mine the rhythmic material not only from p'ungmul but also from the neighboring soundscape of Korean shamanism. When they exhausted their own expertise, they studied informally with specialists or elder teachers. The Songnisan (Songni mountain) research trips to rehearse and to study with village elders were fruitful, and were even documented by Japanese photographer Ichiro Shimizu in a strikingly beautiful photographic book.[41]

The quartet also engaged in an ongoing process of revision. Arrangements of p'ungmul rhythms were subject to editing, expansion, and resequencing. Chapter 2 will provide insight into the fine-tuning of an arrangement that would later become known as "Yŏngnam nongak"—a piece that we will learn more about. In Korean, the terms *chagŏp* (work) and *chŏngni* (organization or arrangement) have been used by quartet members to describe their recursive process. In many ways, this process constituted the SamulNori project's pathbreaking phase of research, experimentation, and (re)creation.

FIGURE 1.6 The SamulNori quartet performing p'an kut inside the Space Theater. Photograph courtesy of Sim Usŏng.

SAMUL NORI'S BIG BANG

What was it about the music or the performances by the quartet that so captivated early audiences? As already mentioned, Kang Chunhyŏk suggested that it was the novelty of SamulNori's seated position, which focused the spotlight on the diversity of rhythms in p'ungmul's regional variants. For others, what piqued interest was the exploratory musical journey on which the quartet embarked—with each concert came a new attempt at creating fresh arrangements from vintage materials. Suzanna Samstag, an American expat who became SamulNori's first managing director, reminisced about the word-of-mouth effect that drew in SamulNori's crowds: "After word got out about SamulNori, the [Space] theater would be totally crowded, standing room only. People would tell their friends to come, and pretty soon there was this group of true believers who were trying to find something sacred" (Suzanna Samstag interview, November 22, 2005).

While the Space Theater remained an important venue and base for SamulNori, demand for the quartet grew exponentially. By 1981, the SamulNori quartet received invitations to perform at other theaters and venues, such as the Cecil Theater (Sesil Kŭkchang), the Sejong Center for the Performing Arts (Sejong munhwa hoegwan), and the UNESCO hall in Seoul. And the group started to receive fees that would mark their move toward professionalization. In 1982, SamulNori made their international debut with a series of events in Japan, beginning in June in Tokyo (SamulNori Hanullim t'ansaeng samsip chunyŏn kinyŏm saŏphoe 2009, 58). This was co-organized by the South Korean government and the Mindan (Korean Residents Union in Japan). Later that year, the quartet traveled to the United States for the first time, performing at music festivals and at theaters in Florida, New York, Boston, Virginia, Washington, DC, and Los Angeles. On November 19, the quartet traveled back to the United States to participate in the Percussive Arts Society International Convention (PASIC), where they made an indelible impression on attendees and fellow percussionists. As SamulNori's success began to extend beyond national boundaries, the quartet garnered both fame and notoriety within South Korea. But rather than narrating the next decade of SamulNori's history here, I turn instead to the quartet's positive reception that fed into SamulNori / samul nori as a global phenomenon.

Journalist Ku Hŭisŏ (or Ku Hee-seo) was an avid fan and supporter of the group. Her writings shaped much of the early reception of SamulNori for the broader Korean public. She was also one of the appointed contributors for Kim Sugŭn's *Konggan* magazine. Ku's essay "Korean Spirit, Korean Rhythm"—written in 1983 for *Konggan*—provided the context for readers first encountering SamulNori through the printed word. She narrated SamulNori's development at the Space Theater as an experimental quartet into a rigorous study group intent on researching and reinterpreting Korea's musical heritage. SamulNori's 1982 U.S. tour highlights were also provided as evidence that the quartet was making headway in American cities. For this, the Korean public should take heed, Ku noted:

> Whether it was by attempting to theorize and actually organize the regional characteristics of nongak's rhythmic cycles, or participate as performers in a *kut pan* [*kut* ritual gathering] for several months in order to learn the rhythms associated with shamanistic music, these performers' efforts are testimony to tears shed during the learning process.
>
> As a result of these valiant efforts, not only have the stereotypical myths about the triteness, monotony, and noisy clatter of nongak (and other traditional percussion music) been completely shattered, but [we hear] the rhythms that have long lived within our *minjung* [people]—this elegance has entered into hearts today and awakened our own voice. (Ku 1983, 98–99)

In the English-language publication *Koreana*, Korean musicologist Han Myung-hee [Han Myŏnghi] echoed this nationalistic sentiment but placed the SamulNori phenomenon in a more sociohistorical context:

> By the end of the 1970s, many Koreans had come to an important point in the process of self-awareness, which included growing interest in Korean Studies and the traditional performing arts. Politically the power structure was pressing heavily on the people's consciousness. Tear gas–filled university campuses, anger, frustration and low morale characterized the consciousness of citizens. It was during these times that SamulNori made its debut and spread its message through the seeming madness. The music provided an antidote to the heartbreak of the era. But interest in the music was not momentary. The music provided a release, an experience of group ecstasy and a way, through nostalgia for the past, for us to find ourselves. (Han, Myung-hee 1993, 35)

To Suzanna Samstag (an important figure in the story of global samul nori), what appealed most about the SamulNori quartet were the electrifying performances. On hearing a particular arrangement for four changgos ("Samdo sŏl changgo karak") in 1982, Samstag recounts that the music "literally tore through my body" (Lee, Katherine In-Young 2004, 37). The four musicians were more or less equal in terms of their training. Onstage, this synergy of talent sometimes resulted in the young musicians trying to one-up each other. The audience became spectators to what was transpiring in performance; witnessing this explosive "turf war" left one breathless with anticipation. Samstag admitted that she was similarly impressed by the physicality of the dancing and the sheer athleticism of the performers—who despite being thin were at the top of their form.

Another "foreign" opinion of the budding quartet came from Beate Gordon (1923–2012), former director of programming at the Asia Society. In an interview I conducted with Gordon at her New York apartment, she mentioned the course of events that led her to invite SamulNori in 1983 to be part of an Asia Society–sponsored tour. Gordon explained that she had heard about the group only indirectly, from a fellow presenter who had observed the quartet perform live at PASIC (Percussive Arts Society International Convention) the year before. Since she was keen on bringing in talented performers from Asia for her series, she decided to take a chance. The risk proved to be one well taken:

> I thought they were superb. I think that their virtuosity, their technique was so thoroughly embedded. I mean, it was just unbelievably strong. You didn't

really have to worry about them at all. . . . In German, one says, *er sitzt*, "it sits." It's in there, it's solid. And they had that.

They were very much the thing that I thought would communicate. And they had that *tsuchikusai* [in Japanese, "rustic earthiness"] thing about them. And I thought that this would come through very strongly, and it did. People were enraptured by them. (Beate Gordon interview, November 23, 2010)

Gordon's sponsorship of SamulNori in 1983 under the auspices of the Asia Society tour stands as the singular launch pad for SamulNori's entry into the "world music" scene in the 1980s. The tour also bore SamulNori's first internationally issued recording, *Samul-Nori: The Legendary Recording by Original Members*, in 1983 on the Nonesuch label.[42]

As evidenced by the sponsorship by powerful individuals such as Kim Sugŭn and Beate Gordon—impresarios both dedicated to the performing arts—auspicious encounters helped to facilitate and propel the SamulNori quartet's development and rise to fame from 1978 until 1993, the year when the quartet disbanded. Modeled after the same tenets of Kim Sugŭn's Konggan Project that aimed to reevaluate Korean culture and history in the face of modernization, the SamulNori quartet negotiated an emphasis on the traditional and regional roots of their own musical research collaborations with a changing urban audience. It was in the Space Theater's culture of innovation that they were given the creative license to undertake such an endeavor. In the process of researching the regional rhythms of p'ungmul, they increased the likelihood that native Koreans would find familiar elements in the sounds of their arrangements. But it was also the "foreign" audience's enthusiastic reception of their dynamic performances as a quartet (in the "classic" line-up of Kim Duk Soo, Kim Yong-bae, Lee Kwang Soo, and Choi Jong Sil) that proved to be a key component in the launching of the quartet and, later, the genre.

TWO

The Dynamics of Rhythmic Form

The word "dynamic" can take on many different meanings in English. We often use it as an adjective to describe people. A person with a dynamic personality is someone who is full of energy and vitality. A dynamic person leaves a lasting impression on others; she is active, quick with ideas, and commands a presence. We also use the term to describe processes of change. A dynamic economy is one that bustles with activity. It has exhibited significant change, perhaps in moving from import-led to export-driven, or in the larger shift from an agricultural to an industrialized economy. While this does not preclude the inevitability of hiccups and downturns, a dynamic economy is more commonly associated with indications of further development and growth. Here, "dynamic" signals active *change* and *progress*. And along similar lines, in academic discourse, the term dynamic can also describe "a force that stimulates change within a system or a process."[1]

In music, there is a common usage for the term, which can either take the form of a noun or an adjective. Dynamics refer to the acoustic volume of a sound. Dynamic contrast in musical performance means performing at higher and lower levels of volume. Or, in other words, it is simply the contrast between loudness and softness. Composers incorporate dynamic markings in the score to indicate the desirable dynamic level for a passage. Dynamics are relative, rather than absolute designations for volume or amplitude. In standard notation for Western classical music, a marking of *pianissimo* followed by a *fortississimo* would instruct the performer to render passages in contrasting levels of amplitude—one passage played very softly and another delivered at an extremely loud volume.

Other fields also claim the word "dynamic." In physics and classical mechanics, dynamics refer to the study of motion and the forces that produce it. In linguistics, dynamic verbs describe actions, whereas stative verbs describe a state of being. Sociologists and psychologists consider group dynamics to analyze social group behaviors and processes. And computer scientists deploy the term in relation to programming, systems, and web pages. While many more examples can be summoned, the point to draw out here is that there is a constellation of meanings for "dynamic." The common ones include motion, change, action, energy, and volume in sound. Even despite the word's multivalence, we know intuitively what dynamic *does not* mean. Dynamic does not mean static. Nor is it dull or monotonous.

I spend time parsing these different meanings because "dynamic" is a word that is commonly used to describe samul nori. First, it is a strikingly frequent descriptor found in books, CD liner notes, programs, newspaper articles, and concert reviews. It is also a word that many people have used when describing their own first encounters with a live samul nori performance. Third, as I explain in chapter 3, South Korea's first national slogan—Dynamic Korea—became sonically linked to the genre in the early 2000s.[2] After many years of hearing this word in relation to samul nori in my interviews and conversations with fans and practitioners, I began to wonder: what *is* so dynamic about this percussion genre? And does this help us to understand how a musical genre from South Korea has come to be adopted and adapted by amateur musical communities around the world? In response to the latter query, this book answers in the affirmative. As for the first, my interpretation unfolds in this chapter.

AN INTRODUCTION TO "YŎNGNAM NONGAK" AND SAMUL NORI

Here I examine a popular samul nori composition called "Yŏngnam nongak" and show how this music is organized. In so doing, I also build the case for how the piece exhibits distinct qualities in its formal structure—qualities that have lent it to circulation or travel across boundaries. I develop an analytic based on "dynamism" and demonstrate that "Yŏngnam nongak" is an example of a dynamic rhythmic form. Other compositions in the samul nori repertory (while they are not the focus of this chapter) share these same formal properties. Rhythmic form, I argue, is central to the samul nori genre, and it is a dynamic rhythmic form that has been central to its mobility.

My attention to form is deliberate. But I do not intend to narrate a story in which form is the sole protagonist, acting alone. This is the farthest from the case. As we have previously learned, the Space Theater was the creative seedbed for the SamulNori project and their explorations of Korean rhythm. SamulNori's process of arranging, rearranging, and recontextualizing rhythmic patterns from p'ungmul led to what eventually would become known as samul nori. Thus, the form that I will describe is interleaved with the musicians who first breathed life into it, and who performed it with such verve and kinetic energy. My formal analysis of "Yŏngnam nongak" takes into consideration the other important actors of the story—the SamulNori quartet and, in particular, Kim Duk Soo. In this sense, *Dynamic Korea* offers an opportunity to witness the pairing of two distinct methodologies that are not usually cast together—ethnography and formal analysis. I contend that there is much to learn from this conversation.

Before moving to the analysis, however, I provide some general background on "Yŏngnam nongak" and its significance in the context of global samul nori. I select this piece for analysis because it is very often the first samul nori composition that beginning students will learn to play as part of an ensemble. (I also return to this piece in chapter 5.) Unlike the "Sŏl changgo karak," which is played exclusively on the changgo hourglass drums, "Yŏngnam nongak" is a representative composition that features the interplay of the four primary instruments of samul nori. SamulNori Hanullim's self-published notation books designate "Yŏngnam nongak" as the first or the "fundamental" piece of the series (Samul-Nori Hanullim 2004). In SamulNori Hanullim's pedagogical system, students must learn "Yŏngnam nongak" before advancing to the more complex pieces known as "Uttari p'ungmul" and "Honam udo nongak karak." The composition provides challenges for the initiate (for example, memorizing the different rhythmic patterns and the sequential order, "feeling" the rhythmic groove, and learning to play as part of an ensemble), yet it is surprisingly surmountable with the proper instruction and adequate practice. In short, "Yŏngnam nongak" is accessible, and it is likely the most performed samul nori composition by amateur ensembles within and outside South Korea.

First, a note on instrumentation. To form a standard samul nori ensemble, four percussion instruments are needed: a double-headed hourglass drum (changgo), a barrel drum called puk, and two gongs—one large (ching) and one small (kkwaenggwari).[3] As earlier mentioned, these are the core percussion instruments (played with sticks called *ch'ae*) that are also featured in p'ungmul. Each instrument in a samul nori ensemble has a different role to play in the musical texture. While a minimum of four musicians on the four different percussion instruments is required for a piece such as "Yŏngnam nongak," instruments such as the changgo and puk can be performed by multiple players. In a group consisting of beginners and intermediates, for instance, students of various levels can select instruments according to one's respective level and strengths. A beginner might opt to learn an instrument such as the puk, which plays more of a supporting role in the ensemble. And a beginning-level student with a good sense of rhythm could take on the ching. Although it has the least active part, the ching serves a critical role in the ensemble by punctuating the primary beats of the rhythmic cycles. Intermediates or beginners could perform on the changgo, which requires some technical proficiency and a capacity for memorizing different rhythmic patterns, known as *karak*. Of the four, the kkwaenggwari part is typically reserved for the designated leader or the person with the most training. The kkwaenggwari player must keep track of the number of beats in a designated karak, the number of repetitions of this pattern, and think ahead toward successive patterns.[4] It is also the job of the lead kkwaenggwari player to provide cues to the other members; these cues signal the last iteration of a cycle and the start of the next one.

As one of the fundamentals of the samul nori repertory, "Yŏngnam nongak" includes features that make it fun and appealing for amateur enthusiasts. There is built-in rhythmic complexity, repetition, an acceleration in tempo toward the end, and the chance to bang away on drums and gongs. Once students are able to play their respective instruments, the process of learning to perform as a group can be a gratifying experience. Each instrument has an independent part (or a different way of rendering a karak) that must be learned separately. But when "Yŏngnam nongak" is played in ensemble formation, the changgo, puk, ching, and kkwaenggwari function together as part of a larger, interdependent unit. Progressing through the various rhythmic patterns, for instance, the four instruments weave into an almost polyphonic musical texture. This texture is not shaped by tonal counterpoint (as heard in conventional Western polyphony), but rather by the timbral sounds produced by four different instruments made of leather and metal. Perhaps this may be best described as a percussive *polytimbral* texture—where distinct percussive sounds interact in a way to produce varied timbral contours. Additionally, a rhythmic "groove" emerges when performers are able to fully synchronize their beats within a cycle.[5] All these combined elements make for an exciting piece to learn and perform.

Thus far, I have been using the term "composition" or "piece" to categorize "Yŏngnam nongak." While this is by no means incorrect, the terms "arrangement" and "adaptation" may be equally valid descriptors. In Korean, the words *chaegusŏng* ("reconfigure" or "restructure") and *chaech'angjo* ("re-create") are frequently used to describe the first musical explorations by the SamulNori quartet in 1978–1982.[6] A more colloquial term, *tch'ada* ("to form or organize"), is also employed by musicians.

The first presentation of what eventually became known as "Yŏngnam nongak" was an arrangement of existing rhythmic patterns drawn from a specific region of South Korea. Yŏngnam (meaning "south of the mountain range") is the former provincial name for the southeastern swath of the peninsula. It is bordered by the expansive T'aebaek Mountains to the north, the Sobaek Mountains to its west, and two disputed bodies of water—one to the east (East Sea / Sea of Japan) and one to the south (Korea Strait / Tsushima Strait). Present-day North and South Kyŏngsang Provinces constitute the Yŏngnam region (figure 2.1).[7] Partly owing to its physical borders, Yŏngnam/Kyŏngsang is known for its colorful dialects (generally characterized by strong accents and dramatic fluctuations in intonation), cuisine, politics, culture, and, of course, music.

The rhythmic patterns featured in "Yŏngnam nongak" hail from a regional style of p'ungmul called Chinju Samch'ŏnp'o nongak. Although it has been associated with other labels, Chinju Samch'ŏnp'o nongak refers to both the name of a regional band and the representative style of p'ungmul performed in the Yŏngnam/Kyŏngsang region. The term nongak (literally, "farming music") is sometimes used interchangeably with p'ungmul.[8] Thus, Chinju Samch'ŏnp'o nongak is understood as the style of p'ungmul practiced in the southern cities of Chinju and Samch'ŏnp'o.

After performing their first arrangement of rhythms from South Korea's central Uttari region, the two main percussionists (Kim Duk Soo and Kim Yong-bae) were encouraged to continue their experimental musical endeavors in the months following. Choi Jong Sil [Ch'oe Chongsil] and Ch'oe Chongsŏk, brothers from the southern port city of Samch'ŏnp'o, were then invited to join the quartet. They replaced Yi Chongdae and Ch'oe T'aehyŏn, who were trained in wind and string instruments, respectively.[9] Raised as percussionists in the nongak tradition of their local town, the Choi [Ch'oe] brothers served as faithful guides for the next (ad)venture—an adaptation of Chinju Samch'ŏnp'o nongak for percussion quartet.[10] The collaboration resulted in an arrangement entitled "Sibi-ch'a samsip-yuk karak" (twelve sections, thirty-six rhythmic patterns) that was premiered in April 1978, and then repeated on March 1, 1979, and renamed "Kyŏngsang nongak."

Chinju Samch'ŏnp'o nongak is one of five regional styles of p'ungmul that

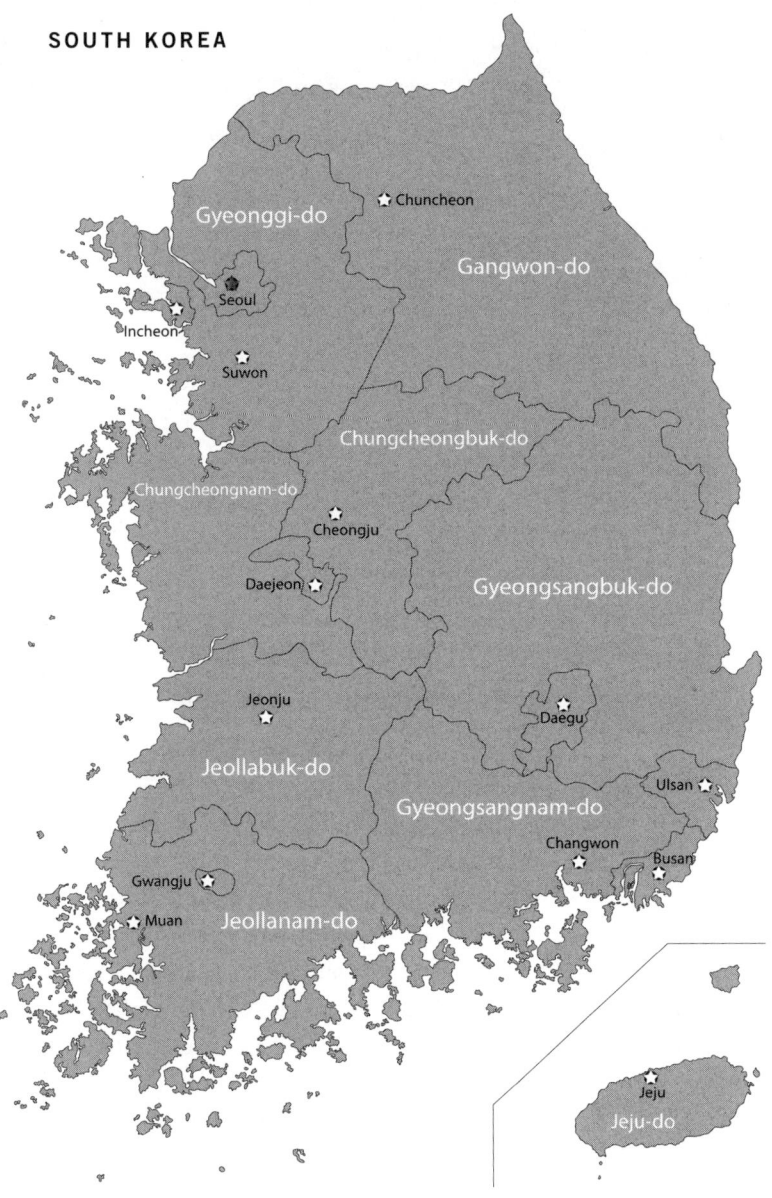

FIGURE 2.1 Map of provinces in South Korea.
© Indos82 | Dreamstime.com

FIGURE 2.2 Minsogakhoe Sinawi program from March 1, 1979.
Photograph courtesy of SamulNori Hanullim.

have been designated as "Intangible Cultural Heritage" by the South Korean government.[11] This style of p'ungmul (also referred to as *maegu kut*) exhibits the historical residue of the role p'ungmul once held within the Korean military. Martial legacies can be witnessed in the retention of particular flags, a bugle-like instrument called the *napal*, tasseled hats known as *sangmo*, and rhythmic patterns that were once used to marshal troops into choreographed formations. The rhythmic patterns are thought to be powerful and energetic, with a general tendency to accelerate and crescendo toward the conclusion of a section. Like other versions of p'ungmul, Chinju Samch'ŏnp'o nongak is performed outdoors, by a large number of musicians and dancers. Performances involve the playing of particular rhythmic patterns (karak), which are repeated as cycles for an indefinite number of times. Depending on the event, a performance can last for several hours. Despite this variability in terms of duration, there is a basic organizational structure to Chinju Samch'ŏnp'o nongak that features twelve sections with distinct rhythmic patterns, functions, and choreographies.

Section 1: *Obangjin*
Section 2: *Ŏllimgut nori—tadŭraegi*
Section 3: *Pŏkku nori (Samch'ae tŏppaegi)*
Section 4: *Kil kunak*
Section 5: *Yŏngsan tadŭraegi*
Section 6: *Mŏt pŏkku nori*
Section 7: *Tŭngmajigut—tadŭraegi*
Section 8: *Anjŭn pŏkku nori—tadŭraegi*
Section 9: *Hohogut*
Section 10: *Kaein yŏngsan kut nori*
Section 11: *Pyŏlkut nori*
Section 12: *Hŏt'ŭngut (hyech'imgut)*

It is this rhythmic repository that the quartet of musicians drew upon to create the seated arrangement of "Kyŏngsang nongak" in 1978. With the elder brother Cho'e Chŏngsok on the lead kkwaenggwari part, the younger Choi Jong Sil on ching, and Kim Yong-bae on puk and Kim Duk Soo on changgo, the quartet performed the arrangement again at the Space Theater on March 1, 1979 (figure 2.2).

The reverse side of the program (not pictured) identifies the different sections that appeared as part of the presentation of "Kyŏngsang nongak":

Section 1: *Ŏllimgut nori*
Section 2: *Kil kunak nori*
Section 3: *Pan kil kunak nori*
Section 4: *Tŏppaegi pŏkku nori*
Section 5: *Pan tadŭraegi*
Section 6: *Chajin ŏllim pŏkku nori*
Section 7: *Yŏngsan tadŭraegi*

[NEW SECTION: PYŎLGŎRI TALGŎRI]

Section 8: *Obangjin nori*
Section 9: *Kutkŏri nori*
Section 10: *Tŏppaegi nori*
Section 11: *Ssangjinp'uri (Hohogut)*
Section 12: *Samch'agut nori (Kaein nori)*

Even for those without a working knowledge of Korean or an understanding of Korean rhythm, a cursory glance at table 2.1 reveals some similarities and many

TABLE 2.1 Comparison of the formal structure of p'ungmul (Chinju Samch'ŏnp'o nongak) and samul nori "Kyŏngsang nongak" versions

SECTION (CH'A)	COLUMN A (P'UNGMUL)	COLUMN B (SAMUL NORI)
	Chinju Samch'ŏnp'o nongak	"Kyŏngsang nongak"
1	Obangjin	Ŏllimgut nori
2	Ŏllimgut nori—tadŭraegi	Kil kunak nori
3	Pŏkku nori (samch'ae tŏppaegi)	Pan kil kunak nori
4	Kil kunak	Tŏppaegi pŏkku nori
5	Yŏngsan tadŭraegi	Pan tadŭraegi
6	Mŏt pŏkku nori	Chajin ŏllim pŏkku nori
7	Tŭngmajigut—tadŭraegi	Yŏngsan tadŭraegi
		Pyŏlgŏri talgŏri
8	Anjŭn pŏkku nori—tadŭraegi	Obangjin nori
9	Hohogut	Kutkŏri nori
10	Kaein yŏngsan kut nori	Tŏppaegi nori
11	Pyŏlkut nori	Ssangjinp'uri (Hohogut)
12	Hŏt'ŭngŭt (hyech'imgut)	Samch'agut nori (kaein nori)

differences between the two columns. Taking into account that the sequential order has been reconfigured in column B, one notices that some sections are identical or nearly identical (e.g., *yŏngsan tadŭraegi; ŏllimgut nori; kil kunak*), whereas other sections bear only a passing resemblance to each other—a mere syllable or word are held in common. One of the most noticeable differences between the two is the inclusion of a new section, called *pyŏlgŏri talgŏri*, in column B. In the program, *pyŏlgŏri talgŏri* appears in parentheses, marked as separate from the rest of the sections. Ironically, this new additional element would later become one of the characteristic sections of the "Yŏngnam nongak" piece, in its global iterations.

The linguistic and sequential differences beg the question: to what extent is SamulNori's "Kyŏngsang nongak" musically derived from Chinju Samch'ŏnp'o nongak? Based on a side-by-side, row-by-row comparison of columns A and B, the two do not appear to be closely related. If one takes into consideration the practice of arranging, and the fact that multiple appellations for the same rhythmic pattern can exist, however, then a different story begins to emerge. Take, for instance, the pairings of *kil kunak / kil kunak nori* and *obangjin / obangjin nori*.

In this case, *nori* (play or entertainment) is employed as a suffix and does not effectively alter the dominant rhythmic pattern used in the SamulNori version. Second, the near match in rows 3 (column A) and 4 (column B): *pŏkku nori* (*samch'ae tŏppaegi*) / *tŏppaegi pŏkku nori* points to a section in the p'ungmul version where musicians using the *sogo* (small handheld drum) perform a spirited, group "solo." The samul nori version employs the *tŏppaegi* rhythmic pattern, which is used in the dance, without incorporating the dance itself. In fact, the name of the section *tŏppaegi pŏkku nori* illustrates this shift in emphasis toward the rhythm over the dance (known as *pŏkku nori*). Lastly, each of the twelve sections in the p'ungmul version can feature one to three core rhythmic patterns. A total of thirty-six different rhythmic patterns, spread out unevenly over the twelve sections, exist in Chinju Samch'ŏnp'o nongak. With this in mind, a wide variety of options are available in the process of musical arranging. A single karak, such as *pan kil kunak*, for instance, can serve as the rhythmic core for one section in SamulNori's arrangement. This contrasts with the p'ungmul version, where the fourth section, *kil kunak*, includes two rhythmic patterns—*kil kunak* and *pan kil kunak*.

Comparisons between SamulNori's "Kyŏngsang nongak" and Chinju Samch'ŏnp'o nongak can proceed at length, accompanied by extensive transcription and analysis. Nathan Hesselink embarked on one such exercise with his meticulous analysis of SamulNori's arrangement of "Honam nongak karak" that derived from a type of p'ungmul practiced in the Honam (Chŏlla Province) region of South Korea. Analyzing the rhythmic patterns shared by both versions, Hesselink concluded that there was an almost identical structural coherence between SamulNori's version and the first movement of the p'an kut section in "Honam udo kut" (Hesselink 2004). By highlighting the shared rhythmic patterns, Hesselink concluded that the SamulNori quartet—despite allegations leveled toward the group of being inauthentic—maintained a strong degree of fidelity (e.g., rhythms, drum strokes, and sequential ordering) to the p'ungmul version. SamulNori's musical allegiance to the source material allowed Hesselink to argue for a more inclusive definition of "tradition," wherein preservation and innovation can coexist in the samul nori repertory (Hesselink 2004, 2012). I agree with Hesselink's assessment. In the section that follows, however, I choose a different path of investigation, which aims to understand *why* the piece known as "Yŏngnam nongak" became so popular among amateur groups around the world. I focus on SamulNori's "dynamic rhythmic form" as one important reason.

MUSICAL ARRANGEMENTS

On closer inspection, SamulNori's "Kyŏngsang nongak" reveals the art of musical arrangement. Musical arrangements, as musicologist Ryan Bañagale describes, "reconfigure an existing piece of music through any number of techniques, including the reorganization or removal of thematic material, the alteration of instrumentation, and the modification of tempo, rhythm, and dynamics" (Bañagale 2014, 3). Not only did the SamulNori quartet adapt the large-scale, outdoor Chinju Samch'ŏnp'o nongak for an indoor stage; they also made specific decisions over the selection, sequencing, and organization of various rhythmic patterns into an arrangement. This was a musical project that involved a fair deal of trial and adjustment and refining over a period of a few years.[12] The changing of the name first from "Twelve sections, thirty-six rhythmic patterns" to "Kyŏngsang nongak" and finally to "Yŏngnam nongak" is an indication that the arrangement evolved over time. Although "Yŏngnam nongak" has come to be understood as a fixed composition that is now notated and part of an established recording history, its origins point to a work in flux, and a creative process of musical experimentation.

An unreleased recording of "Kyŏngsang nongak" from the March 1, 1979, concert at Space Theater serves as an important sonic document of an early version of the arrangement. Just shy of twenty minutes, the recording—which belonged to the private collection of Konggan Sarang's artistic director Kang Chunhyŏk—is at least five to ten minutes longer than other audio versions of "Yŏngnam nongak" that appear on CDs.[13] And unlike other recordings that move at virtuosic speeds, the tempo is moderately paced in the 1979 recorded performance. This is most apparent in the *pyŏlgŏri talgŏri* section, which is repeated twice.[14] Not quite a song, and not quite spoken text, *pyŏlgŏri talgŏri* is a short text that is rhythmically chanted and incorporated into a four-bar, four-beat rhythmic pattern that is repeated as a cycle. The text is not delivered all at once, but rather in individual lines, interspersed with percussion.

In the p'ungmul version, this text was traditionally performed during the Ch'usŏk autumn harvest festival, which falls on the autumnal equinox. It describes a feeling of gratitude for the year's harvest and issues an appeal for yet another bounty in the year following. (This chanted text is featured in the *pyŏlkut nori* section of Chinju Samch'ŏnp'o nongak.) In the 1979 concert at the Space Theater, the chant was articulated in a manner similar to how it is performed in the p'ungmul version—with clear enunciations at a slightly brisk but measured tempo. The dynamic level or volume remains relatively constant. In a few years' time, this chanted portion was to be renamed as *pyŏldalgŏri* and began to increase drastically in speed in performances by the SamulNori quartet. In the 1979 recording, however, we have a better glimpse of the influence of p'ungmul performance practice on the early arrangements of this work.

By the time of the U.S. tour sponsored by the Asia Society in 1983, the arrangement had undergone further revisions. The membership of the quartet had changed slightly by then as well, with Lee Kwang Soo replacing Ch'oe Chongsŏk as the kkwaenggwari player. On the tour, the quartet performed a revised version of "Kyŏngsang nongak," now renamed as "Yŏngnam nongak." Recorded and released on Nonesuch Records, SamulNori's "Yŏngnam nongak" is different in feel from the private recording made just a few years earlier. In a few words, it is more virtuosic and dramatic. And at just seven minutes long, it is also considerably shorter.

As yet another pass at arranging, the 1983 version of "Yŏngnam nongak" was the result of incessant revision. One such adjustment was the elimination of an entire section called *hohogut* from the previous version. In the p'ungmul version, this section is marked by the exclamation of non-lexical syllables "ho-ho" followed by two drum strikes. It is believed that this once served as a signal when p'ungmul was used for martial purposes (Hesselink 2006, 167). The vocalizations are coordinated with two spinning jumps in succession, as the musicians walk in a circular formation during this particular section. With its linkage to specific physical choreography, *hohogut* proved an interesting segment to arrange for a seated quartet. In the 1979 recording of "Kyŏngsang nongak," the musicians chose to retain the vocalizations while playing the core rhythmic pattern, which alternates between compound and duple meters. The cycle is repeated a total of eleven times and accelerates slightly toward the final iteration. Stripped of its choreographic element, however, the 1979 performance of *hohogut* sounded stilted and had a stop-and-go feeling to it. In refining the work, SamulNori struck *hohogut* from the arrangement. The quartet made other such decisions that eventually resulted in a more streamlined and, as I will argue, more dynamic arrangement.

SamulNori's "Yŏngnam nongak" is smartly arranged music that includes an ebb and flow of musical activity. As described above, this was the result of a process of arranging that developed organically over the span of a few years. It was only later on, after recordings and notation emerged, that "Yŏngnam nongak" came to be thought of as a stand-alone, "fixed" composition. But even so, the arrangement/work has retained a degree of flexibility in performance that other canonic compositions resist. Musicians can mutually agree upon the number of repetitions per rhythmic pattern, and thus can expand or contract the length of the piece. This accordion-like effect accounts for the discrepancies in timings of "Yŏngnam nongak" recordings by the SamulNori quartet and also Kim Duk Soo's SamulNori Hanullim group.[15] With this variability, then, what remains identifiable about the arrangement is the rhythm-based form of "Yŏngnam nongak."

I define rhythmic form as a type of musical form whose foundation is based on the sequence of rhythmic configurations. These rhythmic configurations can be conceptualized or represented in a number of different ways—social function, gesture, choreography, timeline, meter, texture, pattern, and/or cycle. They can also be yoked to Western harmony, as Grosvenor Cooper and Leonard Meyer investigated in *The Rhythmic Structure of Music* (1960). In the case of samul nori, the formal structure is organized by the sequential arrangement of individual karak (rhythmic patterns) that are then repeated as cycles. Since the rhythmic patterns are derived from a genre that integrates both music *and* dance, the karak correspond to sections within p'ungmul that have choreographic counterparts. Karak generally do not appear more than once in the sequence. Samul nori's form is thus a sectional or episodic one.

As a rhythmic form, samul nori arrangements such as "Yŏngnam nongak" are not subject to the rules of Western harmony and its structuring principles. Nor are they organized by the developmental progression of melodic or modal material. They are guided instead by the selective arrangement of karak that, in combination, create a musical form with distinct sections. Within this sectional form, there is a multifaceted kind of dynamism—as described at the beginning of this chapter—that can be observed.

I now return to "Yŏngnam nongak," the SamulNori arrangement that transcended its regional roots by going global. I analyze its formal properties and consider the reasons why this piece became popular among amateur enthusiasts around the world. I draw heavily from three sources for this analysis—the aforementioned recording made during the 1983 U.S. tour sponsored by the Asia Society, a notational booklet published by SamulNori Hanullim in 2004, and two video recordings (VHS) that were produced by the Overseas Koreans Foundation and the Korean National University of Arts in 1999. The latter was part of a "Learning Korean Culture Series" that was geared toward overseas Koreans interested in learning samul nori. The two-video set was distributed to Korean cultural centers and organizations outside Korea and was not intended for commercial sale. All three sources exist outside their original format (e.g., dubbed recordings of the CD, photocopies of the notation, and YouTube uploads of the video) and circulate online and in informal networks outside South Korea.[16]

The three sources share a similar version of "Yŏngnam nongak" in terms of formal structure:

Section 1: *Kil kunak*
Section 2: *Pan kil kunak*
Section 3: *Tadŭraegi*
Section 4: *Yŏngsan tadŭraegi*
Section 5: *Yŏngyŏlch'ae*
Section 6: *Pyŏldalgŏri*
Section 7: *Ssangjinp'uri*
Section 8: *Maeji*

A side-by-side comparison with the 1979 "Kyŏngsang nongak" recording shows how the ongoing process of musical arrangement resulted in even further revisions (table 2.2).

In this new configuration, the 1983 arrangement omits a few sections while adding two new ones—*yŏngyŏlch'ae* and *maeji*. The new additions are consid-

TABLE 2.2 Comparison of the formal structure of "Kyŏngsang nongak" (March 1979) and "Yŏngnam nongak" (Nov. 1983)

"KYŎNGSANG NONGAK"	"YŎNGNAM NONGAK"
Ŏllimgut nori	Kil kunak
Kil kunak nori	Pan kil kunak
Pan kil kunak nori	Tadŭraegi
Tŏppaegi pŏkku nori	Yŏngsan tadŭraegi
Pan tadŭraegi	Yŏngyŏlch'ae
Chajin ŏllim pŏkku nori	Pyŏldalgŏri
Yŏngsan tadŭraegi	Ssangjinp'uri
Pyŏlgŏri talgŏri	Maeji
Obangjin nori	
Kutkŏri nori	
Tŏppaegi nori	
Ssangjinp'uri (Hohogut)	
Samch'agut nori (Kaein nori)	

The Dynamics of Rhythmic Form **45**

ered less as stand-alone sections drawn from the p'ungmul source, however, than as transitional and concluding passages for the new arrangement. The 1983 "Yŏngnam nongak" still retains core rhythmic patterns that can clearly be traced back to Chinju Samch'ŏnp'o nongak. But by 1983, it also begins its journey in becoming identified as a classic "composition" in the samul nori repertory. It is this version that is learned and practiced by amateur enthusiasts within and outside South Korea.

For the beginner just getting a hold of basic technique, there are challenging rhythmic patterns to learn and memorize in "Yŏngnam nongak," like the opening *kil kunak* pattern. Some beginning students also often find the traditional method of learning patterns by oral transmission difficult—favoring the use of notation over imitating and remembering drumming syllables. In contrast, karak such as *pyŏldalgŏri* are rather simple to pick up and fun to play in an ensemble. Since karak are typically learned separately and then patched together, I contend that the modular structure makes it easier for beginners or non-musicians to learn. While there is complexity to the rhythms, there is also a great deal of repetition built into samul nori "compositions" and the learning process. In the next section, I discuss the different formal properties of SamulNori's popular "Yŏngnam nongak" arrangement/composition. Rather than developing complicated analytical models to explain how "Yŏngnam nongak" works, I rely instead on the materials that are most readily available for SamulNori's global fan base—SamulNori's recordings and its pedagogical materials that were developed specifically for samul nori enthusiasts.

RHYTHMIC FORM OF "YŎNGNAM NONGAK"

The two-video set produced by the Overseas Koreans Foundation (OKF) is a valuable resource for beginning students of samul nori. Titled *A SamulNori Class with Kim Duk Soo*, the videos feature SamulNori's founding member Kim Duk Soo providing lessons on the core pieces in the samul nori repertory (Overseas Koreans Foundation 1999). Kim also presents historical context for the samul nori genre. As the instructional videos aim "to provide a systematic teaching device for overseas Koreans in learning their cultural roots," the lessons are all given in Korean and subtitled in English.[17] The two videos are organized into three parts: (1) What is samul nori?; (2) The basic *anjŭnban*, the "seated performance"; and (3) The basic *sŏnban*, the standing performance. "Yŏngnam nongak" is the subject of part two. For this lesson, Kim explains the piece's rhythmic form—

FIGURE 2.3 P'ungmul choreography for *kil kunak*.

taking time to systematically address each karak/section individually. He provides some historical context for the rhythmic pattern and the p'ungmul choreography that correlates to it. This is followed by a demonstration of the karak by former members of SamulNori Hanullim (now known as Samul GwangDae). A complete performance of "Yŏngnam nongak" is then presented to the viewer at the conclusion of part two.

In the video, Kim explains that "Yŏngnam nongak" begins with a nod to its military origins, with a karak known as *kil kunak*. Translated literally as "road military music," *kil kunak* is a representative rhythmic pattern from Chinju Samch'ŏnp'o nongak. In the distant past, it was used in military processionals. Unlike some of the other karak that are more appropriate for dance, *kil kunak* is tailored for walking or processing. In the back of the 2004 notational booklet that was published by SamulNori Hanullim, we see a graphic that looks similar to figure 2.3.

The figure depicts an aerial view of the choreography that a p'ungmul band follows during the *kil kunak* section. As the musical leader of the group, the kkwaenggwari player leads the musicians and other performers in a ground formation known as *chinbŏp* that winds from one side to the other. The movement of musicians gradually segues into a circular formation, which is depicted by the direction of the arrow in the figure. The number of times the *kil kunak* pattern repeats as a cycle is at the discretion of the lead kkwaenggwari player.

The Dynamics of Rhythmic Form **47**

With the danced, choreographic element excised from "Yŏngnam nongak," the SamulNori quartet played rhythmic patterns such as *kil kunak* in a seated position onstage. The elimination of dance and large-scale choreographies from SamulNori's seated works (*anjŭnban*) adjusted the focus to the sonic dimension of musical performance. This shift enabled the development of a kind of technical virtuosity that eventually became synonymous with the SamulNori quartet. The rhythmic patterns also developed more complexity in their variations.

We can observe this in the 1983 Nonesuch recording, where the *kil kunak* pattern—repeated a total of twelve times—becomes especially intricate and difficult during the tenth, eleventh, and twelfth iterations of the cycle. The changgo (played by Kim Duk Soo) and the kkwaenggwari (played by Kim Yong-bae), in particular, render increasingly minute subdivisions of beats or what can also be described as rhythmic "grace note" figures. These additional percussive strokes fill in the cycle (one *kil kunak* pattern) and create a denser sonic texture. By the last cyclic iterations of the *kil kunak* pattern, the opening section has increased in dynamic level and in intensity. This is not a surprising move, given the quartet's level of musicianship and technical mastery of their respective instruments. The signature lineup—Kim Duk Soo, Kim Yong-bae, Lee Kwang Soo, and Choi Jong Sil—were all masters of percussion who were also driven by a competitive spirit that emerged when they performed together. We hear Kim Yong-bae, for instance, match the speed and intensity of the kkwaenggwari part with Kim Duk Soo's virtuosic display on the changgo.

The ching and the puk parts also become louder and more active with the repetition of cycles in *kil kunak*. In the beginning of "Yŏngnam nongak," the *kil kunak* cycle is performed quietly, at a slow and stately pace. By the time we get to the tenth iteration of the cycle, which is played much faster, the strikes on the ching draw closer together and become more insistent and aggressive. The reverberations create a near-hypnotic ringing effect, and build to a climax by the end of the twelfth cycle, only to segue into a new rhythmic pattern. The deep resonant sound of the ching and the almost shrill, brassy timbre of the kkwaenggwari—in combination with the two drums—create a complex, polytimbral texture that is foregrounded in the last iterations of *kil kunak*.

Based on SamulNori's notation for "Yŏngnam nongak," the basic *kil kunak* pattern is shown in figure 2.4.[18] The notation includes all four parts—kkwaenggwari, ching, changgo, and puk. Since the changgo is a double-headed drum, the changgo notation reflects that it should be played on both left and right sides.

While one complete iteration of *kil kunak* lasts a lengthy thirty-six beats,

	1	2	3	4	5	6	7	8	9	10	11	12	13	14	15	16	17
Kkwaenggwari	O	O o O	O	O o O	O	O o O o O	O	O o O o O	O	O o O o O	O	O o O o
Ching	O			O			O			O			O			O	
Changgo	●	|●	●	|●	●	●|◉	●	●|◉	●	●|◉	●	●|◉	●
	O	O	O	O	O	O	O	O	O	O	O	O	O	O	O	O
Puk	O	o	o	O	o	o	O	o	o	O	o	o	O	o	o	O	o

18	19	20	21	22	23	24	25	26	27	28	29	30	31	32	33	34	35	36
O	O		o	O o O		O o O o O o O		O		O		O	
	O				O					O		O		O	
●	|◉	|●	●		●|◉	|●	|●	●		●		●		●
O	O	O	O	O		O	O	O	O	O		O		O		O
o	O		O	o	O		O	o	O	o	O		O		O		O

FIGURE 2.4 *Kil kunak* notation.

FIGURE 2.5
"*Wŏn-pang-kak*"
metric indicator
for *kil kunak*.

SamulNori's notation typically breaks down the pattern into fifteen smaller units, which are then grouped into three pairs of three beats and three trios of two beats (3+3/3+3/3+3/2+2+2/2+2+2/2+2+2). The forward slashes represent these groupings of threes and twos. Im Dong-chang [Im Tongch'ang] — a composer-pianist who befriended the SamulNori quartet in the 1980s — is credited with creating a notational system for samul nori's rhythm-based compositions (Im Dong-chang interview, August 6, 2010). Im also developed a design for visually representing the metric organization of a rhythmic pattern. Within the outline of three overlapping circles, Im placed numbers, referred to as "*wŏn-pang-kak*," that correspond to the number of beats and pulses within a rhythmic cycle.

The image is placed to the left of the notation for each percussion instrument. Somewhat nonintuitive at first glance, the graphic is described with clarity by Nathan Hesselink: "*Wŏn*, the 'largest encompassing entity,' now represents the cycle in its entirety, i.e. a *hanbae* (unit) or 'one bar' (in Western musical terms). The next smaller division of *pang*, or 'pillar which divides the entity,' is equated with a beat or 'pulse,' called a small *hanbae*. Divisions of the beat or 'units' are equivalent to *kak*, the smallest *hanbae* of a rhythmic cycle."

Using the image shown in figure 2.5 (called a "metric visual indicator") as an

The Dynamics of Rhythmic Form **49**

example, Hesselink explains further: "When placed at the beginning of a bar of notation, this figure indicates a single cycle (*wŏn* = 1) composed of four beats (*pang* = 4), each beat further composed of three smaller divisions (*kak*: 3 × 4 beats = 12), similar in surface structure to the Western meter of 12/8. Importantly, this metric visual indicator reinforces in the sensitive learner the broader connections that exist between rhythm, the performer's body, the sound of the instruments, and mankind's place within the cosmos" (Hesselink 2012, 97).[19]

In *kil kunak,* then, the numbers correspond to one unit/*hanbae* (*wŏn* = 1) composed of fifteen beats (*pang* = 15), with each beat subdivided into thirty-six smaller beats or pulses (*kak* = 36). The changgo, however, has a more active part (*wŏn* = 1 / *pang* = 15 / *kak* = 72) that plays even smaller subdivisions of the beat as the pattern is repeated. Although SamulNori's notation indicates that there is an acceleration and crescendo in this section, it does not include all the possible variations that can be played on the changgo or kkwaenggwari. Nor does the notation specify the number of repetitions for the pattern (as this decision can be determined by the performers).

In the 1983 recording, *kil kunak* is repeated twelve times, and lasts a total of two minutes and thirty seconds. Within this short amount of time, the performers engage in a memorable rendering of *kil kunak*—one that features an intensification in energy, crescendo in dynamic level, increase in number of percussive strokes played, and noticeable acceleration in tempo. It can be argued that it is in this rendering of *kil kunak* where the SamulNori quartet makes its professional departure from Chinju Samch'ŏnp'o nongak, achieving a level of technical prowess that is physically impossible to attain in p'ungmul. Even in comparison to the 1979 recording of "Kyŏngsang nongak," SamulNori's 1983 interpretation of *kil kunak* seems to have surged forward in speed, momentum, and energy—setting a new standard for the quartet's performances and what would later come to be known as the samul nori genre. After the twelfth iteration of *kil kunak* in the 1983 recording, the intensity suddenly ebbs after the seamless transition into the next pattern, the *pan kil kunak*. This dramatic shift in energy is an important characteristic of the sectional form of "Yŏngnam nongak."

In terms of metrical structure, the *pan kil kunak* pattern is organized around four primary beats (*pang* = 4), which are further subdivided into twelve beats (*kak* = 12). The ching marks the first beat of the pattern or cycle. (In the 1983 recording, *pan kil kunak* is repeated twenty-two times.) The twelve beats are then grouped accordingly: (3+3/2+2+2).

In part two of *A SamulNori Class with Kim Duk Soo*, Kim states that while the

	1	2	3	4	5	6	7	8	9	10	11	12
Kkwaenggwari	O	o	o	O	o	o	O	o	O		O	
Ching	O											
Changgo		⊙	⊙		⊙	⊙		⊙			●	●
	O			O			O		O			
Puk	O			O			O		O			

FIGURE 2.6 *Pan kil kunak* notation.

rhythm itself may be simple to learn, it is important for performers to understand and feel the correct pairing of stressed and unstressed beats. This, Kim Duk Soo observes, is akin to the particular intonation employed in the Kyŏngsang dialect (noted for its use of pitched accents and fricatives). Because of the metrical shift between three and two beat-units in *pan kil kunak*, there is a slight moment of syncopation that can be heard in the puk, changgo, and kkwaenggwari parts (e.g., beat four, or beat nine if counting the smaller subdivisions). This syncopation is emphasized or accented by the changgo, kkwaenggwari, and puk (see figure 2.6).

SamulNori's *pan kil kunak* is markedly different in feel from *kil kunak*. Unlike the *kil kunak*, the *pan kil kunak* maintains its tempo and does not accelerate. And whereas *kil kunak* grows increasingly complex, dense, and virtuosic, *pan kil kunak* does not feature variations and seems to relish its syncopated "groove." In the 1983 recording, the pattern is repeated twenty-two times (1:30–2:15). It is only on the last iteration of the pattern when the kkwaenggwari player gives a signal that indicates that a new cycle follows immediately afterward.

In Chinju Samch'onp'o nongak, *pan kil kunak* is one of the patterns played in the *kil kunak* section—fourth of the twelve different sections. In terms of p'ungmul choreography, *pan kil kunak* often picks up where *kil kunak* leaves off. SamulNori Hanullim's notational booklet uses the S-shaped image (figure 2.7) to explain how the circular formation that is created by the end of *kil kunak* weaves into the sinuous shape. The "S" line divides the circle into two equal parts, and the shape resembles the *t'aegŭk* design—an important Taoist symbol that expresses the concept of yin-yang (opposing yet complementary forces) in nature. In Korea, the *t'aegŭk* symbol is featured prominently in the center of the South Korea flag.

The third section of "Yŏngnam nongak" introduces a rhythmic pattern known as *tadŭraegi*. (The *chinbŏp*/ground formation for this pattern reverses the direction of the *taegŭk* shape that was outlined in *pan kil kunak*.) Equivalent in length

The Dynamics of Rhythmic Form **51**

FIGURE 2.7 P'ungmul choreography for *pan kil kunak*.

to *pan kil kunak*, this karak also has a similar metric organization: (*wŏn* = 1; *pang* = 4; *kak* = 12). Unlike the previous pattern, however, the twelve beats are grouped in four units of three (3+3+3+3), and the phrasing shifts from an emphasis on four primary beats to only two. Kim Duk Soo notes that this contraction from four to two impels a different intake and release of breath, which he calls *hohŭp*.

Translated into English as "breath" or "breathing," *hohŭp* was developed as a pedagogical concept and a series of techniques by SamulNori. It draws a holistic connection between the body, breathing, movement, and rhythm. For its importance in the global transmission of samul nori, I include an extended description from SamulNori's first *Korean Traditional Percussion* workbook (English edition):

> Perhaps the single most important technique that a student of SamulNori's should master is how to breath [sic] correctly. When our breathing techniques become natural and fluid, then correct body position, instrument playing technique and finally proper perception or feel for the rhythm becomes natural also. In this portion of the workbook, basic breathing technique or *hohŭp* and some simple practice exercises to make the technique comfortable for the student will be introduced. . . . Those who have studied traditional [Korean] music will already have an understanding of this phenomenon, but others who have watched SamulNori perform might have wondered how the musicians, without

reference to a written score[,] maintain the proper tempo, and even how they manage to start and finish together and not trespass the boundaries of a certain rhythm they play. The reason, the musicians will tell you, is that staying in time together is the same as maintaining the same *hohŭp*. Breathing correctly ensures that the circle we are creating in our consciousness with *wŏn, pang, kak* and physically by saying *hana-a* does not become, for an instance, an ellipse.

As was mentioned before, the student should begin to think in circles, rather than straight lines. Begin to become comfortable with the idea of a circle and circular motion. As the student progresses in his study of the *samul* instruments, he will find that the instruments themselves are all circles and spherical in construction and that the ribbon of our *sangmo* [tasseled hat] traces only curves and parabola. (Korean Conservatorium of Performing Arts 1990, 18)

In the *tadŭraegi* rhythmic pattern, the quicker intake of breath is coordinated with the upper body moving in an up-and-down motion, all performed at the same pace. SamulNori pedagogue and musician Kim Dong-won [Kim Tongwŏn] has described this integrated movement as "vertical bounce," which is applied even to the seated samul nori compositions (Kim Dong-won, personal communication, June 16, 2013). By performing these deliberate bobbing movements while playing, students are taught to "feel" or embody the rhythmic pattern and synchronize with other members of the ensemble.[20] With the *tadŭraegi* rhythmic pattern—which features a faster paced *hohŭp*—"Yŏngnam nongak" begins a deliberate move toward compression in its form—a move that can best be observed when examining the work as a whole.

A rhythmic pattern called *yŏngsan tadŭraegi* follows suit in the fourth section (*wŏn* = 1; *pang* = 4; *kak* = 12). The duple emphasis in *tadŭraegi* then is contracted even further in the next pattern. In the SamulNori video, Kim ex-

	1	2	3	4	5	6	7	8	9	10	11	12
Kkwaenggwari	O	o	o	O	o	o	O	o	o	O	o	o
Ching	O			O			O			O		
Changgo		●	●		●	●		●	●		●	●
	O			O			O			O		
Puk	O			O			O			O		

FIGURE 2.8 *Yŏngsan tadŭraegi* notation.

plains that in this new section, the phrasing or hohŭp of the pattern shifts from two (tadŭraegi) to one (yŏngsan tadŭraegi).

Figure 2.8 illustrates a steady stream of beats played on the changgo and the kkwaenggwari. And both puk and ching support the ensemble by playing on the first, fourth, seventh, and tenth beats in a cycle that is subdivided into twelve equal beats. In order to help beginning students understand the feeling of the rhythmic pattern, Kim encourages the viewers of the video to zoom out and to think of the larger, overall structure of "Yŏngnam nongak." Whereas the opening *kil kunak* pattern is stately, expansive, and builds in complexity, each successive cycle (*pan kil kunak, tadŭraegi, yŏngsan tadŭraegi*) gradually becomes concise and more compact. As Kim Duk Soo notes, the hohŭp also changes significantly as the performers proceed through the different patterns. By the time performers reach *yŏngsan tadŭraegi*, the hohŭp has shifted to a brisk feeling in "1." In other words, all instruments in the ensemble emphasize the first beat (called *mŏri pak*) of the rhythmic pattern. This sets up a section where two instruments (changgo and kkwaenggwari) play in synchrony, supported by the remaining two. Like the last repetitions of the opening *kil kunak* pattern, the dynamic level increases in this section. *Yŏngsan tadŭraegi* is followed then by a transitional section (*yongyŏlch'ae*) that serves to establish the tempo for the next pattern, *pyŏldalgŏri*.[21]

As mentioned earlier in this chapter, *pyŏldalgŏri* originated from chanted segments in the *pyŏlkut nori* section of Chinju Samch'ŏnp'o nongak. With its agrarian themes and prayers for a good harvest, it was a chant that was performed during the Ch'usŏk fall harvest holiday. Interpreted by SamulNori, however, the chant is incorporated into a tightly knit rhythmic pattern that has now become the most recognizable section in the "Yŏngnam nongak" piece. Although the translation of the chant was included in SamulNori's official program notes, the connection to the agrarian origins of the chant has mostly been lost. In many performances of "Yŏngnam nongak," the agrarian-themed chant is delivered at a breakneck speed, to the point where the text is rendered nearly unintelligible. The shouted lines of the chant, crescendo, and accelerando all serve to heighten the energy of this particular section.

Pyŏldalgŏri is a straightforward rhythmic pattern that begins slowly and quietly and then propels forward in speed in its later repetitions. Unlike the other patterns we have seen, the *wŏn-pang-kak* graphic indicates that *wŏn* = 4, *pang* = 16, *kak* = 32. Here, the cycle is divided into four units of four beats (sixteen total beats). Smaller subdivisions in the changgo and kkwaenggwari result in thirty-

	1	2	3	4	5	6	7	8	9	10	11	12	13	14	15	16
Kkwaenggwari	O	O	O	o	O	O	o	O	o	O	O	o	O	o	O	O	o	O	o	O	o	O
Ching	O				O				O		O		O			
Changgo	●	●	|●		|⊙	|⊙	|●		|●		|●		|⊙	|⊙	|●	
	O	O	O	O	O	O	O	O	O	O	O	O	O	O	O	O
Puk	O	O	o	o	O	o	o	o	O	o	O	o	O	o	o	o

FIGURE 2.9 *Pyŏldalgŏri* notation.

two beats. In the video, Kim Duk Soo demonstrates the feeling of the rhythmic pattern, which is coordinated with the breath and movement of the body. To emphasize the duple meter, Kim walks with purpose while voicing the drumming syllables. The rhythmic pattern is repeated several times before the text is introduced, which Kim explains was a traditional chant that was performed by his ancestors, passed down through the generations.

By the time the performers reach the spoken portion of *pyŏldalgŏri*, the tempo has sped up considerably. The chant is not delivered all at once, but line by line. After each line of text, the first eight beats of the *pyŏldalgŏri* rhythmic pattern (see figure 2.9) are played. A call-and-response between vocal and instrumental parts thus takes place:

1. Hanŭl pogo pyŏrŭl ttago, ttangŭl pogo nongsa chikko; *instrumental response
   Look up at the sky and seize the stars, look down at the ground and till the earth.
2. Olhaedo taep'ungiyo, naenyŏnedo p'ungnyŏn ilse; *instrumental response
   This year's harvest is abundant, next year let it also be so.
3. Tara tara palgŭn tara, taenat kach'i palgŭn tara; *instrumental response
   Moon, moon, bright moon, moon as bright as daylight.
4. Ŏdŭm soge pulpich'i uri nerŭl pich'wŏ chune!; *instrumental response
   In the darkness, your light gives us illumination!

By the time the performers reach the concluding line, which is an invocation, the piece has built to a fever pitch (figure 2.10). There is a large crescendo and ritardando on the final words "gives us illumination." Many samul nori ensembles (including the SamulNori quartet and SamulNori Hanullim) are criticized for playing this too fast—prizing speed over an appreciation for the text's meaning.

The Dynamics of Rhythmic Form 55

	1	2	3	4	5	6	7	8	9	10	11	12	13	14	15	16	
	하늘	보고	별을	따고	땅을	보고	농사	짓고	O	O	O o	O	O o	O o	O o	O	Kkwaenggwari
	Hanŭl	pogo	pyŏrŭl	ttago	ttangŭl	pogo	nongsa	chikko									
	올해	도	대풍	이요	내년	에도	풍년	일세	O				O				Ching
	Olhae-	do	taep'ung	iyo	naenyŏn-	edo	p'ungnyŏn	ilse									
	달아	달아	밝은	달아	대낮	같이	밝은	달아	●	●	|●		|⊙	|⊙	|●		Changgo
	Tara	tara	palgŭn	tara	taenat	kach'i	palgŭn	tara	O	O	O	O	O	O	O	O	
	어둠	속에	불빛	이	우리	너를	비춰	주네!!!	O	O	o	o	O	o	o	o	Puk
	Ŏdum	soge	pulpi-	ch'i	uri	nerul	pich'wŏ	chune!!!									

FIGURE 2.10 *Pyŏldalgŏri* notation with text.

As one of the only portions of spoken text within the samul nori repertoire, the *pyŏldalgŏri* is somewhat of an anomaly. On one hand, it demonstrates samul nori's clear relationship to p'ungmul and Korea's agrarian past through the use of the chant. On the other hand, we witness SamulNori's transformative touch—taking what was once a ritualistic chant and arranging it into an exciting rhythmic pattern that becomes the climax of the piece. In videos of the SamulNori quartet, the performers' bodies bob up and down, arms pumping, as they move to the beat. Then comes the bellowing of the text. Whereas most of *pyŏldalgŏri* is designed to accelerate, the final line is drawn out for dramatic effect.

This rhythmic flexibility and creation of musical tension point to a guiding aesthetic in traditional Korean music. "*Naego, talgo, maetgo, p'ulgo*" can be translated into English as "produce, stir up, fasten, unbind." Folklorist Kim Inu aptly described this concept in relation to Korean music: "A sound is considered complete when these conditions have been met, based on the underlying principle of tension and release. That is to say, the interplay of tension [*kinjang*] and release [*iwan*] is the life of a sound. Although 'producing' (playing with it little by little, skillfully) and 'heating up' (drawing out the energy that has just been produced and making it hot) a sound are of course important in the creation of tension, they are both equally needed for release" (Hesselink 2006, 111).[22]

In a practical context, "*naego, talgo, maetgo, p'ulgo*" refers to a certain degree of flexibility that a performer can engage in during the course of performance. The set of contrasts or binaries (tie and loosen) relates most directly to when the regular beat is slackened and then resumes its normal speed. This is somewhat similar to the concept of Western rubato—the temporary suspension of the beat in order to create an expressive effect in performance. In Korean music, however, the aesthetic is much broader in scope and connects to more pervasively held East Asian concepts of opposing yet complementary forces in nature.

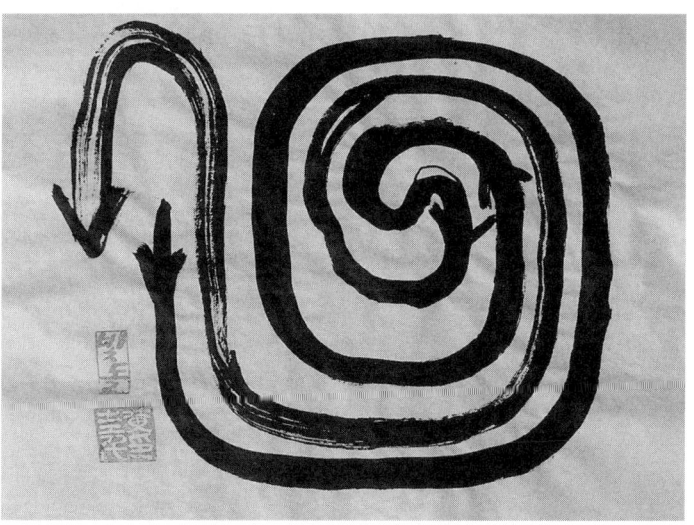

FIGURE 2.11 P'ungmul choreography for *pyŏldalgŏri* and *ssangjinp'uri* 1.

At the same time, navigating between two poles leads to a ratcheting up of tension in the music that is often highlighted by the performer. If one plays with an exceptionally rough touch on a string instrument, it will then be contrasted quickly with a more lyrical mode of playing. Or, in the dramatic form of *p'ansori* (storytelling through song), a vocal passage that features an especially raspy timbre will likely be contrasted with one less gruff. The way in which a performer renders the tension-and-release aesthetic ultimately reveals the artistry of the performer. It is also points to the "dynamic" features found in Korean music, and in a piece such as "Yŏngnam nongak."

After *pyŏldalgŏri* (which sometimes elicits applause from the audience), a multipart section called *ssangjinp'uri* follows immediately, without break. *Ssangjinp'uri* 1 is a simple pattern that features a call-and-response between kkwaenggwari and the remaining instruments. In the notational booklet, we see that the p'ungmul choreography for *ssangjinp'uri* 1 is graphically depicted at first as a snail formation, leading from the *pyŏldalgŏri* (figures 2.11 and 2.12).

The choreography indicates that the p'ungmul ensemble branches out into two separate lines during *ssangjinp'uri* 2 (figure 2.13).

The word *ssangjinp'uri* translates to *ssang* (two or double), *jin* (lines), and *p'uri* (to loosen or release). *Ssangjinp'uri* 2 is organized into *wŏn* = 2, *pang* = 8, *kak* = 24. Kim Duk Soo notes that the rhythmic pattern is felt in two groups of four beats each. After the dramatic buildup of *pyŏldalgŏri*, this section has a more playful

	1	2	3	4	5	6	7	8	9	10	11	12	13	14	15	16	17	18	19	20	21	22	23	24
Kkwaenggwari	○			●		○	○		○	●	○		○	○		○	○		○		○	●	○	
Ching	○												○											
Changgo	●			●		⊙			⊙		●		⊙			⊙			●		⊙		●	
	○						○			○			○	○			○	○		○		○		
Puk	○			●			○		○				○	○			○	○		○		○		

FIGURE 2.12 Notation for *ssangjinp'uri* 2.

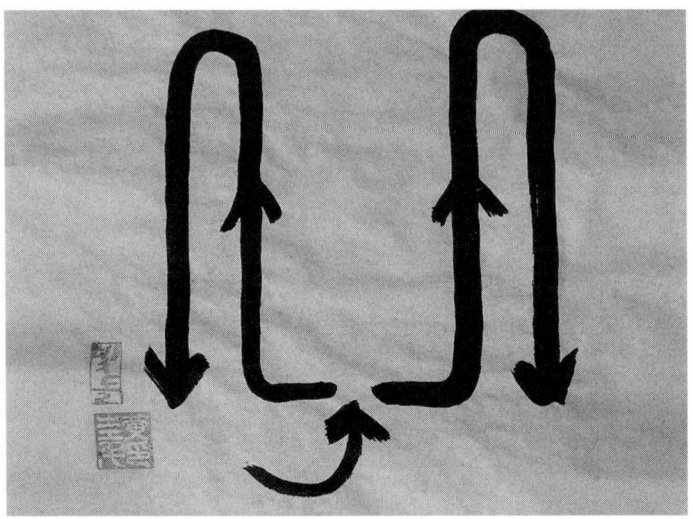

FIGURE 2.13 P'ungmul choreography for *ssangjinp'uri* 2.

and relaxed feel to it. There is a total of six related rhythms in the *ssangjinp'uri* section included in the notational booklet. Similar to the progression of earlier patterns—*kil kunak* to *pan kil kunak*; *tadŭraegi* to *yŏngsan tadŭraegi*—the different *karak* in this section also feature a general tendency to become shorter and simpler as each consecutive rhythm is introduced. Table 2.3 illustrates this move toward concision. The piece ends with a section called *maeji*. "*Maeji*" is derived from the verb *maetta*, which signifies "tying up" or "closure." Again, an accordion-like expansion and contraction take place while the volume and intensity are dialed up for an exciting finish. A brief call-and-response between the kkwaenggwari and the ching drives the energy forward, followed by the kkwaenggwari and changgo playing a steady stream of beats until the conclusion. At the conclusion of "Yŏngnam nongak," the sound of the ching's last beat reverberates for several seconds, ringing into the listeners' ears.

TABLE 2.3 Analysis of "Yŏngnam nongak" rhythmic form

"YŎNGNAM NONGAK" (7:06)	TIME STAMP	NO. OF REPETITIONS	ACCELERATION AT END	MARKED INCREASE IN VOLUME
Kil kunak	0:00	12	yes	yes
Pan kil kunak	2:30	22	no	no
Tadŭraegi	3:18	12	no	yes
Yŏngsan tadŭraegi	3:30	48	no	yes
Yongyŏlch'ae	4:11	transitional passage	no	
Pyŏldalgŏri	4:18	10 (before chant)	yes	yes
Ssangjinp'uri 1 and 2	5:08	4; 10	yes	
Maeji	6:37	transition to end	yes	yes

A DYNAMIC RHYTHMIC FORM

Theorist Joshua Mailman has written prodigiously of temporal dynamic form in Western music. His dissertation argues that musical form should be interpreted as dynamic or as the "retrospective contour of the flux of intensity of qualities" (2010, vii). He aims to challenge oft-held views of musical form as architectonic or structural. While Mailman's choice of repertoire and analytical approaches and methods differ radically from my own, I have benefited from his insights as a music theorist and from his broad-reaching meditation on "dynamism" in relation to musical form. In particular, Mailman's working definition of dynamism theory as an analysis that "asserts motion, change, process, or energy (potential motion, change, or process) as existing in the course of a piece or a performance, as it elapses" (2010, 8) is useful for my own inquiry that fastens formal analysis to ethnography.

I have spent time describing the different rhythmic patterns of "Yŏngnam nongak" in order to explain how the piece is put together as a musical form. It is, in many ways, an illustrative example of "dynamism" at play. If we think back to the discussion that opened the chapter, the word "dynamic" (and its noun form) can signal a variety of things—motion, change, action, energy, and volume in sound. A "dynamism theory," as Mailman posits, then considers this in relation to musical form. I contend that "Yŏngnam nongak" exhibits these qualities of movement and energy shifts in its dynamic rhythmic form. I attribute this partly to the fact that "Yŏngnam nongak" draws its source material from p'ungmul, a multifaceted performance genre that integrates dance and movement with music. But it is also in SamulNori's expert arrangement of the various rhythmic patterns from Chinju Samch'ŏnp'o nongak that "Yŏngnam nongak" exerts a dynamic musical form. This can be observed in the *naego-talgo, maetgo-p'ulgo* (produce–stir up, fasten-unbind) aesthetic that is applied to the sequential ordering of rhythms that brings out contrasts in volume, speed, and metric organization. The rhythm-based form of "Yŏngnam nongak" is thus guided by the relationship of contrasting yet complementary forces.

In describing similar musical aesthetics found in melodic music, noted Korean composer Hwang Byung-ki [Hwang Pyŏnggi] explained that "melodies need to be repeatedly 'tightened' and 'loosened.' Tightening means gathering *him* (strength or energy), somewhat like compressing a spring. Many different techniques are used to accomplish this; perhaps the most impressive method is to produce a sense of strain by increasing the rhythmic density and then, after a climax, reducing it" (Hwang Byung-ki 2001, 816). In several places within the form of "Yŏngnam nongak," we notice intensification effects applied to volume, rhythmic density, meter, and tempi. Over the course of the piece, these effects produce a constant sense of dramatic activity—of motion. The 1983 SamulNori quartet recording of "Yŏngnam nongak" is a perfect demonstration. There are significant contrasts in dynamics—swelling from loud to soft in the span of only a few beats. It is this dynamic process—of moving from one end of the spectrum to another in terms of volume/amplitude, tempo, and degrees of intensity—that often captivates audience members.

Yet, what makes "Yŏngnam nongak" accessible to enthusiasts around the world are the rhythmic patterns—simple enough for an amateur to learn—that are repeated and then patched together to create a composition with a distinct form. Both repetition (rhythmic cycles) and difference (multiple rhythmic patterns) are built into the composition. This modular formal structure helps beginners to process and learn individual sections while simultaneously providing a template for the composition. One of the SamulNori quartet's greatest achievements was to create a dynamic, rhythm-based form that became accessible and legible across cultural boundaries. In the next chapter, we will learn how samul nori's dynamism and growing popularity became an attractive quality to the South Korean government at the turn of the twenty-first century.

THREE

Dynamic Korea and Samul Nori

Samul nori's rhythm-based form proved a significant factor in its ability to traverse international borders. I contend that the design of its form was one that elicited interest while also providing a point of entry to enthusiasts who were eager to try their hand at the foreign percussion genre. This rhythmic form was one of samul nori's greatest assets. But samul nori's story of globalization was also due in large part to the support (both financial and otherwise) that it received from the South Korean government. As the SamulNori quartet began to tour regularly in Europe and the United States in the 1980s, the state took note and thought of ways to both promote and ride its wave of success. SamulNori was invited to take part in several government-sponsored events, some of which were high profile. The quartet accompanied the South Korean representatives who were charged with lighting the Olympic torch for the 1988 Seoul Summer Olympics, for instance. And a few years later, SamulNori was invited to perform at the 1993 Taejŏn Expo, where it led over one thousand drummers in a spectacular percussive display for the international exposition.

When amateur samul nori ensembles began to crop up outside South Korea, the South Korean government supported certain efforts by SamulNori (and later, SamulNori Hanullim) to develop pedagogical materials for the purpose of transmission. Videos and notation books were created and translated into different languages. Mentioned in chapter 2, the video lecture series *A SamulNori Class with Kim Duk Soo* was subtitled into English and underwritten by the Overseas Koreans Foundation—a wing of the Ministry of Foreign Affairs (Overseas Koreans Foundation 1999).[1] This type of state endorsement followed after the positive reception of SamulNori abroad. Or in other words, it was SamulNori's recognition earned *outside* Korea that gave the quartet and the genre a cachet that was then deemed valuable by the state. This phenomenon is not unique to Korea. As David Novak mentions in his ethnographic study of Noise, the Japanese phrase *gyaku yunyu*, or "reverse importation," similarly refers to the domestic validation that artists and athletes receive after attaining fame outside Japan (Novak 2013, 14–15). In SamulNori's case, the South Korean government's endorsement of the popular quartet and genre also proved beneficial to the state.

This chapter centers on the state's cultivation of samul nori as a sonic symbol of South Korea. I employ South Korea's first official nation-branding campaign as a case study to reveal the ways in which the music of samul nori was linked with the "Dynamic Korea" brand and how the state used samul nori's overseas success to trumpet its own dynamic image as a modern, economically viable nation-state. In some ways, samul nori was viewed as one of South Korea's first successful musical exports—well before the advent of K-pop and the much-touted Korean Wave. In this chapter I further expand on the idea of dynamism. Whereas the previous chapter considered samul nori's dynamic rhythmic form, chapter 3 explores dynamism in relation to South Korea's promotion of samul nori. First, I explain why the sounds of samul nori appealed to a modern state with an ongoing image problem.

ENDURING NAMES, INDELIBLE IMAGES

Long before presidential councils on nation branding were formed, Korea has had to reckon with its image to the outside world. For most of the Chosŏn period (1392–1910), Westerners generally viewed unified Korea as an isolated country, uninterested in trade relations. When the peninsular nation slowly opened its doors to the West at the close of the nineteenth century, two monikers made their way into circulation. Appearing in travel writings and armchair ethnographies, the monikers "Land of the Morning Calm" and the "Hermit Kingdom" bespoke Western perceptions of Korea as a quiet and remote country in the Far East. Over time, these two images would come to define a premodern Korea to Westerners.

Two books on Korea, written in English and published during the 1880s, securely established the nicknames. Boston-bred Percival Lowell's *Chosŏn, the Land of the Morning Calm: A Sketch of Korea* was not the first to use the words "morning calm" in print for a Western readership, but was the first text to significantly foster such a depiction (1886). Derived from the English translation of the two Sino-Korean characters that constitute "Chosŏn"—the name by which

Korea was known from 1392 to 1910—morning calm was a poetic turn of phrase from the compound formation of the words for "morning" and "fresh." Huajeong Seok notes that the phrase ("originating from a Westerner's imaginative translation") became a point of departure in Western writings on Korea (2013, 263). Morning calm was employed as an evocative descriptor of Korea by travel writers, diplomats, and missionaries just before the turn of the twentieth century.

A man of many talents, Percival Lowell served as a U.S. diplomat to the Chosŏn government in the late nineteenth century. After already having traveled extensively in Japan, Lowell wrote about his experiences and observations in Korea. *Land of the Morning Calm* covered a range of topics—from geography and climate to aspects of society such as the patriarchal system. Early on in the text, he provided the English translation for Chosŏn and, more importantly, the specific imagery used to accompany it: "The sun rose for them in the peaceful splendor that wraps the morning hours there even to this day, and the sunbeams fell into the valley between the hills and nestled on the land. 'Morning Calm' they called it; and it seemed not so much a name as its very essence. The drowsy *quiet* of the spot lulled them to rest, and they fell asleep, passed away.[2] They were in the world, yet it was to them as if it had passed away. And so they slept on for ages" (1886, 7).

As if stumbling upon the discovery of uncharted territory, Lowell marveled at a culture that seemed otherworldly and impervious to the laws of time. He wrote,

> Like the palace in the fairy tale, everything remained as it had centuries before. Change knew them not, and time stood still. Individuals passed away and were forgotten, but the race seemed immortal. No alien might approach the place; and their neighbors to the north and to the west seemed quite disposed to respect their seclusion, exacting only a tribute for the privilege of being left alone. . . . And so it came to pass that we have here a most remarkable phenomenon, a living fossilization—the preservation intact in this world, the law of whose very existence is change—of the life, the thought, the manners, the dress, of centuries ago. In the Koreans of to-day we are not only looking upon what is strange, we are looking upon what has once been and has elsewhere passed away. (1886, 7)

American Congregationalist minister William Elliot Griffis penned *Corea: The Hermit Nation* (1882) after living in Japan during the early 1870s. Griffis had served as an administrator and an educator in Japan but had never set foot in Korea. As a self-acknowledged armchair researcher, Griffis defended his role as a compiler of sources "who views the whole subject and reduces the many impressions of detail to unity" versus travel writers like Lowell, who merely see "but a portion of the country at one time" (1882, viii).

The Hermit Nation was a synthesis of the then extant literature on Korea, with many materials culled from Japanese sources. This reliance in turn shaped Griffis's analyses and commentary. In an introductory passage describing onomastics (the study of the history and origin of proper names) and geography, for instance, Griffis moves from an unsentimental tone to a foreboding one with an imperialist subtext.

> The native name of the country is Chō-sen (Morning Calm or Fresh Morning), which French writers, always prodigal in the use of vowels, spell Tsio-sen, Teo-cen, or Tchao-sian. The Chinese call it Tung kwo (Eastern Kingdom), and the Manchius, Sol-ho or Solbo. . . . It hangs down between the Middle Kingdom [China] and the Sunrise Land [Japan], separating the Sea of Japan and the Yellow Sea, between the 34th and 43d parallels of north latitude. In its general configuration, when looked at from the westward on a good map, especially the magnificent one made by the Japanese War Department, Chō-sen resembles the outspread wings of a headless butterfly, the lobes of the wings being toward China, and their tops toward Japan. (1882, 3)

At the time of the writing of the text (1877–1880), Griffis was also well aware of Japan's new cultural and political projects aimed at expanding its influence and power in the Far East. It was no secret that one of Japan's pressing political agendas was the incorporation of its closest neighbor to the west—the reclusive Hermit Kingdom.

While Lowell viewed Korea's isolationism as a curious time capsule preserving an exotic, antiquated past, Griffis saw a backward and reclusive state, in need of intervention: "Why should Corea be sealed and mysterious, when Japan, once a hermit, had opened her doors and come out into the world's market-place? When would Corea's awakening come? As one diamond cuts another, why should not Chō-ka (Japan) open Chō-sen (Korea)?" (1882, vi). If Japan had learned to escape isolationism and open its doors to the Western world, then surely its smaller, hermitic neighbor could be coaxed out of its shell, toward the light of modernity. Concluding his first chapter, Griffis wrote: "While the last of the hermit nations awaits some gallant Perry of the future, we may hope that the same brilliant path of progress on which the Sunrise Kingdom has entered, awaits the Land of Morning Calm" (1882, 10).

The metaphorical imagery conjured by Griffis's Hermit Nation—a reclusive state that was still cloaked in darkness from civilization and progress—was the same logic and rationale that Japan used for its imperialist conquests at the turn of the twentieth century. By 1910, Korea was officially annexed by Japan. The "Hermit Nation" as euphemism suggested not only a country in isolation, but one that was developmentally stunted as a result of its lack of contact with the outside world. Even Lowell's representation of Korea as Land of the Morning Calm—penned with a sense of exploratory wonder—evoked a nation quietly biding its time, oblivious of the sounds of modernization and industrialization occurring just outside its doors.

The pair of nicknames and their associated images have had unusual staying power. Numerous books, magazines, articles, and blogs still make use of the appellations that were first (in)famously applied by Lowell and Griffis. "Morning Calm" serves as the masthead for the weekly newspaper of the United States Forces Korea, as well as the monthly in-flight magazine for South Korea's major airline, Korean Air. In contrast, the Hermit Kingdom or "Hermit Nation" hewed to more of its original associations as set by Griffis. What changed was the context and application. No longer was it the nickname for the isolationist peninsular nation just before the dawn of the twentieth century, but rather the go-to descriptor for the reclusive and mysterious Communist state that developed north of the thirty-eighth parallel. With almost seamless precision, the Western press successfully accomplished a metonymic coup; the Hermit Kingdom that once referred to premodern Korea now almost exclusively pointed to North Korea and its policies of *juche* (*chuch'e*) or self-reliance. U.S. media outlets continue to deploy the label, in reference to North Korea.

A BRAND-NEW IDENTITY

Remarkably, even a century after their first iterations, the accompanying images of placidity and reclusion left by Morning Calm and Hermit Kingdom have proven hard to shake off. This is irrespective of the tremendous changes that occurred on the Korean peninsula during the twentieth century. After Korea's liberation from Japanese rule in 1945, the division of the peninsula at the thirty-eighth parallel and the formation of North and South Korea led to two competing ideological visions, with communism taking hold in the north and a U.S.-backed nominal democracy in the south. The Korean War (1950–1953) took a devastating toll on both sides, resulting in years devoted to recovery and reconstruction efforts. While North Korea became increasingly isolationist after the conflict, South Korea, on the other hand, coupled the process of rebuilding with export-led industrialization under the Park Chung Hee [Pak Chŏnghŭi] regime (1963–1979). By the 1980s, even in the midst of massive nationwide democratization struggles, the South Korean economy was steadily building its automotive industry. And a decade later, significant growth was seen in automotive, manufacturing, and IT industries, earning South Korea the title phrase of the "Miracle on the Han River."

After the 1997 IMF financial crisis hit South Korea, the incoming Kim Dae Jung [Kim Taejung] administration (1998–2003) attempted to stabilize the economy through various structural reforms. Within just a few years, the South Korean economy recovered. It was roughly at the same time, in the late 1990s, when the early Korean Wave, or Hallyu, started to take shape in parts of East Asia. Kim Dae Jung's administration observed the growing interest in South Korean films, dramas, and popular music outside South Korea and supported the development of the South Korean cultural industry as a new economic policy (Jeon, Won Kyung 2013, 108–9). The rising influence of the Korean Wave and the global recognition of brands such as Samsung and LG gradually came to be at odds with the long-held images of Korea as a quiet and unassuming nation. In other words, Morning Calm was no longer tenable as a descriptor for South Korea's market economy at the turn of the twenty-first century.

In light of these developments, the South Korean government began to think carefully about the image it wanted to project to the world, and a series of discussions on "image making" took place during the late 1990s. The opening of the 2002 FIFA World Cup in South Korea and Japan became an opportune moment to promote a new image for South Korea, and an "extensive search was made to find the best possible slogan for defining Korea" (Korean Overseas Information Service 2007, 4).[3] Public relations experts were consulted on English-language slogans, and an open call for submissions was even sent out to the general public. In late 2001, a decision was issued by the Kim Dae Jung administration. Rendered in English script, "Dynamic Korea" was designated as South Korea's first official national slogan. For those who were present in the stands or the streets during the 2002 World Cup in Seoul, Dynamic Korea did indeed seem like an apt descriptor for the intense passion and energy coming from South Korean fans. The slogan was meant to symbolically convey more than just homegrown enthusiasm for football, however. A brochure published by the Korean Overseas Information Service in September 2007 gave a conceptual overview of the Dynamic Korea campaign, which by then was considered a full-fledged "nation brand." The brochure identified some of the central reasons as to why "dynamism" was the perfect word to encapsulate South Korea's new identity in the twenty-first century.

> The achievements made in cultural, economic, scientific and political sectors have their roots in the *constantly evolving dynamism* of Korea and its people, a dynamism which has endured for thousands of years.[4] Dynamic Korea represents the vibrant spirit; the heritage of the Korean people that will be passed to future generations. It embodies the unshakable moral strength that has overcome so much hardship, as well as a vision which proactively explores the future.
>
> - [South] Korea has risen from the ashes of the Korean War to achieve remarkable economic development over the past half-century.
> - A modern democracy, founded after overcoming the heartrending pain of foreign occupation and national division, is eagerly working towards reunification.
> - [South] Korean popular culture, based upon unique national traits, is spreading around the world, taking advantage of the Hallyu (Korean Wave) phenomenon.
> - [South] Korea is emerging as a technological powerhouse in the 21st century. (2007, 5)

A byline of "the Hub of Asia" was sometimes used in conjunction with the primary slogan. Taken as a whole, the slogan(s) projected grand aspirations and an extension of the *segyehwa* (globalization) policy that was first brought into play during the Kim Young Sam [Kim Yŏngsam] administration (1993–1998). By the time of the 2002 World Cup, the successive Kim Dae Jung administration had enacted neoliberal economic reforms and sought to highlight South Korea's new position as an undisputed player in the global economy. A new international airport had been built in Inch'ŏn the year before, and the government began to envision a future for Seoul as a global hub city. With ambitious plans laid, the South Korean government needed next to "provide the world [with] a differentiated image of [South] Korea in this fast-paced 21st century" (Korean Overseas Information Service 2007, 14).

The Dynamic Korea slogan reflected a new self-awareness and a rhetorical challenge to the images of calmness, stasis, and isolationism that were summoned

FIGURE 3.1 "Kim Duk Soo's Dynamic Korea" program. Courtesy of SamulNori Hanullim.

by Morning Calm and Hermit Kingdom. Although the latter two were not slogans in the same way that Dynamic Korea was, the image-recall functions were nonetheless similar. All three were intended to represent a quintessential Korean character to the West. In the case of Dynamic Korea, however, it was South Korea that began to take control of its own image and, hence, call its own shots.

DYNAMIC KOREA, DYNAMIC SAMUL NORI

The Dynamic Korea slogan and branding campaign found a sonic counterpart in the genre of samul nori. In March 2002, months before the opening of the FIFA World Cup, Kim and members of the SamulNori Hanullim organization were chosen by the Korean Overseas Information Service to be the official music troupe to represent South Korea's cultural events during the competition (Hong Sŏngsik 2002). The official World Cup anthem that year, composed by the Greek composer Vangelis, also featured the music of Kim Duk Soo's SamulNori group and Japan's renowned taiko ensemble, Kodo Drummers. Quick to jump on the Dynamic Korea brandwagon, Kim Duk Soo produced an ambitious show that ran from June 1 to 20, 2002, at the Hanjeon Artspool Center (Hanjŏn Ach'ŭp'ul Sent'ŏ) in southern Seoul (figure 3.1). The show was perfectly timed to synchronize with the festivities surrounding the opening of the World Cup (May 31 to June 30, 2002).

Of its many sponsors, Kim Duk Soo's Dynamic Korea received support and funding directly from various divisions within the South Korean government (e.g., the Ministry of Culture and Tourism, the Korean Government Information Agency, and the Korea National Tourism Organization).[5] Kim carefully designed the program to highlight a variety of genres of Korean folk music and dance to appeal to foreign visitors. An excerpt from the bilingual program notes stated, "The essences of traditional Korean song, dance and music have been brought together to form one magnificent show. . . . Throughout his life, Kim Duk Soo has worked towards introducing and spreading Korean performing arts all over the world. 'Dynamic Korea' . . . is sure to bring excitement to both foreigners and Korean citizens" (Hanjeon Artspool Center 2002, 12).

KIM DUK SOO'S DYNAMIC KOREA PROGRAM

1. Spirit of Korea: "Ssikkim" [solo dance]
2. Drums of Korea: "Ilgohwarak" [percussion ensemble]
3. Voice of Korea: "The Rabbit Story" [p'ansori excerpt]
4. Rhythm of Korea: "Samdo nongak karak" [samul nori]
5. Beautiful Korea: "Puch'ae ch'um" [fan dance]
6. Dynamic Korea: "P'an kut" [samul nori]
7. World Cup Korea: "A-he-hŏ" [newly composed song with percussion accompaniment]

Likely inspired by the branding concept behind "Dynamic Korea," each part of the program was prefaced by a pithy and symbolic phrase. "Voice of Korea," for instance, was linked to a segment called "The Rabbit Story," drawn from the p'ansori epic of Sugungga (Tale of the underwater palace), and "Beautiful Korea" featured an all-female dance ensemble performing the colorful fan dance.[6] While Kim Duk Soo's Dynamic Korea may have resembled the Korean traditional music (kugak) variety programs presented at places like the National Gugak Center (Kungnip Kugagwŏn) and Chongdong Theater (Chŏngdong Kŭkchang), the value accorded to percussion music was made explicit in the English portion of the program notes:[7]

Korea can suitably be referred to as a nation of percussion. Indeed, percussion has been used for over thousands of years in all aspects of life from village festivals and sacrificial rites to labor-oriented and even military purposes. Without percussion, festivals and rituals would have been lacking a fundamental ingredient.... The late 1970s sparked a renaissance in Korean percussion, which culminated in the formation of SamulNori. SamulNori, which describes a genre of percussion as well as serving as the name of [South] Korea's leading traditional performance group, literally means "the play of four things." For over twenty years, SamulNori have performed throughout the world and have acclaimed international fame [sic]. Audiences have gasped in awe, finding it hard to express the feeling they perceived with the music and experience of SamulNori descended onto them. (2002, 5–6)

On June 19, 2002, I attended the penultimate performance of Kim Duk Soo's Dynamic Korea in southern Seoul. Given that the South Korean football team had just defeated Italy the day prior, the excitement in the theater was palpable. When two of the "greatest hits" of the SamulNori repertory—"Samdo nongak karak" and "P'an kut"—were performed, viewers reacted with shouts, cheers, and applause, and true to the program notes, even the occasional gasp. Kim Duk Soo himself contributed to the atmosphere of excitement. Taking the microphone to give the obligatory remarks (*maent'ŭ*), Kim made sure to drive home the point that Dynamic Korea resonated on many different levels—from the complex rhythms heard in the evening's performance to the fever-pitched, patriotic fervor of Korean football fans. Moreover, South Korea's qualification into the quarterfinal match was seen as an allegory for the country's entrée into global markets as an innovator in digital technology.[8] Kim led the audience in a few cheers that were already being chanted at FIFA games and introduced the concluding number "World Cup Korea." All performers appeared onstage, singing a chant composed by Kim in 1999 called "A-he-hŏ," accompanied by the sounds of the samul nori instruments.[9] This segued into what is commonly called the *twip'uri* segment, where audience members took to the stage, circling around with the dancing performers and drummers.

Kim Duk Soo's vision of Dynamic Korea was not limited to a three-week run, however. In fact, the sounds of Korean percussion could be heard in the sports arenas, as Kim Duk Soo and members of the SamulNori Hanullim organization appeared prominently in the stands for Korean matches during the World Cup. The percussionists were accompanists for the de facto cheerleading squad of the matches—the South Korean public.

Instead of the canonic pieces of the samul nori repertory, the percussionists adapted basic rhythms to accompany the chants or longer cheering (or "support") songs (ŭngwŏn'ga). Although the millions of fans in the stands and the streets were fully equipped to cheer on their favorite team, the sounds of the samul nori percussion instruments (whether prerecorded and broadcast, or performed live) were folded into the sonic texture and added to the intensity of the cheers.[10]

On the whole, South Korean chants are exceptionally rhythmic, and South Korean fans are no strangers to embodying the rhythms. Fans fervently clap their hands or strike pairs of plastic-tube noisemakers to the basic pulse. Known in the United States as ThunderStix or ClapperStix, the ŭngwŏn maktae p'ungsŏn actually trace their origins to South Korea in the early 1990s, for use in baseball games (Sandomir 2002). During the 2002 World Cup, these plastic idiophones were ubiquitous props for South Korean football fans. Unlike the buzzing monotony of the vuvuzelas of the 2010 South African World Cup, however, the ŭngwŏn maktae p'ungsŏn were *rhythmic* noisemakers.

If there was one signature chant of the 2002 World Cup, it would have been the simple yet memorable "Taehan Min'guk"—the country's name in Korean. Literally the "Great Han People's Nation," Taehan Min'guk is translated more commonly as the Republic of Korea (South Korea's legal name). During the matches, the chant thundered throughout the stands and streets, articulating a sense of collective identity while conveying strong currents of ethnic nationalism. The Red Devil Corea National Football Team Supporters Club (the Pulgŭn angma) claimed "Taehan Min'guk" as their own sonic slogan.[11] According to anthropologist Rachael Miyung Joo, the Red Devils prided themselves on promoting a fan culture that used distinctive Korean symbols: "Their chants emphasized the use of *Han'guk mal* (Korean spoken language) and incorporated elements of traditional folk culture, including songs like 'Arirang,' traditional dress, and Korean drums" (Joo, Rachael Miyung 2006, 50). Savvy with social media, South Korea's most organized and dedicated football fan club had a stroke of luck when a major telecommunications company (SK Telecom) agreed to sponsor a Red Devils commercial that was designed to instruct the viewing public on how to perform the "Taehan Min'guk" chant properly—complete with choreographed gestures of outstretched arms.[12] During the 2002 World Cup, the chant was performed by millions of South Korean fans—honorary Red Devils—often at the drop of a hat.

In the same spirit of didacticism, SamulNori Hanullim produced an instructional video called "Samul nori chants: Program for utilizing traditional rhythms for the World Cup cheers" (*Samul ŭngwŏn: Wŏldŭk'ŏp ŭngwŏn ŭl wihan chŏnt'ong ridŭm hwallyong p'ŭrogŭraem*). The video received financial backing from the Ministry of Government Administration and Home Affairs and the Red Devils. Appearing at the start of the video, Kim Duk Soo states: "SamulNori [Hanullim] and the Red Devils have teamed up to create the most quintessential 'Korean'-sounding chants. These samul nori chants can be performed by anyone, being rhythms that are simple, *dynamic*, and energizing—thus enabling us to summon up a fighting spirit.[13] Please join us in learning these samul nori chants and join together in uplifting our nation's spirit" (SamulNori Hanullim 2002).

Kim uses the Korean word for "dynamic"—*yŏkdongjŏgin*—to describe these "Korean"-sounding rhythmic chants that are both easy to learn and galvanizing to perform. This is an important assertion by Kim Duk Soo that reminds us of the central claim of this book—that samul nori's dynamic rhythm-based form was critical in its global transmission. But it also speaks to the ways in which "dynamism" emerged as a positive quality that the South Korean government coveted as it sought to redefine its image through nation branding. The 2002 World Cup was a perfect venue for the South Korean government to roll out this new image.

After Kim Duk Soo's introduction, the video then turns to the former educational director of SamulNori Hanullim, Kim Dong-won [Kim Tongwŏn].[14] He explains the function of each rhythmic chant, as well as the provenance of some of the rhythmic patterns. Many of these patterns are featured in samul nori but hark back to regional variants of p'ungmul. Explanations are followed by demonstrations of the actual rhythms and chants. A few of the examples include "A-he-hŏ," "Arirang," "2-3-4-Han'guk," and "Taehan Min'guk." And although the "Taehan Min'guk" chant is not a South Korean invention, it is nonetheless featured prominently as an essential Korean chant on the instructional video.[15] On the video, the chant begins with the rhythmic motive of five beats (articulated through the clapping of ThunderStix and accompanied by samul nori instruments), followed by the shouting of the syllables *tae, han, min*, and *guk*. Members of the SamulNori Hanullim team and "stand-in" fans perform a gesture (outstretching of the arms) on the first and third syllables of the phrase.

In contrast to the SK Telecom "Taehan Min'guk" chant commercial that aired on South Korean television, it is improbable that the SamulNori Hanullim video was widely viewed by the South Korean public. The video was not commercially available but distributed only to individuals and civic and cultural institutions.[16] And even though there was an attempt to compose effective chants for the South Korean football fans, not all of the *ŭngwŏn'ga* that were featured on the video actually made it into the stands. A folk song–inspired chant ("Kkwae ch'i na ch'ing ch'ing"), for instance, that was intended to be shouted immediately following a scored goal never caught on among fans. And a variation of the "Taehan Min'guk" chant that employed a rhythmic pattern known as *yukch'ae* also never took hold. Even despite these shortcomings, the production (and government backing) of the video itself attests to Kim Duk Soo's concerted efforts to transpose the energy levels felt in samul nori performances to a specific site of engagement—an international sporting event where the world's eyes and ears would be focused on South Korea (figure 3.2).

In June 2002, several million South Korean fans flocked to the arenas and streets to form a unified front for Team Korea. When South Korea unexpectedly advanced to the semifinals, against all odds, the nation became transfixed by the sporting event. Estimates place several million people in the streets of Seoul alone during the seven South Korean matches (Korea.net: Gateway to Korea 2002). Fans donned red T-shirts en masse to symbolize their support for the South Korean football team. Aerial photographs document the sea of crimson that transformed the visual landscape of Seoul, most notably the iconic Kwanghwamun thoroughfare. Coupled with the frenzied cheers, it did seem that the entire country—which often suffers from divisive regional politics—was magically transformed into a single collective body during the World Cup.[17]

The allusion to communist ideology notwithstanding, the Red Devils and their newly subscribed fans wore their patriotism on their sleeves while simultaneously voicing their love of the team and the country. If ethnic nationalism could have a soundtrack, it might have sounded like the mantras of "O p'ilsŭng K'oria" (O, victory Korea) and "Taehan Min'guk," accompanied by the thumping of ThunderStix. The rhythmic chanting in unison enabled the performance of a collective identity, a phenomenon that ethnomusicologist Joshua Pilzer dubs a kind of "entrained nationalism" (Pilzer 2011). I contend that this bodily entrainment was facilitated by the sounds of percussive rhythms, especially in the case of the Dynamic Korea campaign. The instructional video produced by SamulNori Hanullim, for example, reveals a targeted approach to harness the mobilizing potential of rhythmic chants for collective expressions of nationalism. And as heard in the stands of the 2002 World Cup, the sounds of Dynamic Korea—cheers, chants, claps, and shouts accompanied by drums and noisemakers—were energetic and loud in volume. These sonic articulations of "dynamism" in action contrasted sharply with the calm and quiet images associated with Korea's former sobriquets.[18] By the turn of the new millennium, the message

FIGURE 3.2 Samul (nori) chants for the World Cup—videocassette cover of instructional video. Courtesy of SamulNori Hanullim.

became loud and clear. South Korea had awoken from the morning calm of its slumber and isolation and was ready to assert its brand-new, competitive identity.

SOUTH KOREA'S NATION-BRANDING STRATEGY

The "nation brand" is a concept that was first developed by British consultant Simon Anholt in 1996. Anholt contended that the perceptions (whether they are founded in fact or fiction) of a country's image work in much the same way that product brands function. For a commercial brand to be financially successful, it must have a reputable name value. The perceptions that are formed about a country, Anholt contended, "can have a significant impact on the way that overseas consumers view their products, and the way they behave towards those countries in sport, politics, trade, and cultural matters" (Anholt 2003, 109). By the same token, those perceptions will "affect their propensity to visit or relocate or invest there; their willingness to partner with such countries in international affairs; and whether they are more likely to interpret the actions and behaviors of those countries in a positive or negative light" (109). Thus, the image of a country is a powerful index of how other nation-states perceive and treat it.

Although Anholt has emphatically reiterated that his central idea has always been of the "nation brand" and not of "nation branding" (e.g., the ways in which a nation-state can employ marketing strategies to actively shape international opinions of a country's brand image), it seems that the practice of "branding" has come to stay (Anholt 2011). Melissa Aronczyk's *Branding the Nation: The Global Business of National Identity* examines how nation branding has become a worldwide phenomenon and a professional transnational practice in the early twenty-first century (2013). Countries now routinely enlist corporate branding consultants to help ameliorate their image—particularly if it is a negative one. Aronczyk asserts that the goal of nation branding is "to make the nation *matter* in a world where borders and boundaries appear increasingly obsolete" (3). Moreover, the project of nation branding is seen as a way to promote a clear and coherent national identity and to "animate the spirit of its citizens in the service of national priorities" (3).

In South Korea, the government unabashedly took the concept of nation branding to heart. Discussions surrounding a nation-branding strategy began with the Dynamic Korea campaign during the early 2000s. Under the Ministry of Commerce, Industry, and Energy, a task force was first assembled to assess how South Korean brand-name products were perceived internationally (Anholt 2011, 34–35). Eager to quickly recover from the 1997 IMF crisis, the Kim Dae Jung administration imposed a series of economic reforms aimed at restructuring the ways in which South Korean conglomerates operated. One of these reforms forced the conglomerates (known as *chaebŏl*) to streamline operations and focus only on core industries, such as mobile and digital technology. Increasing the brand *value* for companies such as Samsung and LG was deemed critical for generating growth in South Korea's export-driven economy.

But conceptualizing the South Korean nation as a brand was a more complex and emotional process. What impelled South Korea to embark on nation branding in the early 2000s was not just an aspiration to be competitive in the global economy, but a desire to be valued and admired by other countries. This desire was in fact linked to South Korea's sensitivities over its own self-image—an assessment that was deeply imbricated with South Korea's anxieties over how it was being viewed by other countries. The sobriquets bequeathed to nineteenth-century Korea sustained a long life, which in turn shaped Western perceptions of Korea for well over a century. The images of calm quietude and isolationism survived the Korean War (1950–1953) and the vast economic, political, and social transformations that occurred on both sides of the peninsula. Although South

Korea's hosting of the 1988 Summer Olympics was an important debut on the world stage, the event's motto of "Harmony and Progress" failed to stick.[19] And despite well-intentioned efforts by the government to shed the associations with Morning Calm and the Hermit Kingdom, the Western media continued to use the old monikers in their coverage of the "coming out" event. South Korea thus deployed an aggressive marketing strategy for its image makeover before it cohosted its next major international event in 2002.

When nation branding gained traction as a viable practice, South Korea was already primed to adopt it. The nation's first official slogan—designated in 2001 as Dynamic Korea—melded into South Korea's national brand by the mid-2000s. During the Roh Moo Hyun [No Muhyŏn] administration (2003–2008), a National Image Committee (Kukka Imiji Wiwŏnhoe) was newly formed and charged with the task of upgrading South Korea's image and reputation (Kukka pŏmnyŏng chŏngbo sent'ŏ 2005). Guided by the belief that a country could raise its international reputation by strategically marketing its core values and assets, government officials, policy makers, and those involved in the PR sector set to work on the task.

Since Dynamic Korea had already been promoted as a national slogan prior to the World Cup, the next step was to further develop the concept of dynamism. The aforementioned 2007 brochure published by the Korean Overseas Information Service outlined five tenets of South Korean dynamism: (1) functional dynamism (hardy, energetic nature); (2) emotional dynamism (rich and unique culture); (3) intellectual dynamism (wealth of knowledge and technology); (4) spiritual dynamism (solid moral character); and (5) Confucian dynamism (unique Confucian tradition) (Korean Overseas Information Service 2007, 6–10). The brochure also made the surprising move of directly connecting Dynamic Korea to the Morning Calm moniker:

> The basic concept of Dynamic Korea has its origin in "The Land of the Morning Calm."
>
> Dynamic Korea is a future-oriented slogan based on its traditions and characteristics. Korea has been known as the Land of the Morning Calm for generations, but the phrase "Morning Calm" does not simply indicate stillness, mystery, or passivity. As the Indian poet Rabindranath Tagore pointed out in his 1929 poem, "The Lamp of the East," Korean dynamism includes not only moderation and stillness but also limitless potential and high spirits that illuminate the morning of the world:

In the golden age of Asia
Korea was one of its lamp bearers,
And that lamp is waiting
To be lighted once again
For the illumination of the East.[20]

Dynamic Korea represents the harmony of this calmness and dynamism. It symbolizes the aspiration of the Korean people to further develop their limitless passion and energy and *take their place on the world stage*.[21]

Whether the five-pronged brand of dynamism or the Morning Calm / Dynamic Korea origin narrative could be traced to logic or heavy-handed marketing is best left to the reader to judge. What I intend to draw out here is the expanding range of semantic meanings of "dynamism" during the mid-2000s. Rhetoric similar to the brochure began to appear with more frequency and persistence, especially when it described the Dynamic Korea nation brand. A series of tourism and promotional videos produced by the Korea Tourism Organization (KTO; formerly the Korean National Tourism Organization) all featured the catchphrase and the branding concept. One video in particular stands out. At thirty-four seconds, "Dynamic Korea — Listen" intersperses excerpts of various percussive sounds — the playing of a Buddhist wooden fish drum, the traditional method used to launder clothes (using two sticks), and samul nori — with visuals. The description of the promotional video on the website states, "Brief glimpses of Korean culture appear throughout this video: art performances, demonstrations of food preparation, as well as modern percussion performances."[22]

By the mid-2000s, branding had become de rigueur. Municipalities at the local and regional levels followed suit and created their own brand slogans. Examples include "Colorful Daegu [Taegu]," "Dynamic Busan [Pusan]," and "Powerful Pohang [P'ohang]." Perhaps the most well-known was the "Hi Seoul, Soul of Asia" brand slogan endorsed by the Seoul Metropolitan Government in 2007 (*Chosun ilbo* 2006).[23] To make matters more complicated, other organizations and governmental agencies such as the KTO also took on ambitious branding projects.[24] Pak Ch'ŏrhyŏn, current marketing brand director at the Korea Tourism Organization, clarified to me that the branding strategies for the KTO differed from ones that were put forth by the South Korean government (Pak Ch'ŏrhyŏn, personal communication, 2013). While there were attempts to harmonize with the national slogan of "Dynamic Korea," the KTO also issued its own mottos and

Dynamic Korea and Samul Nori **77**

slogans. In 2007, the KTO debuted "Korea, Sparkling," at the cost of 5 billion wŏn (Do, Je-he 2010). The slogan was conceived by Anholt himself, who had been appointed as a brand policy adviser to the South Korean government. After being the subject of much ridicule for evoking associations with effervescent drinks, however, the tourism brand was replaced by yet another slogan. As of July 2014, "Imagine your Korea" is the current tourism brand slogan of the Korean Tourism Organization. And in July 2016, "Creative Korea" was designated as the new nation brand slogan (Kwon, Mee-yoo 2016).

THE DARK SIDE OF DYNAMIC

In the quest to stake out the perfect branding image for the nation, Dynamic Korea was abandoned after a few years' time. On January 22, 2009, the Lee Myung-bak [Yi Myŏngbak] administration (2008–2013) announced the inauguration of the first-ever Presidential Council on Nation Branding (Kukka Pŭraendŭ Wiwŏnhoe). Lee proclaimed in a speech on South Korea's Independence Day, "If the nation wants to be labeled as an advanced country, it will be necessary to improve its image and reputation significantly."[25] In his first year as chair of the presidential council, Ŏ Yundae advocated the nomination and selection of a new "national brand" to replace Dynamic Korea. Of the many slogans that were coined and marketed by various agencies and municipalities, Ŏ claimed, nothing seemed to effectively capture the "Miracle on the Han River" and South Korea's burgeoning information technology market. He also noted the polysemous meanings that were embedded in previous slogans and mottos—meanings that sometimes worked against the strong and positive image that the Korean government was trying to cultivate. After the launch of the "Korea, Sparkling" campaign, some journalists and PR consultants began to deride the brand for its associations with carbonated beverages (Breen 2008). And while "Dynamic Korea" handsomely aligned with the vibrant and visionary agenda that the South Korean government stood for in 2002, the word "dynamic" was believed to evoke both positive and negative connotations. According to Ŏ, "dynamic" could also conjure images of the violent protests during South Korea's democratization movement or the tense situation between North and South Korea (Pak 2009). As a way to avoid possible misconceptions and allusions to dark or tense periods of South Korean history, the Dynamic Korea brand was officially retired in 2009. During his tenure, Ŏ suggested "Miraculous Korea" as a suitable alternative. This was passed over, however, for the short-lived "Korea, a Loving Embrace."[26]

While, on the one hand, the medley of slogans speaks to the constant search and negotiation for South Korea's quintessential branding image, I contend that the Dynamic Korea campaign also provides us with an opportunity to consider how the meanings of certain (musical) sounds can have broad implications in social and political situations. Elsewhere I have described how the promotion and demise of the branding campaign were linked to semantic ambiguity over the word "dynamic," and also to powerful sonic registers (Lee, Katherine InYoung 2015). Here, I intend to draw out the ways in which the percussive sounds associated with samul nori were grafted onto the branding of Dynamic Korea. If we think of "dynamic" in terms of volume or amplitude, then the sounds of rhythmic chanting (aided in part by SamulNori Hanullim's collaboration with the Red Devils fan club) during the World Cup certainly added another layer of sonic meaning onto a dynamic Korea. But perhaps most significantly, the Dynamic Korea campaign reveals how the South Korean government deemed the sounds of samul nori as useful in its highly curated image makeover. What better way to challenge the old images of placidity and reclusion than with an unapologetically boisterous percussive music? Moreover, since the samul nori genre had become successfully transmitted outside South Korea, it stood as a symbol of South Korea's outward-looking stance. Even after the Dynamic Korea campaign was retired, there continued to be various levels of state support for SamulNori and the samul nori genre. While the examples are numerous, I provide the Dynamic Korea case study as a reason as to why South Korea was invested in promoting positive aspects of its culture abroad.

FOUR

Global Encounters with Samul Nori

During the 1980s, SamulNori's tours in Europe, Japan, and the United States left in their wake a legion of newly converted fans. The quartet's dynamic performances of virtuosity and vigor often captivated critics and attendees on first listen. At times, it seemed as if the drumming alone unleashed a powerful and direct connection to foreign audiences, with no need for cultural translation. In a *New York Times* review of the quartet's performance at New York's Asia Society in 1983, critic Jon Pareles characterized the performance as a "spectacular din." SamulNori performed pieces that would start with a "fairly simple beat or an annunciatory rush of sound," leading to sections of differing tempi that eventually culminated in a "hurtling, ecstatic momentum" (1983). Pareles was quick to note, however, that the highlight of the performance for him was the danced *p'an kut*, the finale of the program. Here, the members of the quartet left a memorable impression by drumming complex rhythms while simultaneously dancing in "light, skipping steps, together in a circle and individually in eye-boggling spins and leaps" as "whirling plumes on their hats traced streaks in the air" (1983). Lewis Segal, dance critic for the *Los Angeles Times*, raved that SamulNori's "ratchety attacks, gunshot accents, eight-part cross-rhythms — sudden death terminations" revealed a folk music of "primal power and technical sophistication" (1985). In the same glowing review, Segal predicted that SamulNori would become "stupendously popular." The driving force of the percussion music coupled with the visuals of whirling white ribbons, acrobatic twirling, and graceful dance movements formed the ingredients for a complete sensory experience. In these performances non-Korean audiences were witness to a musical tradition that was visceral yet enchantingly distant.

It was often at this first encounter with SamulNori that indelible impressions were formed. For many first-timers, the experience of viewing a SamulNori performance was simply an introduction to Korean percussion or, more broadly, to East Asian music. For others, the *music* of that first encounter resonated long after the performance, piquing the curiosity of those interested in Korean percussion and eventually giving way to a discovery of the quartet's recording history. And for other spectators, the encounter was a life-changing one — an important juncture that would lead to a long-term engagement with learning how to play Korean percussion music. The salience of this moment rests in the transformation from a state of observation to an active state of learning and performance. In the case of a few individuals, this conversion from fandom to a desire to become a samul nori practitioner led to numerous trips to Korea to train directly at the Puyŏ SamulNori School. And a handful of avid fans known as "SamulNorians" have made the decision to devote their lives to musical performance, focusing specifically on Korean percussion.[1]

In this chapter, I give attention to some of these musical encounters as they have emerged in myriad transnational contexts. While one important subfield of music scholarship considers the fraught musical encounters that occurred within colonial or imperialist histories, here I am guided in part by recent studies of cross-cultural encounters in relation to global music genres (to name a few, Condry 2006; Lauševic 2007; Wallach, Berger, and Greene 2011; Bigenho 2012; Silverman 2012; White 2012; Helbig 2014; Spiller 2015). Anthropologist Bob White describes "global encounters" as "situations in which individuals from radically different traditions or worldviews come into contact and interact with one another based on limited information about one another's values, resources, and intentions" (2012, 6). These encounters can be limited in terms of their frequency or duration or characterized by constancy and repetition. Like White, I interpret global encounters in broad terms. I view these less as singular meetings between strangers from different parts of the world than as a process of cross-cultural exchange that is often asymmetrical. In the plural form, "encounters" can be ongoing and can also serve as fertile ground for developing a commonly shared interest — in this case, percussion music. The global musical encounters with the quartet and the second-generation SamulNori Hanullim troupe have been at the heart of the samul nori genre's popularization and transmission outside South Korea. Sites of performance have often been central to these musical encounters.

The encounter itself does not always privilege a person-to-person interaction. As Tim Taylor and Steven Feld have previously pointed out, many encounters with world music have been mediated by the experience of listening to audio recordings—objects that are inextricably linked to capitalist enterprises and the music industry (Taylor 1997; Feld 1994, 2000). One can first encounter the music of Senegal through a CD by Youssou N'Dour, and not necessarily by attending a live performance by N'Dour. In a similar vein, other avenues of discovery have emerged over the three decades since SamulNori's debut. First musical encounters with SamulNori can be introduced vis-à-vis more informal networks of sharing: dubs of SamulNori's recordings, digital mp3 files, YouTube videos uploaded by users, and photocopies of the notation developed by SamulNori Hanullim.[2]

In this chapter I present some of the more exceptional encounters that have resulted in life-changing circumstances, alongside the more casual ones. These narratives offer a glimpse into globalization as it works at a very small-scale, personal level. Through ethnographic observation and interviews conducted with samul nori practitioners based primarily outside South Korea, I examine the different points of entry into their encounters with SamulNori and/or the samul nori genre. Often, these entry points are guided by people's first impressions of samul nori's dynamism. These encounters then lead to subsequent journeys of discovery with samul nori's rhythm-based form and Korean percussion music. Whether it was the experience of watching a SamulNori performance on a stage in Berlin or the circulation of cassette tapes and workbooks among U.S.-based college Korean percussion groups, it is clear that these encounters are all global in some sense.[3] Increased networks of connectivity and international travel have facilitated the rapid circulations of people, media, and texts. Yet, as these narratives of "global encounters" reveal, it is most often at the individual level or in a modest constellation of individual networks that cultural exchanges are fostered across national boundaries. And in the case of samul nori groups that have sprung up in places outside South Korea, it is the individual encounter with SamulNori (or SamulNori Hanullim) that is both formative and generative.

My former status as the overseas coordinator for SamulNori Hanullim employees provided me with a wealth of opportunities to tap into a broad network of international samul nori fans—some of whom I had met while working in Korea in the early 2000s. The personal connections I have cultivated with many SamulNorians over the years (and the conversations I have shared with them) are critical to my own understanding of how SamulNori / samul nori is experienced by Koreans but also by many non-Koreans. I profile some of these global encounters with SamulNori, delimiting my analysis to those individuals whom I met in South Korea between 2003 and 2009. Furthermore, I focus only on people who participated in some capacity at the 2008 World SamulNori Festival in Puyŏ, South Korea, an event at which I volunteered. All my interviewees attended the festival and competition as members of samul nori groups representing four different countries: the United States, Mexico, Switzerland, and Japan.

In this chapter, I give definition to the initial "encounter" as it elicits subsequent cross-cultural interactions and leads to an engagement with learning how to play samul nori. In the case of Suzanna Samstag—the subject of the first profile—this encounter would not only change her life but also alter the course of SamulNori's history. It is important to note that these global encounters are not intended to be comprehensive histories, extending into the present day. As with most musical groups, membership changes over time. This fluid membership can impact group dynamics, choices of repertoire, performance practice, and even cause a group to disband. Thus the following profiles serve more as snapshots and introductions to the global encounters with SamulNori / samul nori. These profiles also provide the necessary context for chapter 5, where I closely examine the World SamulNori Festival of 2008—a large-scale event that culminated in the convergence of all profiled individuals in South Korea. I center my analysis primarily on the opening event of the festival for both its symbolic currency for the SamulNori Hanullim organization (in affirming the global reach of the samul nori genre) and its remarkable literal and figurative "homecoming" of sorts for these international samul nori ensembles.

I turn now to several global encounters with SamulNori / samul nori that have had lasting repercussions.

SUZANNA SAMSTAG, A PIVOTAL FIGURE

As one of SamulNori's true insiders, Suzanna Samstag represents a vital link to international audiences and the ways in which they first learned about the "drummer-dancers from Korea."[4] In fact, the global spread of samul nori and SamulNori's overseas success can be attributed to Samstag's dedication as their first managing director (figure 4.1). How did an American woman (then in her twenties) end up managing South Korea's most famous musical quartet for over ten years? The answer lies in Samstag's own first encounter with SamulNori.

Fresh out of undergraduate studies at Georgetown University, Samstag first arrived in Korea in 1980 as a Peace Corps volunteer. Assigned to work as a tuberculosis control specialist, she participated in home visits and health education programs throughout the country. When her tour of duty unexpectedly ended a

FIGURE 4.1 Suzanna Samstag with her two children, Sang-hyuk (*left*) and Jiyun (*right*), at the World SamulNori Festival, October 2008. Photograph by author.

year early because of Peace Corps budget cuts, she was presented with the options of returning to the United States, relocating to Tonga, or renewing her Korean visa for the remaining year (Harris 2004, 405). She elected to stay in Korea and enrolled at Seoul National University (SNU) as a graduate student. Samstag's first year at SNU was devoted to Korean language study, and it was in 1982 that her Korean language teacher took her class to see a performance of Korean music at the Cecil Theater (Sesil Kŭkchang) in Seoul.[5] Little did she know at the time that attending the concert would be a life-altering experience. According to Samstag, the ensemble that performed that evening consisted of "four wiry guys" playing traditional Korean percussion instruments, who "were at the top of their form" (Lee, Katherine In-Young 2004, 37). After hearing the newly unveiled "Sol changgo karak" (rhythmic pattern performed on four changgo drums), Samstag recounted that the force of the music "literally tore through my body" (37). She noted that there was a healthy dose of competition among the musicians, who sought to prove their worth to one another. The audience became spectators to the turf war that was transpiring onstage. The young musicians, in their late twenties, were the members of the newly solidified SamulNori quartet (Kim Duk Soo, Kim Yong-bae, Lee Kwang Soo, and Choi Jong Sil).

The visceral reaction to the sounds and sights of samul nori proved to have a significant impact on Samstag. In a published interview, she reflected that it was the physicality of the dancing that attracted her most to SamulNori. During her youth she was a gymnast, and she was offered college scholarships to pursue competitive gymnastics. She opted for academic studies, but ended up coaching the women's gymnastics team at Georgetown University. After seeing SamulNori perform, Samstag—who had no prior background in music—became determined to try to learn Korean percussion music. Since she had already studied a bit of *t'alch'um* (Korean masked dance drama), she believed she could approach the music of SamulNori through her background in dance and gymnastics.

> When I saw them perform [on changgo], I wanted to go and learn how to play this instrument, even though previously I had never had an interest to play a musical instrument. I found out where their studio was and gathered up the courage to go there. These four guys had no interest in teaching anybody, however—especially not a foreigner who could hardly speak Korean, so they gave me the blow-off. I was determined not to give up, though. I came by all the time and attended all of their performances. I was the ultimate groupie! Finally, they conceded and let their driver teach me, and so I said okay because I just wanted to learn.
>
> I arrived at the studio every day at 6:00 a.m., which turned into 7:00 usually, as the driver wouldn't show up for the first hour, forcing me to sit on the steps outside their rehearsal space until the guy showed up. The driver knew some of the music, but he wasn't trained and he didn't know how to teach. I tried as best I could for months and months, though, until finally I said, "You know, why don't you give me a key and I'll come in and practice by myself until you get there." (Harris 2004, 409–10)

Samstag's persistence eventually paid off. The quartet allowed her to practice in the small office/studio (in the A-hyŏn district of Seoul) during the early mornings. In gratitude, she would tidy up the office for the quartet members. She divided her time between her studies at SNU and the SamulNori studio. One day when the group was away on tour, Samstag took it upon herself to organize the paperwork in the office; documents and files were so entirely neglected that they overflowed out of the desk drawers that housed them. Growing up in the United States, Samstag had worked in her father's law office and had experience with clerical work. She applied these skills to the project at hand:

First thing I did was organize all of their papers and put them in the filing cabinet. And they [SamulNori] were like, "Oh thanks." . . . To them, it didn't really mean anything. To me, it was like, this is the key to your future—answering letters and communicating with people who are writing who want to work together. If you just tell me what you want to do, I'll type it up and send it back. Remember we were communicating at pretty basic levels for a while. But they didn't see the importance in all this correspondence yet. Then I think they realized later on, that this is how you ran a business—you had someone answering letters. (Suzanna Samstag interview, September 6, 2009)

SamulNori's first U.S. tour in 1982 was partly arranged by the South Korean government. After this tour, the quartet began to receive inquiries from Western presenters. Since the musicians were not able to read English, and the quartet did not have an agent at the time, the letters were left unanswered. Samstag took it upon herself to answer the letters—typed in English, much to the surprise of foreign presenters.

The Asia Society was funny because they didn't believe in letters. They'd send telegrams. Well, I mean, in their logic, they were dealing with a lot of people or groups where regular addresses or postal systems weren't good in their countries. . . . The first letter I ever wrote for them [SamulNori] was in 1983. There was this young woman working for the Asia Society named Karen. And she said, they were so surprised—all that time they were communicating with telegrams and vague phone calls. And all of a sudden was this very neatly typed letter [in English]. (Samstag interview, September 6, 2009)

Soon thereafter, Samstag found herself handling all the correspondence with international presenters. She became SamulNori's first agent and managing director at the tender age of twenty-four. In his autobiography Kim Duk Soo paid tribute to Samstag for her decade-long involvement with the quartet: "She was the first person to pave the way for SamulNori's internationalization" (Kim Duk Soo 2007, 190). Samstag not only handled the daily affairs of business but also served as acting manager for all SamulNori's international and domestic performances from 1983 to 1994. As tour manager, Samstag wore many hats, from overseeing the tour schedule and operating the lights at shows to interpreting for the group. When SamulNori began integrating workshops and residencies into their international tours, Samstag also served as drumming instructor and interpreter. She was responsible for nearly all the English-language publications, from the promotional materials to the initial SamulNori workbooks.

Had it not been for Samstag's initiative, persistence, and management acumen in the early 1980s, it is almost certain that SamulNori would not have catapulted so quickly to international attention. SamulNori provided the raw goods, and Samstag facilitated the quartet's overseas engagements. She also helped to curate an image for the group through her flair for writing; Samstag was the author of SamulNori's English program notes.[6]

The years of international and domestic touring and dealing with temperamental personalities eventually took their toll, however, and Samstag decided to leave not long after the quartet disbanded. Before she departed, she negotiated a contract between Kim Duk Soo's newly formed SamulNori Hanullim artistic troupe and Herbert Barrett Management—an American artist management company based in New York. (The SamulNori quartet did not have North American representation but worked closely with Ryo Hommura of Planet Arts Company in Tokyo for their Japanese performances.) It was around this time that Samstag was scouted for a position at *Newsweek*. She then served as chief editor of *Newsweek* (Korean Edition) from 1994 to 2001 and coordinated weekly with the New York office in the planning of news coverage.

A long-term expatriate, Samstag still lives in South Korea with her two children. She is often called upon to advise on issues related to Korean music and culture. The SamulNori Hanullim organization invited her to serve as a judge during the 2008 World SamulNori competition. At the time of this writing, she is senior adviser to the president of the Daesung Group (an energy company) and a consultant for the Korea Foundation.

SHINPARAM, UNITED STATES

Shinparam identifies itself as a traditional drumming group of the Korean American community in the Twin Cities of Minneapolis–Saint Paul, Minnesota, and as a group that plays "p'ungmul on the prairie" (figure 4.2).[7] Since its founding in 2004, the group has been composed of a diverse mix of second-generation Korean Americans, Korean adoptees, adoptive parents, international Korean students, and non-Koreans with an avid interest in Korean drumming. Shinparam was founded partly as a publicity and outreach project of the *Korean Quarterly* newspaper, a publication that serves the interests of the Korean American and Korean adoptee communities of the Twin Cities and the upper Midwest. Sarah

FIGURE 4.2 The American group Shinparam at the Dragon Festival in Saint Paul, Minnesota, in 2006. *From left*: Stephen Wunrow, Sarah Lee, Martha Vickery, Madeleine Soon Young Wunrow, Jennifer Yang Hee Arndt, Eunhee Yang, Sangho Sam Kim, Lia Bengtson, Peggy Olsen, Han Yong Wunrow, Rami Cha, Shirley Sailors. *Front row* (bride and groom): Ami Nafzger and Aron Spiess. Photograph courtesy of Stephen Wunrow.

Lee, the group's first leader (2004–2006), chose to render the English translation of the group's name Shinparam with the poetically evocative phrase "wind of inspiration."[8]

Shinparam's Facebook group page states that its goals are to "develop members' proficiency in the tradition of *poongmulnori* [*p'ungmul nori*]: marching and dance choreography with drumming" and the "more modern samul nori (a seated concert-style of traditional drumming)."[9] Membership is open to anyone (teens and adults) with an interest in Korean percussion. Since its inception, the group has had two leaders, Sarah Lee and Sangho Kim. Lee and Kim previously learned selected aspects of the p'ungmul and samul nori genres in Chicago and South Korea, respectively, and both were graduate students at the University of Minnesota at the time of their involvement with Shinparam. In September 2016, Kim stepped down as the leader, because of a job relocation.

The person most responsible for spearheading Shinparam in its initial configuration, however, is Martha Vickery. Since 1997 Vickery and her husband,

Stephen Wunrow, have devoted their time to publishing the *Korean Quarterly*, a periodical newspaper that includes stories and critical analysis on Korean and Korean American–related issues, book and film reviews, photo essays, and resource and event listings for the Korean American and Korean adoptee communities.[10] As editor, Vickery writes a majority of the feature stories and oversees the content of the quarterly, which averages between ninety and a hundred pages an issue. Wunrow serves as the publisher, photographer, designer, and director of advertising. The nonprofit publishing project—now over nineteen years old and recognized with numerous awards—has been a labor of love for the couple.

Vickery and Wunrow have three children, two of whom are adopted from South Korea. Over the years, they had acquired SamulNori recordings through their interest in all things Korean. Vickery admitted, however, that she knew little about the samul nori percussion genre until they became affiliated with the Korean Institute of Minnesota (KIM). In the mid-1990s, the Korean language institute and cultural center received an instrument grant from the Overseas Korea Foundation that allowed them to purchase sets of samul nori instruments. When Vickery learned that samul nori lessons would be offered only to children enrolled at the school, she was admittedly disappointed. Vickery and Wunrow toyed with the idea of starting up a group to help publicize the *Korean Quarterly* and to create interest in and appreciation of Korean music.

On January 31, 2004, Vickery took her family to see a SamulNori Hanullim performance (led by Kim Duk Soo) at Saint John's University in Collegeville, Minnesota.[11] Knowing of Kim's status as a master musician, Vickery encouraged many friends in the Korean community to attend. According to Vickery, she was surprised to find that the auditorium was "jam-packed" even in the midst of a true Minnesotan blizzard (Martha Vickery interview, June 11, 2009). The performance was "fabulous" and sparked a renewed interest in her community drumming group idea. After SamulNori Hanullim's performance, Vickery began actively recruiting members for a start-up Korean percussion ensemble. She persuaded Sarah Lee, then a first-year medical student at the University of Minnesota, to lead the group in the fall of 2004. The Korean Institute of Minnesota lent the group samul nori instruments and costumes and also provided a rehearsal space.[12] By the fall of 2004—just a few months after Vickery and Wunrow's first encounter with SamulNori Hanullim—Shinparam had eight regular members.

Sarah Lee, a second-generation Korean American, taught the group of beginners based on what she had learned as a member of the Loose Roots Korean-American drumming group at the University of Chicago (1997–2001) (Sarah

Lee, personal communication, July 8, 2010). According to Vickery, when Lee first started teaching the group, she "was making up her own pieces, stringing beats together, just to teach us beats and transitions" (Vickery interview, June 11, 2009). Lee often consulted with Paul Namhoon Kim, a member of the Chicago-based IlGwaNori drumming troupe (Shinparam's mentor group of sorts) as to what to teach the Minnesota group next. By the summer of 2005, the Shinparam group had already performed at three local events: a Lunar New Year's event for the Korean school in February 2005, a multicultural celebration held at the University of Minnesota Medical School benefiting the Native American free clinic in Minneapolis, and the *Korean Quarterly* fund-raiser and community outreach event, "Spring Thing," held on April 30, 2005 (Vickery, e-mail communication, May 20, 2005).

In June 2005, upon a nomination by the author, the Shinparam group was selected to participate in the fourteenth annual SamulNori Kyŏrugi (festival and competition) in Puyŏ, South Korea.[13] The Shinparam team sent nine members to Korea during the last week of September 2005. The members who traveled to Korea were Jennifer Arndt, Sam Breitheim, Sarah Lee, Shirley Sailors, Martha Vickery, Stephen Wunrow, and Emma, Madeleine, and Han Yong Wunrow. At sixty, Sailors, a Euro-American with connections in the Korean community, was the eldest member of the group; at ten years old, Han Yong Wunrow, Vickery and Wunrow's adopted son from Korea, was the youngest. Kyung Un Ro [No Kyŏngŭn], a native Korean who had been an exchange student staying at the Wunrows' home earlier in 2005, joined the group when they arrived in Puyŏ.

Although the team was inexperienced and rather green for the competition, it attracted a great deal of publicity from Korean media outlets (e.g., KBS TV, the *Korea Herald*, *Joongang Ilbo*, and Arirang TV). Much was made of the group's diversity in terms of ethnic background and age. Reflecting on the group's first trip to Korea, Vickery said, "We got a lot of press that time, because we had children in our group, and children who were pretty good, you know, for just being Americans.... Everybody's kind of the same level ... but everybody kind of focused on the kids ... adopted Koreans and Korean Americans and Caucasians in the group together was kind of a media draw" (Vickery interview, June 11, 2009). Vickery also remarked that it was exciting to meet other Korean and foreign samul nori groups at the festival and to be included as part of a global samul nori community. She profiled several of the groups in the Winter 2005–6 issue of the *Korean Quarterly* (Vickery 2005–6a and b).

Attendance at the 2005 SamulNori Kyŏrugi was an eye-opening experience for the group. In a blog entry published by the *Korean Quarterly*, Sarah Lee chronicled some of these revelations.

> We were all so nervous, since our team is only a year old, and others have been together for six or more years. I was especially stressed, because as the teacher and choreographer, I knew that not every bit of knowledge I had passed on to my team members was traditionally accurate, in terms of what has been passed from one drummer to the next in the 5,000 years of Korean history. After all, my drumming skills had been thoroughly filtered through Korean American ears and minds before being taught to me. I had never been taught by the Korean masters. . . . I was strangely comforted talking to other international teams who are also struggling without access to a bona fide Korean drumming expert. . . . I want our beats to be in synch with others across the world so we can join together, so we must learn the textbook-traditional way. However, I agree with a Korean-German born fellow drummer, that it is futile (and perhaps vain) to seek the pure Korean way for our groups. Our group, Shinparam, will always have an undeniable American flavor, from how we move when dancing with our drums to the arrangement of the drumming beats. The way one plays Korean drums, reveals a lot about one's personality, so I'm glad that our music is a reflection of who we are. I came back with enough memories for a couple lifetimes, strong beats in my heart, and not just a new perspective on drumming, but on life in general. I will take Duk Soo Kim's advice, and not to strive only for correctness but to inspire and give *shinparam* [the wind of inspiration] to those around me. (Sarah Lee, as quoted in Vickery 2005–6b, 75–76)

At the beginning of 2006, the leadership of the group transitioned from Sarah Lee to Sangho (Sam) Kim. Lee was no longer able to balance the duties of leading the group with her obligations as a medical student. A native Korean, Kim had joined Shinparam during the fall 2005 semester, after coming to the United States to begin a doctoral program in electrical engineering at the University of Minnesota. Kim's experiences in amateur drumming circles in Korea gave him the requisite skills to serve as the next teacher for the group (Sangho Kim interview, June 28, 2010). During his undergraduate career at Pusan National University he had been part of a drumming circle and trained at transmission camps (called *chŏnsu*) that specialized in Pusan Nongak. As part of his required two-year military service to the Republic of Korea, he was also recruited to perform as a percussionist in the *munhwa sŏnchŏndae*—"cultural propaganda units" of the South Korean military that broadcast propaganda and music across the Demilitarized Zone (DMZ) to North Korea.[14]

Upon first seeing the Shinparam group rehearse, Kim felt a strong desire to assist the group in becoming more technically proficient at drumming. Unlike Lee, Kim mainly taught from SamulNori Hanullim's set of notation workbooks that the group had purchased during their trip to Korea. They learned many of the standard items of the samul nori repertoire: "Yŏngnam nongak," "Uttari p'ungmul," "Sŏl changgo karak," and "Samdo nongak karak." Kim maintained the Shinparam website (now defunct) and shared notation and audio recordings of the samul nori pieces with the group.

During their trip to Puyŏ in September–October 2005, Shinparam also met Kim Dong-won [Kim Tongwŏn], SamulNori Hanullim's former education director. The following year Kim was invited by Vickery to lead drumming workshops for the group in Minnesota. He returned in 2007 to perform for *Korean Quarterly*'s tenth anniversary event and has maintained a connection with the group. Individual members have also traveled to Korea for short-term to long-term stays, most often combining language study with lessons in Korean drumming.[15] Shinparam has also expanded its repertoire to include more p'ungmul (in their word, "standing") set pieces such as "P'ungnyu kut."

Since 2006, Shinparam has maintained an active performing schedule, with an average of one performance a month. According to Sangho Kim, the group is now well known in the Twin Cities area and receives regular requests to perform at events and festivals. In 2008 the group was invited for the second time to participate in the World SamulNori Festival in Puyŏ, South Korea. As of September 2016, Kim departed Minnesota for a job in California and stepped down as leader. Shinparam still continues to rehearse and perform.

SWISSAMUL, SWITZERLAND

Swissamul was an all-female group based in Basel, Switzerland, during the mid- to-late 2000s (figure 4.3). They described themselves as an "ensemble of drummers . . . dedicated to the fiery energy and vibrant dynamism of Korean drum music known as 'SamulNori.'"[16] The members were all Swiss nationals and ranged in age from forty to fifty-eight. Swissamul could be described as a musical community of affinity, in that none of the members share ethnic ties to Korea.[17] Their connection to Korea was cultivated primarily through their fascination with Korean percussion. In 2008, the members included group leader Suzanne Nketia,

FIGURE 4.3 The Swiss group Swissamul at the World SamulNori Festival in October 2008. *From left:* Hildegard Eichmann, Suzanne Nketia, Nathalie Baumann, Bettina Marugg, and Hendrikje Lange. Photograph by author.

Hendrikje Lange, Hildegard Eichmann, Bettina Marugg, Nathalie Baumann, and Gudrun Emminger. As a group, Swissamul performed in Korea three times, at the SamulNori Kyŏrugi festival and competition in 2002, 2005, and 2008. All members of Swissamul participated in samul nori workshops organized by Nketia at the Musik-Akademie Basel. These workshops were taught by samul nori pedagogue Kim Dong-won. Most members also made numerous trips to Korea to study at the Puyŏ SamulNori School.

During its active years, Swissamul closely aligned itself with samul nori. Since samul nori requires a minimum of only four performers on four different percussion instruments, it was well-suited to the group, which had only five to six regular members. Nketia typically played the lead kkwaenggwari part, as she had the longest exposure to samul nori. Although all members were proficient at playing the changgo, each specialized in one instrument. The group's website lists as part of Swissamul's repertory "Yŏngnam nongak," "Uttari p'ungmul," and "Sŏl changgo karak." Two additional pieces, "P'ilbong nongak" and "Kyŏnggi todanggut," from the p'ungmul and *musok* (shamanic) traditions, were later added. According to Lange, Swissamul considered their primary teacher to be Kim Dong-won. Sent originally by SamulNori Hanullim, Kim traveled almost yearly to Basel to lead weeklong samul nori workshops at the Musik-Akademie Basel since 1996.

Swissamul's somewhat reluctant leader, Nketia, has led a life dedicated to dance and music. Originally trained as a classical ballet dancer, Nketia moved to London in her twenties in order to "find a dance which touch[ed] her soul" (Nketia interview, August 11, 2009). There she became acquainted with a pan-African dance troupe and began to take lessons in various styles of West African dance (e.g., Ga, Ashanti, and Ewe). Nketia eventually transitioned from ballet to performing West African dance and spent over twenty years becoming immersed in Ghanaian dance and its culture.[18]

In the late 1980s Nketia was first exposed to Korean percussion through a rhythm-based workshop led by Austrian musician Reinhard Flatischler.[19] Flatischler studied several forms of percussion in India, Korea, Cuba, and Brazil. Building on the concepts and practices from various percussion genres, he developed the TakeTiNa Rhythm Process in 1970. In an interview with the author, Nketia reflected on her first point of entry into Korean percussion vis-à-vis Flatischler: "He developed a system of teaching rhythm—which he had experienced in different cultures—like India, Korea, Brazil, or Cuba. . . . The body and the voice are connected. And for me, it was a good method to learn rhythm in a deeper way" (Suzanne Nketia interview, August 11, 2009).

Through Flatischler, Nketia was introduced to Korean rhythm and the sounds of Korean percussion. What moved her most, however, was witnessing a live performance by the SamulNori quartet. In 1990 Nketia attended a performance at the Mühle Hunziken in Rubingen, Switzerland. Members Kim Duk Soo, Lee Kwang Soo, Choi Jong Sil, and Kang Min-seok (who replaced Kim Yong-bae in 1984) performed at this concert with the jazz group Red Sun as part of a three-week Red Sun / SamulNori European tour.[20] Afterward, she felt inexplicably moved and compelled to learn more about the Korean percussion genre. Nketia was first and foremost impressed that the performers were both expert musicians and dancers. She stated simply: "The music touched me differently. Most of the European drummers—they don't have hohŭp. And African drummers, they have hohŭp, in another way. And that it [hohŭp] was taught. I learned it, and this impressed me very deeply. *And I think this was the reason—why samul nori could take me*" (Nketia interview, August 11, 2009).

When an opportunity to travel to Seoul presented itself in May 1991 to her partner, Michael Huber, Nketia decided to accompany him as a way to try to meet with the SamulNori group.[21] Nketia inquired with SamulNori's manager, Suzanna Samstag, about the possibility of visiting the SamulNori rehearsal space. Samstag was able to arrange for Nketia to sit in on rehearsals and lessons at the Nanjang Studio in Sinch'on, an area in northern Seoul. For two weeks she took lessons from composer-pianist Im Dong-chang [Im Tongch'ang] and Kim Dong-won, and she also joined in on group lessons that were often led directly by Kim Duk Soo and Lee Kwang Soo.[22] In many ways, this experience at the Sinch'on Nanjang planted the seeds of her long-standing relationship with the SamulNori community.

Despite having a difficult experience acclimating to life in Seoul, Nketia decided to continue pursuing her interest in Korean drumming by attending a SamulNori workshop in Berlin in April 1992.[23] The workshop was led by Kim Duk Soo, Lee Kwang Soo, Choi Jong Sil, and Kang Min-seok, and assisted by Samstag. The quartet took note of Nketia's enthusiasm and invited her to participate in the fourth SamulNori Kyŏrugi competition and festival in 1993. Initially turned off by the idea of participating as a solo performer in a competition, she was reassured by Samstag that the festival would be "great fun" and was encouraged to attend. The 1993 Kyŏrugi was held in the large venue of the Seoul Olympic Stadium, originally built for the 1988 Summer Olympics. Nketia performed the "Sŏl changgo karak" as a soloist in the foreigners' category and took second place in the competition. She described her sense of confusion and surprise at the entire experience: "I didn't know what to dress [sic]. So I chose a red dress [laughs]. Everything was wrong when I was there. I realized the costumes, and then, I didn't understand anything. And then it was, at the end, when we did the prizes. I didn't think of a prize at all, and then I won and had to go [onto] the stage. . . . The first time, and second prize. And I received a changgo and a ching [as] my prize. And I was really—I didn't understand the world at all. . . . And I received this letter—and everything I couldn't read. . . . Still, I was so touched" (Nketia interview, August 11, 2009).

After learning that SamulNori was slated to appear at a festival in Geneva the following year (1994), Nketia contacted Samstag and arranged to pick up the group afterward. She organized a samul nori workshop for the quartet in Liestal. She also enlisted help from the wife of the president of the Society for the Korean Community of Switzerland to prepare Korean meals for the group. Nketia admitted that this invitation to SamulNori was both a gesture of appreciation for her experience at the festival and also a way to continue taking lessons. In 1995 she organized a similar weeklong workshop for the group, and in 1996 Kim Dong-won started to come yearly to Basel to serve as sole instructor for the samul nori workshops in collaboration with the Musik-Akademie Basel. By attending the yearly workshops in Berlin (largely attended by members of the Korean German community) and organizing her own events in Basel, Nketia was able to patch together lessons for herself in Europe during the mid-1990s.[24] Soon, others became interested.

Hendrikje Lange inquired about taking changgo lessons from Nketia after hearing her perform in a workshop in 1995. Lange was, in effect, Nketia's first "student." Lange's first encounter with a live performance of samul nori was in 1996, when the Samul GwangDae [Kwangdae] team—then part of the larger SamulNori Hanullim artistic troupe—performed at a music festival in Basel.[25] In an interview with the author, she reflected on this life-changing experience:

> It was really like, how can I say, like a shock. Like an earthquake, when I saw them. I could really never imagine something like that existing of this world. So this was actually the moment when I really took a very strong position: I will go to Korea, and I really want to learn changgo. This is the only thing I really want to learn. Because when I saw this performance I was really crying. I was so touched by the beauty and power. . . . I remember the singing of Park An-ji. Especially his singing was something that was very deeply touching for me. . . . But it was immediately touching my heart directly, even though I didn't understand what it was about. But I felt immediately it was a prayer song.[26]
> (Hendrikje Lange interview, August 14, 2009)

Lange first traveled to Korea in the summer of 1999 to study at the Puyŏ SamulNori School. Later that fall, she traveled with Nketia to perform as part of the SwiKo trio at the Seoul Drum Festival, and in 2001 she joined the newly formed Swissamul ensemble under the direction of Nketia. Other members of Swissamul included Hildegard Eichmann, Bettina Marugg, and Nathalie Baumann. Eichmann and Marugg had both received certification in TakeTiNa instruction and were participants in the 1996 samul nori workshop that Nketia organized in Basel. And Baumann (a research associate with training in urban ecology) first began taking lessons in 2000 from Kim Dong-won and Nketia.

Swissamul's members have traveled to Korea together and individually, to study at the Puyŏ SamulNori School. Their last trip to Korea as a group was in 2008, in order to attend the World SamulNori Festival in Puyŏ. In the summer of

2009, when I was finishing my field research, Eichmann and Marugg studied for a few weeks in Puyŏ. Marugg and Lange also forged close ties with the Kŭmsan Buddhist Temple in Kimje and often combined samul nori training with Buddhist meditation retreats. In April 2010, Swissamul performed together with Kim Dong-won, at the Musik-Akademie Basel. The concert was titled "Korean Music between Tradition and Modernity."[27]

In 2010, Swissamul's membership changed when Hendrikje Lange left her job as a psychomotor therapist in Basel and relocated to Seoul in order to pursue further studies in Korean percussion. Lange started to train intensively at the Puyŏ SamulNori School in the fall of 2010 and began the arduous process of preparing for the entrance audition to a two-year master's program in Korean performing arts. In January 2012 Lange was admitted into the Korean National University of Arts (K-Arts). She became the first non-Korean to be accepted into a Korean music program through a standard admissions process. Lange's story caught the attention of the Korean media, and she was featured in numerous segments on South Korean television (e.g., YTN and the SBS Lunar New Year special).

Upon graduating from the Department of Traditional Performing Arts (Yŏnhŭi kwa), Lange continued to live and work in Korea until September 2016. One of her positions included a job as the samul nori instructor for foreigners at the National Gugak Center. She also founded the Expats SamulNori Team in 2013. Since recently returning to Switzerland, Lange has resumed working as a psychomotor therapist. At the time of this writing, she hopes to start another samul nori group in Basel.

When I interviewed Nketia in 2009, one year after Swissamul was awarded first prize at the World SamulNori Festival, she was pleased with the current members of the group, who were "willing to go deeper into the culture and the music" (Nketia interview, August 11, 2009). Lange has certainly followed through on this, and in many ways her story merits another profile.[28] It is clear, however, that Nketia's Swissamul group has provided a necessary base for its members to explore Korean percussion traditions and Korean culture further.

CANTO DEL CIELO, MEXICO

Now known as Samulnori Mexico, Canto del Cielo was the name of a samul nori ensemble composed of Mexican nationals that formed in the late 2000s (figure 4.4). To date they are the first all-Mexican female samul nori team to have formed. Similar to Swissamul, Canto del Cielo (Song of Heaven) is a musical

FIGURE 4.4 The Mexican group Canto del Cielo at the World SamulNori Festival in October 2008. *Back row, from left:* Wendy Rodríguez Muñoz, Martha Bermúdez Ortíz, Maria del Carmen Donají Hernández Vélez, Bárbara Cario Martínez, and Ch'oe Namyun. *Front row, from left:* Aidée Santillán Moreno, Mariana Campos Pérez, Viridiana Sánchez Zaragoza, and Ariadna Ramírez Lealde. Photograph by author.

community of affinity.[29] Unlike the Swiss group, however, the original members of the Mexican group were first drawn to Korean culture through their zeal and passion for South Korean dramas that were broadcast on Mexican television in the mid-2000s. Ranging in age from twenty to thirty-five, many of the female members of Canto del Cielo were diehard fans of Korean male actors who starred in Korean melodramas that became associated with the Hallyu (Korean Wave) phenomenon.[30] Viridiana Sánchez Zaragoza (b. 1989), for instance, was president of the Kwŏn Sang'u Mexican Fanclub, and Wendy Rodríguez Muñoz (b. 1975) served as president of the Chang Tonggŏn Fanclub while also overseeing thirteen Mexican-based Hallyu fan clubs (Wendy Rodríguez Muñoz, personal communication, November 23, 2009).[31] The dramas (and their leading male heartthrobs) gradually piqued the members' curiosity about Korean culture and the Korean language.[32]

Many turned to the Centro Cultural Coreano en México (hereafter referred to as the CCC) in Mexico City as a place to take Korean language classes and learn

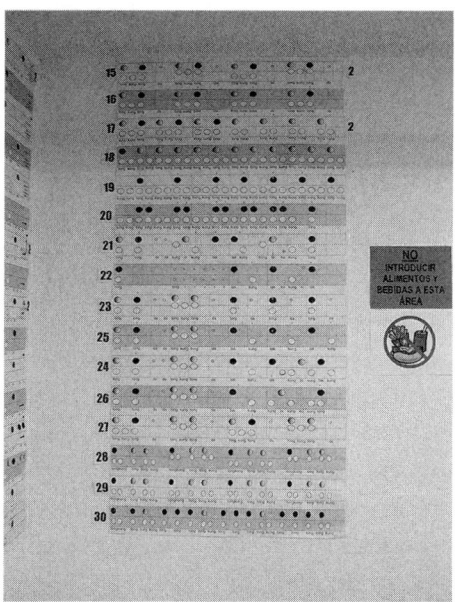

FIGURE 4.5 Samul nori notation "wallpaper" in the rehearsal studio of the Centro Cultural Coreano en México, Mexico City. Photograph by author.

more about Korean culture. It was at the CCC that they were first introduced to the sights and sounds of Korean percussion music by way of a samul nori group (composed solely of ethnic Koreans) who practiced at the center.[33] The CCC is housed in a modest building in the Zona Rosa district that features an office and rooms used as classrooms for language courses.[34] Instruction is offered in both Korean and Spanish languages. Korean students come to learn Spanish, and Mexican natives register to learn Korean. The center also offers classes in *puch'ae ch'um* (Korean fan dance) and t'alch'um (Korean masked dance); many of Canto del Cielo's members have taken classes in the Korean fan dance (Ch'oe Namyun interview, July 15, 2010).

In July 2007 a weeklong samul nori workshop was held at the CCC that attracted several Mexican participants. Lee Chŏng-u, a percussionist formerly affiliated with the SamulNori Hanullim troupe, was sent by the SamulNori Hanullim office in Seoul to lead the workshop. Since the workshop participants had never played Korean percussion instruments before, Lee was charged with the task of beginning from square one. Participants learned fundamental playing techniques, from the holding of sticks to the basic *hwimori* (duple meter) rhythmic pattern.

According to Sánchez Zaragoza, the workshop was a great success and spurred a general curiosity and interest in the samul nori genre. Wendy Rodríguez Muñoz, an active member at the CCC, then spearheaded efforts to form a samul nori group from among workshop participants (Rodríguez Muñoz, personal communication, November 23, 2009). She coined the group's name, Canto del Cielo, which she translated into Korean as *Hanŭl sori* (song of the sky).[35] Since a rehearsal space was already available at the CCC, Rodríguez Muñoz merely needed to ensure membership and a teacher who was willing and able to lead the group. Some workshop participants, such as (Aidée) Santillán Moreno, for instance, had already been involved with Korean dance classes at the CCC and gravitated naturally toward the incipient samul nori group. For samul nori instruction, Rodríguez Muñoz called upon Ch'oe Namyun, a Korean émigré who had lived in Paraguay for seventeen years before settling in Mexico in 2001.

Ch'oe grew up in Yongkwang, in the southern Chŏlla Province of Korea. As a small child he learned p'ungmul from elders in his village (Ch'oe Namyun interview, July 15, 2010). He resumed music much later in his life, after he emigrated to Paraguay for business. He became affiliated with a Korean school in Paraguay, and it was there that he first learned the newer genre of samul nori. Ch'oe continued to practice samul nori as a hobby and recalled that he acquired samul nori notation from the National Gugak Center as a way to learn a wider repertory. After relocating to Mexico City, Ch'oe and his wife opened a Korean restaurant in the Zona Rosa district, where the CCC is also located. He teaches the Canto del Cielo group on the weekends at the center. Referred to as "the Professor" by his students, Ch'oe leads the group by calling out drum syllable patterns while also making use of magnified notation printed on large pieces of paper that are affixed to the wall of the studio (see figure 4.5). The members have a photocopied book of notation to consult as well, drawn largely from SamulNori's notated workbooks.

As of July 2010, the group's repertoire consisted of "Yŏngnam nongak," "Uttari p'ungmul," and a modified piece based on the *hwimori changdan* (duple meter rhythmic pattern). The group also learned parts of the "Sŏl changgo karak." Soon after its formation, Canto del Cielo was already asked to perform at a few high-profile events in and around Mexico City. By way of the samul nori workshop that Lee Chŏng-u led in 2007, Canto del Cielo was nominated to participate in the World SamulNori Festival in October 2008. The participants who traveled to Korea included eight women: Wendy Rodríguez Muñoz, Viridiana Sánchez Zaragoza, Maria del Carmen Donají Hernández Vélez, Mariana Campos Pérez, Bárbara Cario Martínez, Ariadna Ramírez Lealde, Martha Bermúdez Ortíz, and Aidée Santillán Moreno. They were accompanied by Ch'oe, who performed with the group onstage and served as a translator, and by the president of the CCC.

This was the first trip to Korea for all the Mexican team members but Rodríguez Muñoz. In an interview, Sánchez Zaragoza noted that her first impressions of Korea were not all that surprising, since she had been exposed to many aspects of the country through her viewing of Korean dramas. The weeklong stay in the somewhat placid town of Puyŏ, however, provided a more balanced picture, contrasting with the hyper-urbanized Seoul: "So the travel show[ed] me another Korea, if we can say that. . . . The town and the people in the town—that was the most important" (Sánchez Zaragoza interview, June 19, 2010).

Although there was genuine excitement among the members during their stay in Korea, the trip was not without some conflict. International travel, the mores of a foreign country, and being forced to be in close proximity with other group members for the entirety of the trip were cause for some internal friction. Sánchez Zaragoza admitted that prior to October 2008, Canto del Cielo members had never spent long periods of time with each other. In Korea, where the "group formation" was requisite at almost all times during the festival (e.g., the foreign groups were expected to eat all meals together, rehearse, and share room assignments), spending all day in close quarters with the group proved to be challenging for some members. After their return to Mexico, there were some changes in membership. One member cited her obligations to family, and two others chose to drop out for more personal reasons. Despite the turnover, Canto del Cielo (under the new name of Samulnori Mexico) carried on with Rodríguez Muñoz, Sánchez Zaragoza, Cario Martínez, Ramírez Lealde, and Santillán Moreno. As of January 2018, the group continues to perform.

SHINAWI, JAPAN

In 2003, Kenichi Yanaka (b. 1983) was a sophomore at Waseda University in Tokyo. During the fall of that year he was invited to participate in a cultural exchange program that was organized for college students from Korea and Japan. Yanaka and twenty other Japanese students, including a woman named Yuki Goto (b. 1983), went on an all-expense-paid trip to Korea for one week. The objective of the program, sponsored by the Korean government under the rubric of the "Korea-Japan Year of Friendly Exchange," was to learn about and experience Korean culture firsthand. For three days the Japanese college students stayed in Puyŏ, in central Korea. There they learned about one of Korea's most popular genres of Korean "traditional" music and engaged in an intensive three-

FIGURE 4.6 The Japanese Shinawi team at the World SamulNori Festival in October 2008. *From left:* Kyosuke Uchida, Mayumi Abe, Yuki Goto, Yuko Noguchi, and Kenichi Yanaka. Photograph courtesy of Kenichi Yanaka.

day course in samul nori at the Puyŏ SamulNori School. This was Yanaka's first time encountering the samul nori percussion genre. Among the other activities planned for the program (e.g., visiting cultural heritage sites and an elementary school), the samul nori intensive workshop proved to be the highlight of the trip for him (Kenichi Yanaka interview, August 14, 2010).

In the beginning of 2004, Yanaka began to discuss with friends the possibility of starting up a college *sa-kuru* (circle) at Waseda University based on the Korean percussion genre that he had learned in Puyŏ.[36] Without any experience except for the brief three-day course at the SamulNori School in Korea, he sought help first from Kim Kyŏng-nan, a graduate of Waseda University who five years earlier had been a member of the university's first samul nori club. A Zainichi Korean (ethnic Korean residing in Japan), Kim had been a driving force of the group during her university years. As is common in college clubs, the group eventually folded, however, after members graduated. Upon meeting Yanaka, she encouraged him to reinstate the samul nori sa-kuru and donated a set of instruments to him. Kim gave Yanaka basic lessons in technique and rhythmic patterns and also suggested that the new group keep the Shinawi name, which refers to a type of instrumental music in Korea that is largely improvised.[37] Kim was unable to step in as the group's instructor, however, since she no longer resided in the area.

Thus, with a very rudimentary understanding of how to play rhythmic patterns, the Waseda University samul nori sa-kuru took a collaborative approach to learning how to play some of the samul nori pieces. Yanaka recalled that over the years, members consulted SamulNori Hanullim's notation booklets and listened to and viewed audiovisual materials as a way to fill in for the absence of an instructor. Just three months after its formation, the nascent group was invited to perform at an event in February 2004. Under the auspices of another Korea-Japan cultural exchange program, five members of the newly reestablished Shinawi group traveled to Korea and performed a short samul nori piece on the stage in front of the Migliore department store in Myŏngdong. The members who traveled to Korea at that time were Mayumi Abe, Yuki Goto, Yuko Noguchi, Kyosuke Uchida, and Kenichi Yanaka. Similar to the American-based Shinparam group's first appearance at the World SamulNori Festival in 2008, the experience of performing in Korea likewise gave momentum to the group in its early stages.

Since its formation in 2004, the Waseda University samul nori sa-kuru underwent the ebb and flow of membership that most university organizations experience on a yearly basis. About 80 percent of the members were native Japanese, with the remainder Zainichi Koreans. Occasionally, native Koreans who have been exchange students at Waseda University have also joined the group for short periods. In the case of college p'ungmul and samul nori clubs in South Korea, the survival of a group is contingent upon a strong *sŏn-hubae* system.[38] Musical transmission and transferral of institutional knowledge occurs from elder to younger colleagues in a cycle that repeats every two to four years. Groups often find themselves in a precarious position when the number of incoming members willing to train and stay in the group is not proportional to the number of senior leaders. In the case of Waseda University's first iteration of the Shinawi sa-kuru, the group ceased to continue after Kim Kyŏng-nan graduated. In the second iteration, two "founding" members continued to stay active in the group, even after graduation from the university. Thus the group maintained a line of senior members since 2004, which helped to ensure its continuity. Even during a year that Yanaka, the de facto leader, spent studying at Hanyang University in Seoul as an exchange student, the samul nori sa-kuru managed to survive. Yanaka joined the p'ungmul *tongari* (group) affiliated with the university and was able to advance his technique and playing of the four percussion instruments. When he returned to Tokyo, he was able to transmit what he had learned in Korea to the Shinawi group. He mentioned that he also viewed YouTube videos of SamulNori and listened to recordings multiple times to solidify his understanding of some of the standard samul nori pieces.

After graduating from Waseda University in 2007, Yanaka continued to serve in a leadership capacity for the Shinawi sa-kuru, which maintained its institutional affiliation with Waseda University. He declined to take responsibility as the group's leader, however, saying that the group dynamic was a collaborative one. He also insisted that the Shinawi sa-kuru was not a group that strove for perfection in its technique but rather was an informal club centered on "drinking, hanging out together, and enjoying playing drums together" (Yanaka interview, August 14, 2010). At the time of the interview, Yanaka was employed by the Korean company Samsung, at a branch in Tokyo. Because of the demands of his work life in Japan, it was difficult to find time for rehearsals except on weekends. Other core members such as Yuki Goto and Mayumi Abe, who were employed at a postal office and a marketing company, respectively, also had other commitments throughout the week. Thus the sa-kuru rehearsed at Waseda University's student center on Saturday afternoons and stored instruments there. The connection with Waseda remained strong, even despite the graduation of some of Shinawi's core members. A blog administered by Yanaka mentions this affiliation:[39]

SHINAWI (シナウィ)

早稲田大学公認サークル「コリア伝統芸能遊戯団シナウィ」のブログへようこそ★

와세다대학교공인 사물놀이동아리 "시나위" 입니다!
저희는 2004년부터 활동하기 시작하여 지금까지 한국과 일본에서
수많은 공연을해왔습니다. 항상 따뜻한 눈으로 지켜봐주시는
여러분들께 감사드립니다. 공연요청도 기꺼이 응하겠습니다.^^
자세한 사항은 관리자에게 문의해주시기
바랍니다. 감사합니다.

SHINAWI

Welcome to the blog for the Waseda University registered club—Korea Traditional Performing Arts—Shinawi!

We are Waseda University's registered SamulNori club, Shinawi!

From our start in 2004 until the present, we have performed numerous concerts in both Japan and Korea. We thank you kindly for your warm reception. We will gladly answer performance requests. ☺ Please send a detailed message to the webmaster with your request. Thank you.

In the fall of 2008, five members of Shinawi traveled to Korea to attend and compete in the World SamulNori Festival in Puyŏ. For Yanaka and Goto, this was their second time in the city of Puyŏ. Given that all the members were employed at the time, it was not feasible for the Shinawi group to arrive any earlier than the evening of October 7. Many of the other international groups had arrived several days before, in order to take lessons and train at the Puyŏ SamulNori School. The group was unable to participate in the opening event of the festival, having arrived only the night before. They went on to compete, however, in the Kyŏrugi competition.

As of September 2010, the club's roster included seven additional members: Go Kaneda, Masako Takahashi, Yuko Kazuno, Rei Sato, Hiroko Fujii, Midori Hanashima, and Akiyo Wakatani. The group continued to rehearse and perform for college festivals and some local events in Tokyo for a few more years before calling it to a close.

―――――

These five profiles provide a glimpse into some of the more extraordinary international encounters with SamulNori over the past two decades. In many ways, these narratives highlight cross-cultural encounters that have led from an enthusiastic reception of a musical repertory into something that is akin to a musical conversion. As Suzanna Samstag, Suzanne Nketia, and Hendrikje Lange noted in their interviews, the act of listening was not enough for them; all three felt compelled to learn how to play Korean percussion after witnessing their first SamulNori performance. Others such as Wendy Rodríguez Muñoz and Kenichi Yanaka became introduced to the samul nori genre through pedagogical workshops that were sponsored by the SamulNori Hanullim organization and partially funded by the Korean government. Their initial encounters, in comparison to those of Samstag and Lange, seem rather muted. Yet the experience of learning samul nori directly from instructors proved to whet their curiosity about the percussion genre, leading to further investigations in Korean music.

In these first encounters—whether by attendance at a SamulNori performance

TABLE 4.1 Descriptors and phrases used by international fans to describe first encounters with SamulNori the quartet and samul nori the genre.

visceral	groove	harmonious
heart-pounding	blown away	natural
exciting	a turf war	graceful
dynamic	exciting group	emotional
primal	a shock	stress release
hypnotic	an earthquake	fun to play
spellbinding	fabulous	bonding experience
	powerful	

These terms are drawn directly from my interviews with samul nori enthusiasts.

or through other means—the common descriptors and phrases uttered by interviewees and fans tend toward the dramatic (see table 4.1). Viewed in another light, some descriptions seem to involve vivid terms that cast SamulNori / samul nori as an exoticized Other. And more conspicuous still is the marked presence of many female interviewees who have been enraptured by a foreign music that was traditionally associated with only men. While it may be of interest to readers to learn more about the popularity of SamulNori / samul nori in relation to exoticism or to its gendered fan base, I leave this line of analysis to future researchers. I am most interested here in the sensory first impressions that comment on dynamism, motion, energy, or the somatic. For international audiences first encountering SamulNori (or SamulNori Hanullim) onstage without any prior knowledge of Korean music, the energy and excitement created by the performers were both palpable and unforgettable.

When fandom then transforms into active musical learning and practice, novices of samul nori bring with them a desire to re-create that dynamism for themselves. In an interview on Arirang TV in 2005, Shinparam member Stephen Wunrow commented on the ineffable yet paradoxically expressive quality of samul nori from the perspective of an amateur performer: "There's something about the music—something about the actual rhythms and the beats of samul nori, I think, educates you about Korean culture in a way that's not with your head, but more with your heart." And Swissamul founder Suzanne Nketia stated simply: "[the power of samul nori] comes from the movement. The movement comes first and then the music. Or the music is movement" (Nketia interview, August 11, 2009).

———

As a whole, these profiles offer alternative ways of considering cross-cultural musical interactions not as part of monolithic processes of globalization but from the perspectives of the individual encounter with samul nori. These global encounters with samul nori are idiosyncratic. But at the same time, there are some common threads in terms of what this music has done to move people. And eclipsing mere spectatorship, the story of samul nori's global flows is one that has become intertwined with the formation of amateur music-making communities around the world. This is significant. In the next chapter we will encounter some of these samul nori groups again—but in South Korea.

FIVE

Transnational Samul Nori and the Politics of Place

> Beyond providing a chance to simply reflect upon the past thirty years, this year's festival creates a place for international samul nori enthusiasts to assemble their energy and spirit together to think productively about how the music of samul nori can generate new cultural or societal values in the future. . . . *Samul nori is no longer solely our own asset.*
>
> Kim Duk Soo, 2008[1]

We know now that samul nori has made an impact. It has transcended its origins as an organic, experimental musical collaboration to become a global music genre. This transformation happened because of a number of factors: SamulNori's international touring schedule, positive audience reception and life-changing encounters, the South Korean government's support of this musical export, the circulation of recordings and notation, and the pedagogical mission of SamulNori Hanullim. But mostly, as I have argued, the dynamism of samul nori's rhythm-based form has contributed to its appeal and to its transmission around the world. Its rhythmic form has helped to draw in first-time listeners and afforded its global journeys. And its rhythmic form is what gives guidance and structure to students and fans-turned-practitioners as they learn how to play Korean instruments for the first time.

But at the risk of painting too rosy a picture of samul nori—absent shortcomings and cultural politics—I also address the limits of samul nori's story of globalization. I have drawn out the point that what we now consider the "samul nori genre" emerged from an intensive process of research, revision, and adaptation by the SamulNori project. In their first years as a group, the SamulNori quartet took on projects that involved the creation of several musical arrangements. What eventually became notated and popularized as the core repertory of samul nori represents just a small slice of the quartet's musical output over time. While "Yŏngnam nongak" and "Samdo nongak karak" are examples of arrangements that were learned by groups outside South Korea, there are other arrangements that never "went global" in the same way. The text-based narrative prayer known as *pinari* is one such example.

In this chapter, I give attention to an important event that featured two SamulNori arrangements—"Yŏngnam nongak" and "Pinari." I show that the two types of forms (rhythm-based and text-based) had different effects and purposes in the conceptual planning of an event that was the centerpiece of an international samul nori festival. Whereas one was deployed to demonstrate global reach, the other was intended to emphasize local heritage and culture. And as it turned out, the two forms also revealed different levels of engagement among the international practitioners of samul nori. A detailed description and analysis of the event, which took place in 2008 in Puyŏ, South Korea, will first be preceded by some important context for it.

The year 2008 was a milestone in SamulNori's history. It marked the passing of thirty years since the first groundbreaking performances by the four musicians at Space Theater. It also recognized the impact of the quartet's formation and the subsequent emergence of the samul nori genre. Many projects were planned to celebrate the thirtieth anniversary, including the publication of a commemorative book, the convening of an International SamulNori Symposium in January 2009, and the reunion tour of the "original" SamulNori quartet. Underwritten by Credia Korea, the highly publicized tour brought together three of the four surviving members of the quartet—Kim Duk Soo, Lee Kwang Soo, and Choi Jong Sil.[2] Nam Kimun (formerly of the Seoul-based Namsadang troupe) stepped in as the fourth performer, replacing Kang Min-seok, who had declined to participate.[3] Touted by the Korean press as the SamulNori "Dream Team," the ensemble of seasoned performers played to Korean audiences who were curious to witness this rare assemblage of the "founding fathers" of SamulNori. Posters used to promote the tour featured slick images of the four musicians in black tie, as well as in the standard attire that is associated with the samul nori genre (figure 5.1).

The first performances of the tour were held at the Sejong Center for the Performing Arts (Sejong Munhwa Hoegwan), one of Seoul's premier venues for the

Transnational Samul Nori 109

FIGURE 5.1 The "Founding Fathers of SamulNori," an image used to promote the SamulNori thirtieth anniversary concert tour in 2008. *From left:* Lee Kwang Soo, Choi Jong Sil, Nam Kimun, and Kim Duk Soo. Photograph courtesy of SamulNori Hanullim.

arts. Although there was a great deal of hype surrounding the concerts, reviews of the performances were lukewarm. While many younger fans were dazzled by the collective star power of the performers, critics and older fans complained that the musicians were no longer in sync with one another, leading to underwhelming performances (Samstag 2008a, 75; Joo Jay-youn, personal communication). The simple yet telling Korean expression "The breath [hohŭp] was not together" was whispered frequently by insiders who expressed disappointment at the event. In many respects the reunion concerts that "commemorated the birth of SamulNori" were more of a symbolic gesture than a bona fide attempt to re-create the past. Still, the reunion of three of the four principal members—who had not parted on the best of terms—represented a significant moment in SamulNori's history.

Later that same year, Kim Duk Soo's SamulNori Hanullim organization hosted the World SamulNori Festival and Competition in the county of Puyŏ. The three-day event, held October 10–12, featured more than seventy participating teams and was prefaced by a weeklong workshop for eleven international samul nori teams from nine different countries (see table 5.1). The workshop was held at SamulNori Hanullim's own school, known as the SamulNori Hanullim Puyŏ Educational Institute (SamulNori Hanullim Puyŏ Kyoyugwŏn). The event brought together a record number of international participants and attracted national media attention because of the thirtieth anniversary year.

While the reunion tour applauded the legacy and accomplishments of the SamulNori quartet, the World SamulNori Festival celebrated the outward transmission of the samul nori genre and the emergence of international samul nori ensembles over three decades. Because of the singularity of this event—a commemorative occasion with international samul nori teams converging at the same time and place on the native terrain from which samul nori was conceived—I devote a substantial portion of this chapter to it.

BACKGROUND TO THE SAMUL NORI FESTIVAL

September 27–29, 1989, marked the first SamulNori competition and festival for amateur samul nori ensembles (Joo Jay-youn 2010, 63). Held at the Seoul Olympic Stadium (designed by Space Theater impresario and architect Kim Sugŭn), the event took place one year after South Korea hosted the 1988 Summer Olympics in Seoul. Since then, the SamulNori Kyŏrugi Hanmadang (SamulNori Competition and Festival) has largely remained an annual event, typically held in the fall.[4] Venues have included a variety of locations in South Korea: the

TABLE 5.1 International samul nori teams represented at the World SamulNori Festival, October 10–12, 2008

Belgium	Mujigae (Brussels)
China	Lilac (Harbin)
France	Samul over the Rainbow (Paris)
Germany	Senari (Berlin)
Japan	Shinawi (Tokyo)
	Han Taep'ung (Osaka)
	Ch'ŏngsa Ch'orong (Amagasaki)
Mexico	Canto del Cielo (Mexico City)
Russia	Sakhalin Korean Culture Center (Sakhalin Island)
Switzerland	Swissamul (Basel)
United States	Shinparam (Minneapolis–Saint Paul, Minnesota)

National Gugak Center (1991), Ch'anggyŏng Palace (1995), Tŏksu Palace (1999), Yangpy'ŏng athletic field (2000), and Yongmunsan (2001–2004).[5] The selection of the festival site has mostly been contingent on the availability of funding from regional governments and local city offices. From 2005 to 2008 the county of Puyŏ in the southern Ch'ungch'ŏng Province hosted the SamulNori competition and festival.

At the heart of the SamulNori Kyŏrugi Hanmadang is a contest in which samul nori teams perform in two rounds of competition over the course of three days. The noun form *kyŏrugi* in fact relates to the verb *kyŏruda*, meaning "to compete" or "to vie (for)." Although there is a category of competition for semiprofessional teams, SamulNori's Kyŏrugi celebrates and encourages participation from all walks of life. The majority of these amateur teams come from schools, universities, civic organizations, and cultural clubs throughout South Korea. All teams, amateur and semiprofessional, compete in various categories for prizes, with the most coveted being the President's Award. Based on recommendations and applications from participants, the SamulNori Hanullim organization also invites a handful of international teams to attend the competition. In past years these teams have typically received partial or full reimbursement for airfare from the Ministry of Culture, Sports, and Tourism and coverage of accommodations and meals by SamulNori Hanullim.[6]

The main thrust of the competition has always been the contest for amateur samul nori groups, which culminates in an awards ceremony on the closing day. Although each evening of the Kyŏrugi has featured performances by either Kim Duk Soo's ensemble or professional musicians (usually appearing in the "Friends of SamulNori" Saturday concert), the evening events are more of a postlude to the day's rounds of competition. For the past several years the sequence of events in a SamulNori competition and festival has followed a standardized and efficient schedule. Held over one weekend from Friday to Sunday in order to maximize attendance, the Kyŏrugi has typically drawn several hundred participants in a given year. In the application process prior to the festival, groups elect to compete in one of three basic categories: samul nori, p'ungmul, and *ch'angjak*. The *ch'angjak* category refers to "newly created compositions" that may include works considered as "crossover" or "fusion" with non-Korean instruments or musical idioms.

On the morning of the festival's opening day, representatives from the competing groups draw for order and begin the first round of competition. Teams are organized by the main festival staff into a range of subcategories according to "amateur" or "professional" status and "age"—the latter being delineated into brackets of elementary school, middle school, high school, college, and adult divisions. A separate category for "foreign" teams includes both non-Korean and ethnic Korean samul nori groups that reside outside South Korea. Teams in this category are usually invited directly by the SamulNori Hanullim organization, although some may have been selected to participate through a standard application process.

After the first day of preliminary competition, all participants typically take part in a large-scale processional parade known in local terms as *kilnori* or "street play." The kilnori features all performers involved in the event, including members of the SamulNori Hanullim artistic troupe. It is not a rehearsed performance but rather an informal procession of participants perambulating on the festival grounds while drumming, culminating in a rousing and unified "jam" session. The kilnori is borrowed from p'ungmul and also the namsadang traditions, where musicians process from one area or village to the next while playing and dancing (Hesselink 2006, 165). An allusion to the kilnori is also included in a standard SamulNori program, with the *mun kut* processional that segues into the opening act of the pinari.[7] In SamulNori's interpretation, performers congregate in the lobby just prior to the beginning of a concert and process down the aisles to the stage, where they then perform the pinari.

The first day of the Kyŏrugi also features an opening ceremony with introductory remarks and acknowledgments by Kim Duk Soo and a select group of local officials. The second day resumes with a full schedule devoted to the preliminary round of competition. To give a sense of the scale of the competition, in 2007, for instance, there were fifty-six groups with a total of 702 participants competing in the preliminary round. A panel of four to five judges (one of whom is the artistic director, Kim Duk Soo) then sits through the two rounds of competition.[8] At the close of the second day, while the judges tabulate the scores, there is usually a concert featuring guest artists invited by the SamulNori Hanullim organization. In past years guest performers have included p'ansori artist An Suksŏn and pop singer Han Yŏng'ae.[9] The third day begins with the final round of competition and concludes in the evening with the awards ceremony, hosted by an emcee. The closing ceremony then features performances by the winning teams.

Although the majority of attendees are indeed the domestic samul nori groups appearing in the competition, the festival planning committee goes to great lengths to ensure an enjoyable experience for both local and foreign attendees. The festival grounds house various "Experience Culture" activity stations, photography exhibits, merchant stalls, food kiosks, and a main open-air stage for evening performances. As there are several different events running simultaneously, the festival planning committee requires the assistance of volunteers and also technical staff who are often called on as freelancers. In a report issued by SamulNori Hanullim in November 2007, for instance, the sixteenth SamulNori Kyŏrugi Hanmadang listed fifty-six people as festival staff affiliates (SamulNori Hanullim 2007, 7).

By 2008 the Kyŏrugi competition was a well-established music event, already in its seventeenth iteration. During the previous sixteen years of the contest, the event was referred to as the SamulNori Kyŏrugi Hanmadang, which loosely translates as the "SamulNori Competition and Festival."[10] In October 2008, however, a new English title was bestowed on the event—the World SamulNori Festival. In keeping with the self-congratulatory and laudatory tones peppering the discourse surrounding SamulNori's thirtieth anniversary, the name change reflects a conscious shift in both scope and emphasis placed on the international profile of the 2008 festival. The *2008 World SamulNori Festival: Results Report* states that it was indeed "only fitting to replace the '*kyŏrugi*' moniker with a more apropos 'festival' appellation" because it had expanded its circumference of activities to include a "World Networking Program" and had become a more rounded cultural and international event (SamulNori Hanullim 2008, 5).

ARRIVAL IN PUYŎ

Puyŏ is nestled in the central heartland of South Korea, about two hours away by car from Seoul. In addition to serving as the site for the 2008 World SamulNori Festival, Puyŏ is home to the "SamulNori School," where many people from around the world have come to learn Korean percussion. As the former overseas coordinator for SamulNori Hanullim, I had visited the SamulNori Hanullim Puyŏ Kyoyukwŏn many times. In 2008, I was given a ride to Puyŏ by Joo Jay-youn, the managing director at SamulNori Hanullim and my former boss. When we arrived in the city center, I was surprised to discover that the festival grounds were located right in the middle of a cultural heritage complex in downtown Puyŏ and adjacent to the Chŏngnim temple, a well-known tourist attraction (figures 5.2 and 5.3). A nationally designated cultural property, the historic temple is most famous for its five-tiered granite pagoda, which was constructed in the sixth century, during the Paekche kingdom. Given that the theme of Buddhism plays a role in the opening ceremony's "International Pinari," I include the following description of the temple:

BUYEO JEONGNIMSA [PUYŎ CHŎNGNIM TEMPLE] SITE

Historic Site No. 301

    Located at Dongnam-ri [Tongnam-ri], Buyeo-eup [Puyŏ-ŭp], Buyeo-gun [Puyŏ-kun], Chungcheongnam-do [Ch'ungch'ŏngnam-do]

    This is the site of a Buddhist temple. The temple was built soon after Baekje [Paekche] moved the capital to Sabi (the ancient name of Buyeo [Puyŏ]). The temple used to be a single-storied one typical of Baekje's temples [Paekche kingdom: 18 BCE–663 CE]. . . . In the Goryeo period [Koryo: 918–1392 CE] the temple was called Jeongnimsa Temple [Chŏngnimsa]. This fact was clarified due to the discovery of a roof tifle. The roof tile produced in 1028 is inscribed with the name, Jeongnimsa. . . . A stone statue of the seated Buddha was discovered at the site of the lecture hall.[11]

A new cultural arts complex was built around the original temple grounds in the mid-to-late 2000s. Stone-colored bricks were laid neatly in rows to form wide walkways between stretches of green lawn in the surrounding areas of the site. In the distance were still the familiar low mountainous peaks. The location itself—with its treasured monuments and new cultural heritage museum—seemed to me a peculiar venue for an international drumming festival. As I was to discover, however, the selection of the Chŏngnim site was one that resonated well with the bold objectives of the 2008 festival.

THE OPENING CEREMONY

Not surprisingly, the opening concert of the 2008 World SamulNori Festival turned out to be the most ambitious opening event in SamulNori's history of hosting the competition and festival. In years past, the kickoff event featured Kim Duk Soo's SamulNori Hanullim troupe, sometimes appearing with other kugak performers. This year was to be different. As a way to showcase the globalization of samul nori, all the performers affiliated with international teams were to perform on the same stage.

    The preparations for the opening ceremony began at the Puyŏ SamulNori Educational Institute a few days before the start of the festival. During this pe-

FIGURE 5.2 The Chŏngnim temple and pagoda, seen in the background of the festival's outdoor seating area. Photograph by author.

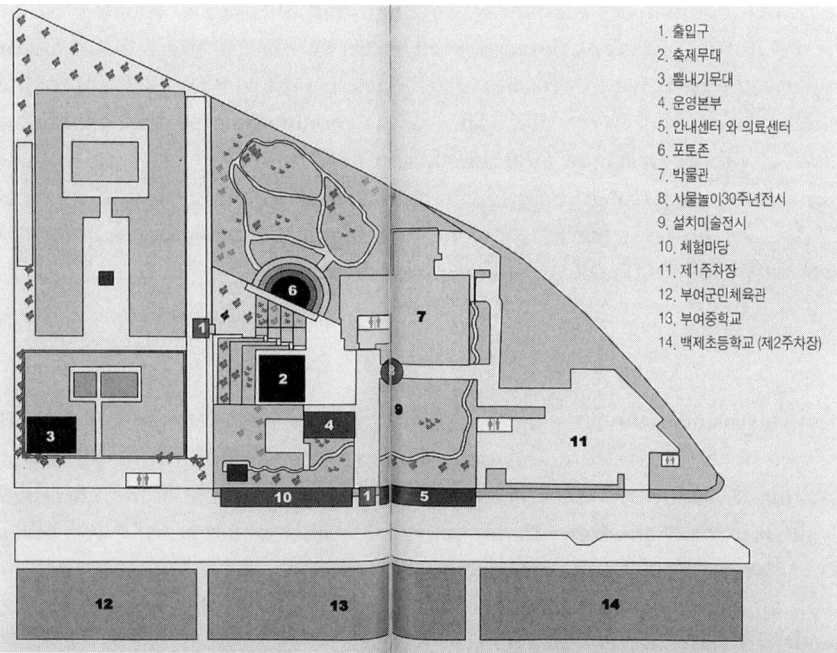

FIGURE 5.3 Map of the festival grounds for the 2008 World SamulNori Festival in Puyŏ, South Korea. The historic Chŏngnim temple grounds (in the upper left corner) were flanked on adjacent sides by two outdoor stages (3, 2). The main stage used during the opening event (2) was located close to the Chŏngnimsaji Museum (7), while other festival components were located on the lawn. Image courtesy of SamulNori Hanullim.

riod, international teams rehearsed their prepared pieces for the competition and received instruction from members of SamulNori Hanullim. The amateur teams also participated in large group rehearsals for the opening concert, under the musical direction of Kim Duk Soo. With the exception of the French team (who were members of a professional theatrical troupe), most participants had never taken part in a large-scale musical production before.[12] Drawing on ethnographic observations and analyses of my field notes and field videos, I now provide an extended narrative description of key moments during the October 10 opening ceremony of the 2008 World SamulNori Festival.

Dusk has fallen. About one hundred meters from the large outdoor stage the performers have gathered near one of the gates for entry to the festival space. They are poised to begin performing at any moment, with colorful flags and instruments in tow. Yet they remain on standby, obligated to wait through the opening comments by the emcee, the English interpreter, and various local officials. They stand inconspicuous to the audience, who have already taken their seats and whose eyes are directed toward the illuminated stage. The only people who notice the curious assemblage of international participants are the stragglers, who file past the entrance and the group of performers. My camera captures them as they quickly brush by. Men clad in black suits point the latecomers to the empty chairs in the back. I am positioned directly in front of the performers, since I am aware of the order of events for the evening. I have a clear view, thanks to the gaggle of journalists and cameramen who take to filming the speakers onstage. At times, I pivot in that direction; the stage appears as beacons of light in the near distance. I want to document as much of this sensory experience as possible—from panning the local audience to focusing in on the person delivering remarks at the podium. When I zoom in to the stage, however, my footage becomes wobbly because of the distance and the unsteadiness of the corporeal tripod. Since the speakers are decently amplified, even from where I stand, I decide to try to multitask.

Scanning back to my original vantage point, I see that Kim Duk Soo has now entered the frame. Of modest stature yet brawny build, Kim's figure cuts a larger-than-life presence to those who know him. He dons a chartreuse *hanbok* accentuated with a red scarf. He speaks to the young college-age volunteers who have been elected as the flag bearers for the evening's event. The casualness of their dress is offset by the flags that they carry. There are ten national flags, representing South Korea and each of the other nine countries from which the festival participants hail. The flag bearers stand in pairs, at the head of the line. Korea and Mexico assume the lead position. In the middle of a set of opening remarks, Kim Duk Soo directs the entire group to inch closer to their starting point. The time is getting closer, but there is still at least one other speaker slated for the podium. It is very clear to me that Kim is anxious to get the *kilnori* on its figurative road.

———

Directly behind the flag bearers is the team of ethnic Koreans (Zainichi) from the Kŏn'guk School in Osaka, Japan. They too bear flags, although theirs are decorated with colorful images of dragons and animals of the Chinese zodiac. Their group is the largest of the international teams, and several members display instruments other than the ubiquitous drums and gongs of Korean percussion.[13] Some of the participants carry conches (*nagak*) and long trumpets known as *napal*, instruments that are not part of contemporary samul nori practice.[14] Rather, these are sonic emblems that intimate more ancient lineal affinities of samul nori, such as the variations of *ch'wit'a* heard in military band processionals and Buddhist instrumental band music. Although the group members are young, they carry themselves with an assured presence, forming a united and impressive front. Some of them start to practice spinning the *sangmo* and warming up their legs for the show. Because they are such a large group, I can only make out silhouettes of the performers who have lined up behind them. The anticipation just before the official start is palpable in the air.

    The signal from Joo Jay-youn (who is the evening's emcee) finally comes, and we then hear the striking of the *ilch'ae* pattern on the barrel- and hourglass-shaped drums, interspersed with punctuated grunts. Three affiliate members of SamulNori Hanullim are the ones leading the musical intro. They stand just behind the team from Osaka. The long, sustained notes on the conch and trumpet then ceremoniously join in, and are followed in quick suit by a blanket of percussive sounds. The audience have now turned their attention to the sounds, which are audible from their far left. The flag bearers have stationed themselves perpendicular to the performers, and move closer to the stage. Their comportment has changed from slouchy to well postured. Meanwhile, the popular "Arirang" tune is cheerfully rendered on the set of melodic gong chimes by the Korean-

Japanese ch'wit'a band. The tempo is an upbeat one, and the performers start to walk in place, bobbing up and down.

"Mun Yŏpsio! Mun Yŏpsio!" booms the stentorian voice of Kim Duk Soo, calling for the festival's symbolic gates to be opened. "Republic of Korea, and the South Ch'ungch'ŏng Province—Puyŏ district! World SamulNori Festival—Chŏngnimsaji [Chŏngnim temple]—Sumo General—Open the gates!" Participants respond with a prolonged "Ye-eeeeeeee."

"From all corners of the world, the [international] samul nori teams have come, with the county of Puyŏ and the Republic of Korea, and the world village, many people gather together and go toward the Chŏngnimsaji. Now we shall enter!" "Ye-eeeeeeee." And with that, the procession begins.

While drumming, the participants now make their way to the stage. I stand in one place, watching as this spectacle of nations passes by. The fully outfitted ch'wit'a band, with their rigid kicks of the legs moving in time with the music, play up the exaggerated embodiment of the martial. They arrange themselves in two straight lines, synchronizing their stylized leg movements with the whole of their group. This contrasts sharply with the relaxed and buoyant spring that the professional SamulNori performers have to their step. The diverse group that follows behind the de facto leaders then sprawls out, not adhering to any explicit sense of order. Groups sometimes appear in clusters, walking together. A few members of the Russian team, for instance, find themselves walking next to the Mexican group and sandwiched in between members of the Swiss team. The formation of performers is not organized by instrument, either. Barrel-drum players appear side by side with small gong players, and then at other times there is an entire row of people playing the hourglass-shaped drums. A visual scan of the loose configurations of performers also brings into relief those who have learned well the embodied practice of hohŭp that emphasizes a holistic connection of the breath to the body when performing. For others, the movements are less natural, and the coordination between playing an instrument and purposefully bending the knees when "walking" appears to sacrifice one action for the other.

With other groups, it is not so much the way in which the body moves but what adorns the body that stands out. The women of the Chinese team from Harbin, for instance, wear patterned *cheongsam* while playing the drums and gongs. And peeking out from just behind them are the nodding outlines of peacock feathers. These belong to the exuberant headdresses of the Mexican team, who wear traditional Aztec dress. From the Russian team, there are two women who are clothed in traditional Russian peasant dress. The other members of their group, however, who are fourth-generation Korean Russians, wear the standard black samul nori outfit with colorful sashes. Likewise, not all groups have opted for the display of ethnic garb. The all-female Swiss team sport a look that is a cross between the modern, modified hanbok and the baggy two-piece attire worn by Korean Buddhist monks. And the American team, which would be hard-pressed to come up with a representative ethnic costume, dress in blue jeans and black T-shirts printed with their group's name.

Cameramen run in front of my camera now, trying to get a good shot of this parade of diversity. The flag bearers have taken their positions in front of the stage, directly facing the audience, while the group of over one hundred performers files in from the left side of the audience proper. A bottleneck forms as the group waits to climb up the one set of stairs onto the stage. As more and more people make their way onto the stage, the movement of people begins to take on a "snail" formation. Growing in density, the crowd squeezes in closer to one another. At the nucleus are the members of the Osaka-based team, visible now only by their *pup'o* feathered hats. Once everyone is onstage, the small-gong players give the signal for the faster-paced duple *hwimori* rhythm. People face the center of the circle and skip sideways to the beat. The spiral of bodies whirls toward the right, and then finishes to immediate applause from the audience.

Instead of bowing toward the audience, however, the group bows to the *kosa* table of offerings, located at the back of the stage. Kim Duk Soo then comes onto the stage with a handheld microphone. The performers continue to drum, rearranging themselves by forming several lines that face the audience. Kim introduces himself and bows respectfully to the audience. He begins his set of introductory remarks: "We celebrate now the thirtieth anniversary of the birth of SamulNori. . . . In this magnificent historical and cultural city of Puyŏ, right here at the Chŏngnimsaji site, we have representatives from all around the world—world Samulnorians—who have all gathered together in this one place." Kim goes on to announce the program for the evening's special event. "Today's first program [of the International Pinari] has no historical precedent. . . . Right now, the world is difficult. The representatives from each international country, in their own native tongues, will pray for peace. And give well-wishes for the city of Puyŏ. . . . So now I ask kindly if the representatives from the Puyŏ local offices will please come up to the stage—perform well-wishes for world peace, and ask for the stability of the economy.[15] [We will now have the] lighting of the candles. Thank you. And thus we shall begin."

PERFORMING PINARI

And with that grandiose introduction, the pinari for the 2008 World SamulNori Festival officially commenced. But unlike other standard performances of this narrative prayer song that opens a SamulNori program, this performance was unusual and, as Kim Duk Soo announced, historic. Never before had an "International Pinari" been attempted, and never before had such a diverse cast of foreign samul nori players been assembled to participate in a large-scale performance of it. The 2008 "International Pinari" was an ambitious undertaking that served as the conceptual backdrop for an elaborate ninety-minute production that reified and artfully manipulated depictions of the local, the national, and the international.

As the sole text-based piece in the SamulNori repertory, the pinari narrates a cross-section of Korea's history, geography, and culture, and a complex composite of spiritual beliefs. Unlike the other standard numbers in SamulNori's repertory, the rhythmic accompaniment actually takes a backseat in this work. In an oft-cited description of pinari penned by Suzanna Samstag for SamulNori's program notes, it is described as "a sweeping prayer song that is used to signal the beginning of a stay at a village. The shaman sings an extensive prayer that recounts the tale of creation and many other aspects of Korean beliefs. It calls on various spirits that live in the village and its homes, asking for a blessing upon the people, the players, and the ground they inhabit."[16] As with their arrangement and adaptation of p'ungmul rhythms into "compositions," the SamulNori quartet also adapted the pinari narrative song into its performances.

In a standard ninety-minute performance where "Pinari" is the opening number on the program, performers typically make an unconventional entrance into the theater from the lobby. This is meant to bear some resemblance to the *mun kut* ritual. The mun kut is usually performed at the gate or entrance to a village by p'ungmul or namsadang troupes. It functions as an annunciation of sorts, and begins with a clarion call asking for the "symbolic" gates of the space to be opened. In the SamulNori version, the performers proceed through the same doors where the audience enters and begin a processional that leads directly to the stage. The four percussion instruments of samul nori are heard in combination with the sharp nasal timbres of the *t'aep'yŏngso* (shawm), as the musicians step gracefully in time to the *chajinmori* (12/8) rhythmic cycle. Meanwhile, the audience's attention has been successfully diverted to the musicians, who eventually assemble in a line formation onstage. The lead singer steps up onto the stage and then begins the pinari, with instrumental accompaniment provided by the other musicians.

While there are many variations of the pinari text and possibilities for improvisation during the course of a performance, the versions performed by Lee Kwang Soo have become models for subsequent generations of samul nori musicians.[17] It was one of Lee's renditions of "Pinari" from which SamulNori Hanullim member Ch'oe Ch'an-kyun drew in his performance for the 2008 "International Pinari."

The first few lines of Lee's "Pinari" cover a lot of territory—in the metaphorical and the literal sense.[18] The text of the prologue (part 1) opens with the creation of the skies and earth, and then moves very strategically to narrate the foundation of the Chosŏn (Yi) dynasty, which ruled from 1392 until 1910.[19] The city of Hanyang (now Seoul) was auspiciously selected as the seat of administration. The Yi dynasty, born immaculately out of the cosmos, brings peace and prosperity to the people of the Chosŏn state. The designation of Hanyang was made in accordance with the principles of geomancy, heeding the correct alignment of the capital with the Samgak Mountain. It is atop the rising phoenix upon which the grand palace of Chosŏn is erected, and facing the phoenix are laid the foundations for six ministries of governance.

천개 (天開)—우주 (宇宙) 하날이요
지개조축 (地開造蓄) 땅 생길제
국태민안 (國泰民安) 법륜전 (法輪轉)
시화연풍 (時和年豊) 돌아들고
이씨한양 (李氏漢陽) 등극시 (登極時)
삼각산 (三角山) 기봉 (起峯) 하고
봉황(鳳凰) 이 생겼구나
봉황(鳳凰) 눌러 대궐 (大闕) 짓고
대궐 (大闕) 앞에는 육조 (六曹) 로다

The sky and the universe open, and the ground of the earth comes into
    formation. The prosperity and safety of a nation's people are cultivated,
    in accordance with the Buddhist scripture.
Peace and bountiful harvest comes to the country year after year.
It was the time of the establishment of the city of Hanyang as the seat
    of administration for the Chosŏn Yi dynasty.

> The Samgak Mountain stands,
> The phoenix rises; and upon the phoenix the grand palace is constructed,
> And in front of the phoenix lie six administrative centers.[20]

"Place" is given central importance in this abbreviated genesis narrative of the Chosŏn dynasty, as it identifies important local sites within the capital city such as the Samgak Mountain and the Han River. The text also describes how the harmonious alignment of mountains and waterways has led to the obvious selection of Seoul as an administrative center—the rising phoenix of the grand palace with the six governing ministries facing it.

After its narrated mapping of the natural environs of Seoul, the text moves into a second section (Salp'uri—part 2) that intimates an undeniable connection to Korea's indigenous shamanistic legacies. In an abrupt change of narrative content, the singer quickly lists the numerous kinds of calamities and adversities—*sal*—that can strike humans during their lifetime. More than twenty-eight kinds of adversities or "negative forces" are named. Some are domestic misfortunes that befall those with an ailing parent or a deceased loved one. Other misfortunes arise from being out of favor with indigenous spirits such as the Mountain God and the Underwater Dragon King. By naming and identifying the different kinds of sal, the singer of the pinari attempts to placate such spirits and deities and also to mitigate some of the adversities people encounter in life. The third section, Ch'ukwŏn tŏkdam, shifts tone by moving into a prayer-like mode. The singer beseeches blessings of well-being for the residents of a house. A refrain that invokes blessings and good fortune is sung by the rest of the ensemble (who also accompany the singer with the *chajinmŏri* pattern). This section of the pinari most resembles the Buddhist chant known as *yŏmbul*.

The pinari is a highly complex, literary text. Even the translation of a few lines of this Sino-Korean text into English requires a referential knowledge of premodern Korean history and culture. While the pinari in and of itself merits a full-length study, the point I underline here is that the introductory passage of the narrative invokes place, religion, and history. As such, it is best understood by people who have a high degree of proficiency in the Korean language. It is perhaps for this reason—the dense literary and religious text—that the pinari is one of the pieces least performed by amateur samul nori groups outside Korea. Simply put, the language and interpretive skills required demand a linguistic and cultural fluency on the part of the singer. On a performative level, the pinari is

Transnational Samul Nori **123**

a challenging piece and can fall flat or lose its efficacy if performed by an inept orator. The singer must be able to memorize and deliver long sections of text, preferably with charisma. Even within Korea the pinari is often excluded from the samul nori repertory that amateur groups learn and perform. It remains a specialty genre, primarily the trademark of Lee Kwang Soo, Park An-ji [Pak Anji] (of the Samul GwangDae quartet), and just a handful of other professional samul nori musicians.

Although various renditions of the narrative chant have been documented and transcribed by Korean scholars such as Kim Hŏnsŏn, and in a master's thesis by Kim Suyong, the pinari text has not been incorporated into SamulNori Hanullim's pedagogical workbooks (Kim Hŏnsŏn 1995; Kim Suyong 2005). The workbooks (of which there are several now) feature notation for only the percussion pieces. It is not easily taught, nor is it easily learned—even by native Koreans.[21] And to the best of my knowledge, only a handful of amateur international ensembles have attempted to perform the pinari on a regular basis. The pinari, then, can be seen as the one piece in the samul nori repertory that has stubbornly resisted "going global." With its specific references to place, the pinari maintains an intimate connection with Korean history and Korean culture. Moreover, the linguistic and performative abilities it requires of the musician make the pinari a work that is largely undertaken by Korean specialists.

THE POLITICS OF PLACE IN AN INTERNATIONAL PINARI

The pinari is a narrative song that savors its provenance. The notion of an international pinari performed by the World Samul Nori teams, then, raises the question of how such a performance negotiates or retains its sense of locality amid the diverse background of its international participants. Would the pinari lose its local flavor? Or would the sense of a Korean locality somehow be strengthened by its international cast of performers? As I learned from my observations of the rehearsals, interviews with the participants and staff, and filming of the opening event, the mapping and performance of place was a meticulously choreographed and constructed undertaking, where identifications of the "local" were grafted onto more sweeping nationalistic proclamations.

Some of the following examples offer insights into how the concept of place was linguistically evoked in the opening section of the "International Pinari" during the 2008 opening ceremony. Again, my field video recording of the event serves as the base for analysis. Ch'oe Ch'an-kyun was the lead singer (and kkwaenggwari player) for this performance. Ch'oe begins with what appears to be a standard rendition of Lee Kwang Soo's version of the pinari text. Just after the relation of the designation of Hanyang as the capital city for the Chosŏn dynasty, however, there is a sudden transition to something different and unexpected.

Rather than continuing on with the narrative, Ch'oe steps back from the microphone. Representatives from each international samul nori group then come up and say a few words of introduction. In the spirit of the pinari's third section, each speaker bestows a set of well wishes upon the Korean audience. Here, a representative from each samul nori team becomes a symbolic spokesperson for a participating country. Since the performers were not expected to learn the Korean text, they spoke in their native languages, albeit with some awkward inflections and cadences. The first person to recite was Stephen Wunrow of the Shinparam p'ungmul troupe, based in the Twin Cities in Minnesota: "We come from Minnesota, land of ten thousand lakes, where the women are strong, the men are good looking, and the children are above average. We wish you peace, friendship, and we thank the heaven and the earth and the people of Puyŏ!"[22] The reference to Garrison Keillor's *Prairie Home Companion* worked as a "local" symbol of Minnesota and, perhaps more imaginatively, as a linguistic morsel of Americana.

Other team representatives spoke in turn and presented similar self-introductions and blessings in Spanish (Canto del Cielo), Russian (Sakhalin Korean Culture Center), French (Samul over the Rainbow), and German (Swissamul). One of the final participants to take to the microphone was the representative from the Osaka (Han Taep'ung) team, a Zainichi Korean affiliated with the Kŏn'guk school as a teacher.[23] "Hello, and good evening!" he began. "We come from Japan. We are a group consisting of second-, third-, and fourth-generation Korean Japanese [members]. We really like Korean culture! And we especially love samul nori!" Although the Korean Japanese representative was also fluent in Korean, he spoke in Japanese.[24] He might have easily delivered the same message in Korean or even attempted to sing a portion of the original pinari text. But it was the sounds of Japanese that most effectively invoked difference within the context of the "International Pinari." In the opening segment of this production, the demarcation of nation-states was thus strategically articulated through the use of different languages within the pinari.

I contend that the selection of the pinari text in the festival's opening event not only served to evoke nostalgia for a cultural high point in Korea's history; it also sought to articulate South Korea's aspirations to be a key player in a twenty-first-century global community. This nationalistic posturing became even more evident during the second half of the performance, when the "International Pinari" unexpectedly segued into a medley of musical performances—a kind of potpourri of geographical diversity framed within the contours of a "local" piece. Teams presented brief performances that were designed to highlight the distinctiveness of their country's culture. This was a deliberate intervention on the part of the festival's chief architect, Kim Duk Soo.

Festival participants themselves were not always attuned to the politics of place that were activated in these various musical and cultural registers, whether because of language barriers or other miscommunication, or simply as a matter of concepts being lost in cultural translation. The selection of representatives for the "International Pinari" chant, for instance, caused much internal turmoil for a few groups in rehearsal. Some participants were reticent to perform onstage as team representatives, while others were unaware of what their role was in the production. On the festival organizers' end, what was most desired was the convincing embodiment of *difference*, as opposed to a virtuosic imitation of the Korean narrative. For this reason, selected team representatives for the pinari were advised by Kim Duk Soo to speak in the language that would best capture a sense of "foreignness" or "otherness." And, in the case of the Russian and the American teams, for instance, Korean adoptees or ethnic Koreans were intentionally not selected, in order to highlight visually the internationalization of the samul nori genre.

In an interview I conducted with a member of the American team, I learned that the group was ill prepared for the variety-show-like segment of the production. Because of a missed communication, the organizers' agenda of having each group perform its own "national identity" was a point unfortunately lost on this group: "We realized our group was very informal. Our group is mostly a way to have fellowship and to appreciate p'ungmul for what it is. . . . I just realized it when we rehearsed in front of Kim Duk Soo. What we were supposed to have prepared . . . right, this kind of traditional piece that reflected our country's tradition; I don't know if you caught on, but we were completely unprepared. . . . Apparently, in some e-mail we should have gotten the message that we were to prepare a very short piece that demonstrated the tradition of our own countries. . . . We just didn't get this message. So Mexico brought their drums . . . [and] everyone had their own [kind of ethnic] deal worked out. And we had nothing. We were panicking. . . . We had prepared to do just an improvised stand-in piece. So we performed, and Kim Duk Soo was not happy with this because we were supposed to be reflective of the United States" (interview with Nik Nadeau, July 1, 2009).

The American group was advised by Kim Duk Soo to perform a seated samul nori piece as an alternative. Although Shinparam would have been hard-pressed to convincingly perform an "American identity" even if they had received the advance notice from the festival planning committee, the episode reveals the cultural politics at play in the conceptualization and production of the "International Pinari." It also speaks to the power differentials that existed as a consequence of the structuring and funding of the event. International samul nori teams were beholden to the wishes of the organizers and the artistic director (who were on their home turf). In the end, SamulNori Hanullim had the upper hand.

The team from Mexico (Canto del Cielo) decided to stage their traditional heritage by preparing an Aztec dance to perform in the "medley" portion of the "International Pinari." Much to the delight of the Korean organizers and the Korean media, the Mexican team came equipped with Aztec headdresses and outfits (figure 5.4). Yet as I learned from an interview with one of the founding members of the group, the Aztec performance came together at nearly the last minute. Viridiana Sánchez Zaragoza explained that the Mexican group was unsure whether it would even be able to travel to Korea until two weeks prior to the festival. Once they received confirmation from SamulNori Hanullim that their airfare would be covered, they scrambled to buy the appropriate outfits and accoutrements: "We went to a person who practices the dance in the Zócalo [the main square in Mexico City]. It's a very popular place, you know? Yeah, in the Zócalo, there's a lot of dance—Aztec dance, dancers. And we asked some of them to teach us the basic steps" (Sánchez Zaragoza interview, June 19, 2010).

Thus, just prior to their departure for Korea, the Mexican samul nori team learned quite expediently and effectively how to perform Aztec culture for the opening event of the World SamulNori Festival. Although they were complete novices in Aztec dance and had rustled up their costumes and choreography in extreme haste, the group members convincingly portrayed their newfound culture to a Korean audience. It seemed, in retrospect, that the Mexican samul nori team had understood Kim Duk Soo's underlying motivations in crafting a showcase of national identities that nonetheless highlighted Korea and its role as a sending country. As the darlings of the Korean media that year, the Canto del Cielo team put on a strong and confident front at the festival, giving everyone

FIGURE 5.4 The Aztec dance performance of Mexico's Canto del Cielo instantly focused the media spotlight on this all-women team, here assembled to be photographed by the Korean press. Photograph by author.

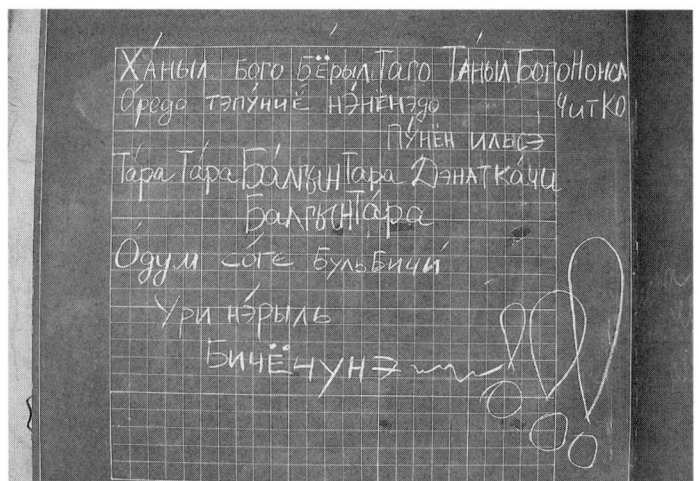

FIGURE 5.5 A Russian transliteration of the *pyŏldalgŏri* chant, inscribed on a chalkboard at the SamulNori Hanullim Puyŏ Educational Institute during the 2008 World SamulNori Festival. Photograph by author.

present the clear impression that for them Aztec dance was an inherited tradition, while Korean samul nori was a comfortable fit as an adopted one.

In the final section of the "International Pinari," all performers appeared together onstage, performing "Yŏngnam nongak." With that piece's status as one of the most recognized and transmitted in the samul nori repertoire, it is not surprising that all the international samul nori teams had learned some version of it prior to traveling to Puyŏ. During the rehearsals in the week preceding the festival's opening ceremony, international participants received training from instructors in order to calibrate a version of the piece for public presentation. It became apparent that some participants needed more review than others. Many also needed a refresher course in the *pyŏldalgŏri* chant. Although some teams had adapted the chant by translating it into their own native language, it was required for the teams to perform the *pyŏldalgŏri* chant in Korean at the opening concert. International participants were drilled on the chant (with some learning it "correctly" for the first time) and its pronunciation, as well as on refining their skills for the instrumental portion of the "Yŏngnam nongak" (see figure 5.5).

Large group rehearsals were held during the pre-festival workshop, led by Ch'oe Ch'an-kyun and Hong Yunki (members of SamulNori Hanullim), and then overseen by Kim Duk Soo in the dress rehearsals (see figure 5.6). The teams were expected to train rigorously for the performance, which was to feature "Yŏngam nongak" as the centerpiece for the final segment of the "International Pinari" production. Although there were stressful moments during the rehearsals, the performance of the "International Pinari" at the opening ceremony was an unequivocal success.

In considering the conceptual architecture of the "International Pinari" musical production for the World SamulNori Festival, the placement and performance of "Yŏngnam nongak" by the international samul nori teams are significant for their strategic representations and constructions of place. Where the first and second segments of the "International Pinari" celebrated difference, and the diverse backgrounds of the international performers, the final segment with the "Yŏngnam nongak" was designed to amplify a *unification* of difference. This was engendered through the collective performance of samul nori—South Korea's most dynamic musical export—by all those who had "imported" samul nori as fans and amateur practitioners. The performance of animated drumming in synchrony and the recitation of the *pyŏldalgŏri* chant, in Korean, by all the international participants (who wore their sartorial markers of ethnicity) made for an impressive display of nationalistic spirit and pride in South Korea's cultural prowess.

FIGURE 5.6 International samul nori teams at the SamulNori Hanullim Puyŏ Educational Institute rehearse "Yŏngnam nongak" under Ch'oe Ch'an-kyun (playing the small gong) for the opening event of the 2008 World SamulNori Festival. Photograph by author.

In the production of the "International Pinari" in the 2008 World Samul-Nori Festival, the global dissemination of the samul nori genre (in particular "Yŏngnam nongak") becomes a pivotal analogy by which South Korea is defined as an exporter of culture and a key player in the global economic market. This was made clear by the discourse surrounding the event and the calculated presentation of diversity as evidence of samul nori's global dissemination. But Kim Duk Soo's visionary outlook of a modern South Korea—produced through the global encounters with samul nori—is ultimately entwined with Korea's history, religion, and culture of yore. This helps us to understand why samul nori's dynamic and portable rhythmic form was presented within the context of a contrasting yet complementary counterpart—the deep-rooted, text-based pinari. Kim Duk Soo instructs the festival participants—through an intensely opaque narrative—of the land and culture whence samul nori emerged. And the site-specific location of the Chŏngnim temple grounds in Puyŏ provided the natural setting for Kim's lesson.

As this review of sample components and aspects of performance reveals, the selection of the pinari as the primary conceptual frame for the 2008 festival's opening ceremony was a choice richly vested in layers of symbolism. Arranging for the most vernacular of all the samul nori pieces to be performed by an international cast of players was an act that not only conveyed the international reach of the local but also served to elevate the status of the national by strategically inflecting the "global." Second, because other pieces in the samul nori repertory are already well rehearsed by teams in Korea and abroad, the performance of the "International Pinari" had a novelty factor that aligned very well with the celebration of SamulNori's thirtieth anniversary. And lastly, the "homecoming" of international participants was a special moment for Koreans to witness the fruits of the widespread transmission of the samul nori genre—on their own native land. Seeing that the pinari is a religious prayer song that is precisely a meditation on place, it was the ideal narrative through which to stage the global encounters with SamulNori, and thus with South Korea, the nation.

Epilogue

South Korean artist Psy made headlines in December 2012 when his "Gangnam Style" became the first video to reach one billion views on YouTube. The music video, featuring a song rapped mostly in Korean, is a satirical poke at the attitudes and lifestyle of the nouveau riche in the Gangnam [Kangnam] district of Seoul. While much of the satire is lost on non-Korean listeners, "Gangnam Style" became a viral sensation because of its zany scenes and catchy "earworm" phrases. The success of the video catapulted Psy (Pak Chaesang) into American popular culture, with appearances on the *Today Show*, *Ellen*, *Saturday Night Live*, and a pistachio nut commercial that aired during the 2013 Super Bowl.

"Gangnam Style" and Psy's imitable "horse dance" also spawned parody videos by the dozens. One of the first to appear on YouTube was called "Hongdae Style." The amateur video featured scenes filmed in the lively neighborhood surrounding Hongik Fine Arts University, interspersed with spoofs of stock sequences from the original video. Known as the seedbed of the indie rock scene in South Korea, Hongdae once was seen as artsy, bohemian, free-spirited—the counterpart to the wealth- and status-obsessed Kangnam region. The makers of "Hongdae Style" parodied the "Gangnam Style" video, but also managed to promote Hongdae in the process. Soon thereafter, YouTube videos proclaiming "Chicago Style" and "London Style" began to emerge, along with American collegiate versions: "MIT Style," "The Oregon Duck—Gangnam Style parody," "Kentucky Style," and "Gunrock Style" (University of California, Davis). Other parodies caricatured figures from popular culture. Still yet, there were the viral videos of flash mobs assembled in Jakarta, Rome, and Paris, performing Psy's infamous "horse dance."

Psy's tongue-in-cheek video elicited an imitative and performative treatment by its global fans. "Gangnam Style" became a musical and choreographic blueprint for use by different types of communities—enabling them to promote their own local identity and culture. While the original audio soundtrack (with the Korean language) was often retained, many of the parody videos altered the "Gangnam Style" sequences in order to bring into relief the markers of their own community. The episodic nature of the video—montages of the galloping "horse dance," the red convertible in the parking structure, and the comic yet slightly discomfiting scene with Psy and comedian No Hongch'ŏl in the elevator—became imitative signposts in many of the parody videos. And the musical form (largely a strophic one) of Psy's "Gangnam Style" hit served as a guiding template for the parodists.

What can the "Gangnam Style" phenomenon tell us about global musical circulations? On one hand, we learn how astonishingly quickly a music video can now go "viral" in the age of social media and the Internet.[1] On the other hand, we bear witness to how a viral video can then become the source material for parodic and creative treatment by individuals from around the world. The global circulation of "Gangnam Style" was not just limited to viewing and listening; it also involved imitation and performance. At once discernible as parodies, these amateur videos often served a dual purpose in the promotion and performance of local identities. For the parodists, knowledge of the Korean language or an understanding of the satirical content of the original video was not requisite: simply an awareness of (and loose adherence to) the sonic and visual contours of the music video sufficed. *Form* becomes a template for action.

Whereas the "Gangnam Style" example speaks to the clarity of parody's form—namely an imitation of the original source—samul nori's global circulations reveal a more nuanced story of how rhythmic forms have traveled across geographical and cultural boundaries. For one, samul nori's global journeys are connected to cross-cultural encounters of various kinds. These encounters go beyond the parodic imitation of a popular music video and often involve establishing a meaningful connection to pedagogues or other SamulNorians. As we learned in chapter 4, some of these global encounters lead to remarkable life changes that involve leaving one's home country and moving to South Korea to take percussion music lessons. And more commonly, other encounters lead to a path of discovery that entails attending workshops and joining social media groups devoted to samul nori and p'ungmul.[2]

Fans-turned-practitioners are drawn to and draw from samul nori's dynamic rhythmic form. Pedagogical materials that SamulNori and SamulNori Hanullim developed and published for a global audience have assisted enthusiasts on their path to learning how to perform pieces in samul nori's instrumental repertory. Similar in some ways to the "Gangnam Style" phenomenon is the fact that amateur samul nori ensembles around the world have often created their own adaptations of pieces such as "Yŏngnam nongak." The Swiss-based Swissamul team, for instance, was featured in a documentary called *The Beauty of Korean Style—Samul Nori*, produced by South Korea's Arirang TV. The documentary (which aired in Korea on September 30, 2009, and throughout parts of Asia) showed the group performing "Yŏngnam nongak" with their own spin—translating the chanted portion of the *pyŏldalgŏri* into German. The narrator's comment is apropos: "As it was with the creation of samul nori, they are participating in the reinterpretation and the re-creation of tradition" (Arirang TV 2009). Other groups have similarly adapted such pieces, creating their own localized versions.

We should remind ourselves that the genre of samul nori emerged organically from a process of musical trial and error, adaptation, and revision. This process—which I have dubbed the SamulNori project—involved the art of musical arrangement. P'ungmul's vast repository of regional rhythms provided the raw materials; the SamulNori quartet arranged these rhythmic patterns into condensed forms that eventually became standardized as "compositions" such as "Yŏngnam nongak." But we also know now that there is a flexibility in the rendering of such compositions in practice. This elasticity—or rather, a flexibility to figuratively breathe in performance—is afforded by samul nori's dynamic rhythmic form. Samul nori ensembles are free to determine the number of repetitions of a rhythmic cycle within the form. There are recommendations, but no set parameters for the exact number of repetitions that are provided in pedagogical materials. And much like SamulNori's recursive process of musical arrangement in the early years of the SamulNori project, many groups make modifications to the form itself—adding or subtracting certain sections to suit their own logistical and creative purposes.

In terms of global flows and global circulations, we have also learned that samul nori's dissemination was certainly aided in part by the support from the South Korean government. Even before the concentrated influx of capital for the marketing and export of Korean popular culture during the crest of the Korean Wave of the 2000s, the South Korean government found ways to assist with samul nori's global transmission. The government supported the publication of notation books and instructional videos, and the Overseas Koreans Foundation established grant applications for organizations and groups to apply for free samul nori instrument sets delivered from South Korea. The rationale was clear. Both the quartet and the genre became a symbol not just of Korea but of a modern and dynamic South Korea. The government sought to promote this particular image in the context of neoliberal economic policies. After all, like its slicker, hipper, K-pop tidal heir of Hallyu, samul nori was also made and branded in South Korea.

This book has argued that samul nori's rhythm-based forms are dynamic. This dynamic rhythmic form is what has helped attract enthusiasts to not only an appreciation for the percussion genre, but a desire to learn and perform it as well. As discussed in chapter 2, the rhythmic patterns that the SamulNori quartet drew upon had a previous social life; these patterns were also intimately associated with movement, dance, communal rituals, and large-scale choreographies. When the quartet fashioned the rhythmic patterns into musical arrangements, many of the patterns still carried these associations of dynamism—a multifaceted dynamism that invites movement, energy, change, and intensification. Arrangements such as "Yŏngnam nongak" and "Uttari p'ungmul" feature a modular formal structure, a more macro progression from complex rhythmic cycles to ones more simplified and compressed, and significant contrasts among tempi, volume, and levels of energy exerted in performance. I posit that the modular formal structure helps beginners to process and learn individual sections while simultaneously providing an architectural template for the composition. The relative simplicity of discrete rhythmic patterns, arranged into a sectional form, gives amateur enthusiasts an opportunity to engage in a musical tradition that may be quite distant from their own. In this sense, I contend that one of the SamulNori quartet's greatest achievements was to effectively design an elegant rhythmic form that—while steeped in local culture and rural rhythms—was able to become legible and audible across boundaries.

Here, form organizes, shapes, teaches, and navigates this otherwise unfamiliar sonic landscape. In its journeys abroad, samul nori's rhythmic form has provided a starting point, a guiding template for people first becoming acquainted with the world of Korean percussion. This, I contend, is the work of samul nori's dynamic rhythmic form.

DYNAMIC FORMS IN CIRCULATION

There are indeed other musical genres that exude their own brand of dynamism, with origin stories and pathways to global transmission differing drastically from those of samul nori. This dynamism captivates first-time listeners and moves them to engage beyond the act of listening. A select few examples include Ewe drumming, Japanese taiko, Brazilian samba, Caribbean *zouk*, and hip-hop. Some of these global genres are intimately linked with dance and movement, and some are wedded to text. What is commonly shared, however, is the prominence and persistence of rhythm. Whether they are conceptualized as distinct patterns and cycles or organized into larger forms, these rhythm-based genres (and forms) can be powerful in their abilities to travel and to become sites for cross-cultural engagement. In certain cases, rhythmic forms can be easier to grasp than other types of musical forms coming from the same culture (e.g., text-based and modal-based). The pinari provides a compelling instantiation of a text-based form that has eluded facile portability.[3]

Returning to the question that first opened this exposition—of what makes one form of music go global and another stay relatively put—I recapitulate that samul nori's dynamic rhythmic form has afforded its globalization. But in thinking of the broader implications of this argument, I aim to convey here that a formalist line of inquiry—in conjunction with ethnography—has analytical purchase for understanding how music moves. This is especially relevant for music and globalization studies.

Motivated by how literary specialist Caroline Levine employs the tools of literary formalism to explore form in social and political contexts, I suggest that music scholars have much to offer in interrogating popular musical forms and their mobility in transnational contexts. How might we apply the tools of our (ethno)musicological trade and examine other forms in circulation—rhythm-based forms that we can find in popular music and dance, and various musical traditions of the world? Although Adorno may have dismissed it, consider for a moment repetition in relation to rhythmic form. Or, as Michael Tenzer and John Roeder explore, "musical periodicity—repetition and its role in musical form" (2011, 4).[4] In a rhythmic context, this can take many guises in world music: cycles, patterns, clave, timeline, groove, riff, and ostinato—to name just a few. Analyzing musical periodicities in tandem with ethnography—considering somatic and sensory experiences of these periodicities across cultures, for instance—can give us new insights into how and why certain musical forms travel.

I believe that this inquiry—understanding how and why certain musical practices go global—can be a productive site for bringing together ethnomusicologists, musicologists, and music theorists in collaborative projects. Recent developments in music cognition and music perception, such as the work on repetition by Elizabeth Hellmuth Margulis (2013) and Justin London's study on the psychological aspects of musical meter ([2004] 2012), also yield new directions in research collaborations that can put the subdisciplines in closer dialogue with one another. Ethnomusicologists, in particular, are well poised to combine nuanced ethnographic and musical analysis to engage in how and why a musical genre goes global, and why it is that rhythm-based forms are so portable and powerful—thereby leading to cross-cultural encounters and the formation of new musical communities.

APPENDIX 1
English Translation of Pinari Text

비나리 (Pinari)[a]

Pinari (Supplication) is a chant for good fortune. This pinari has three narrative sections. The prologue praises the Chosŏn dynasty founder and describes Seoul as a site of good fortune based on geomancy. During the second section, Salp'uri, a singer lists all kinds of malevolent spirits and casts them out. The last section, Ch'ukwŏn tŏkdam (Blessing), prays for wealth, longevity, and good fortune.

KOREAN TEXT WITH SINO-KOREAN CHARACTERS	ENGLISH INTERPRETATION AND TRANSLATION[b]
1. 선고사	*1. Prologue*
천개우주(天開宇宙) 하날이요 지개조축(地開造築) 땅 생길제	The heavens opened and the sky came forth, the earth opened and the land came forth.
국태민안(國泰民安) 법륜전(法輪轉) 시화년풍(時和年豊) 돌아들고	Peace over the land, peace to the people Buddha's teachings everlasting far and wide, bountiful harvest year after year
이씨한양(李氏 漢陽)등극(登極)시 삼각산 (三角山) 기봉(起峰)하고 봉황(鳳凰)이 생겼구나	When the first Chosŏn king named Seoul the capital, he came down on high from the mountain like a phoenix in flight.

봉황(鳳凰)눌러 대궐(大闕)짓고	Sitting on the phoenix, a royal palace
대궐(大闕)앞에는	In front of the palace,
육조(六曹)로다.	six royal ministers.
오영문(五營門)하각사(下各司)內	Created five armies and their troops.
각도(各道) 각읍(各邑)을 마련할제	
왕십리(往十里) 청룡(青龍)이요	Wangsimni to the east is the blue dragon
동구만리(東區萬里)가 백호(白虎)로다	Tonggu to the west is the white tiger
종남산(種南山) 안산(案山)되고	South Mountain becomes Peace Mountain,
과천 관악산(冠岳山)	Kwach'ŏn Kwanak Mountain to the north
화산(火山)이 비쳐	keeps out the flames.
동작동(銅雀洞) 수구(水口)막고	Block the mouth of Tongjak-dong,
한강수(漢江水) 둘러싸니	and the Han River's waters surround Seoul,
여천지(與千地) 무궁이라(無窮)	
원아(源我)는 금여찬데 (今如)	Here today we voice our wishes,
차일(此日)은 사바세계(娑婆世界)	here in the world of humans. Here east of the sea,
남섬부주(南瞻部州) 로다	Here in the great country of Korea is the
해동(海東)이면 대한민국(大韓民國)	(Great Republic of) Korea.
건구건명(乾口乾命) (이름)씨 대주	Owner and Lady,
곤명(坤命)에는 ( ) 부인(婦人)	dwell with parents and children
당상(堂上)부모(父母) 모시고	at your side,
슬하자손(膝下子孫)거느리고	happy for as long as you live.
백년해로(百年偕老) 누려살제	
이댁 가정(家庭) 드시거들	In this house
몽중살(夢中煞) 없을소냐	evil spirits must dwell and
몽중살(夢中煞) 풀고가자	evil spirits must be cleansed.
2. 살풀이 (煞)	2. Salp'uri—Expunging of negative influences
몽중살 (夢中煞) 직성살 (直星煞)	Misfortune of the evil star

살(煞)풀어서 거리살(距里煞)	Misfortune spilt on the roads
원근 (遠近) 도중에	Misfortune of death far from home
이별살이요(離別煞)	Misfortune of leaving friends
부모(父母) 돌아가 몽상살 (蒙喪煞)	Misfortune of dying parents
몽상(蒙喪)입어 거상살 (居喪煞)이요	Misfortune in the midst of a funeral
거상(居喪)벗어 탈상 (脫喪)이라	
장인 삼촌(三寸)의 복채살 (卜債煞)	Misfortune sneaking in with money
동네 방네는 불안살 (不安煞)	Misfortune of uneasy surroundings
이웃지간에 희살살 (戱殺煞)이요	Misfortune of unlucky neighbors
도적 (盜賊)난데는 실물살 (失物煞)	Misfortune of theft
흙을달아 토살 (土煞)인데	Misfortune smeared on the dirt
돌달아서 석살 (石煞)이라	Misfortune rubbed on the rocks
산 나무는 목신살 (木神煞)	Misfortune on living trees
죽은 나무는 동토살 (動土煞)이라	Misfortune on dying trees
산에올라 산신살 (山神煞)	Misfortune in the mountains
들로내리니 들룡살 (煞)	Misfortune in the fields
물로내리니 용왕살이요 (龍王煞)	Misfortune in the water
바깥마당 벼락살 (煞)	Misfortune in the outer courtyard
안마당에는 회룡살 (回龍煞)	Misfortune in the inner courtyard
지붕마루는 용충살	Misfortune while fixing the roof
혼인 (婚姻)대사에 주당살 (周堂煞)이요	Misfortune from the wrong day for a wedding
마루대청 성주님살 (成柱任煞)	Misfortune in the pillar holding up the house
건너방에는 군웅살 (群雄煞) 이요	Misfortune in the parlor

안방을 접어들어	Misfortune in the bedroom
이벽저벽에 벽파살 (劈破煞)	Misfortune for the couple
내외지간 (內外) 공방살 (空房煞)	
애기난데 삼신살 (三神煞)	Misfortune while giving birth
횃대밑에는 넝마살 (煞)	Misfortune clinging to clothes
거리거리 서낭살(城隍煞)	Misfortune from neglecting the village guardians
만경창파 (萬頃滄波)뜬 서낭살(城隍煞)	
무지개 발로 휘어다가	Evil and misfortune, away with them all.
원강천리로 소멸 (消滅)하니	This rainbow banner sweeps them all away.
오늘 여기에 오신분	In this house, for all who came,
만사(萬事)가 대길 (大吉)하고	A thousand things will go well,
백사 (百事)가 여일 (如一)하고	a hundred things will go right.
마음과 뜻과 잡순대로	As you desire,
소원성취 (所願成就) 발원(發願) 이라	your wishes will be heard.

3. 축원 덕담 (祝願 德談)

3. *Ch'ukwŏn tŏkdam*—*A song or prayer that blesses the owner's health, wealth, and happiness*

상봉길경(常逢吉慶)에 불봉만재 (不逢萬災)로구려 만재수야 (滿財數)	Always blessed with good things, avoiding all kinds of disaster and blessed with good fortune.
아아 헤에헤에 헤에헤에 해로누려라	*A-a he-e he-e he-e he-e haero nuryŏra*
어러얼 사랑만 하십소사 나아하	*ŏrŏ-ŏl sarangman hasipsosa na-a-ha*
보오오 에에헤에 헤험이로다	*Bo-o-o e-e-he-e hehŏm iroda*
보오오 오호오 에헤에 . . .	*Bo-o-o o-ho-o e-he-e* . . .
	~~
축원이 갑니다. 덕담이 갑니다. 발원이 갑니다. 건구 건명전에 (乾口 乾命) 이댁	Hear this wish. Hear this blessing. Hear this entreaty.
가중,문전 축원 고사 덕담	Raising this heartfelt prayer for this household,
지성 정성으로 여쭈신델랑	

남의댁 가중 남의댁 동중	even if misfortune befalls
이러니 저러니 할지라도	another house.
건구건명 이댁가중으로	In this house,
드시걸랑	may the fires at night be bright
밤이 되면 불이나 밝으시고여	the water in the day be clear.
낮이 되면 물이나 맑아	
밤이 되면 불이 밝고	At night the fire must be bright
낮이 되면 물이 맑아	in the day the water must be clear.
물과 불은 상극 (相剋)이라	And as these are opposites
원사속경 공양각서(供養覺書)ᶜ	may you keep them in harmony
옥쟁반에 금쟁반 순금쟁반에	for a life of good fortune
진주를 굴린듯	Like rolling pearls
얼음위에도 백로 같소	on a jade platter.
오동나무 상상가지	Like rolling pearls on gold,
봉황(鳳凰)같이도 잘사실제	on a pure gold platter.
	Like a white crane on ice,
	branches on an oak tree,
	live well like a phoenix.
건구건명 이댁 가정	In this house,
천금같은 아들따님	may the son and daughter
성명삼자(姓名三字)로 저 달만 그린듯이	be blessed and live long.
만복(萬福)이라	(refrain)ᵈ
에헤에 사실지라도 늘여서 사대(四代)만	Be blessed with good fortune.
사십소사	Live a long life.
사랑 에헤에 에헤에 어험이로다	*Sarang e-he-e e-he-e ŏhŏm iroda*
보오오오 오호오 에헤에 ~~~~	*Bo-o-o-o o-ho-o e-he-e*
	. . .
건구건명 이댁가정	In this house.
슬하자손 (膝下子孫)거느리고	May children be at your side
태평성대 (泰平盛大)누리실제	for as long as you live.
작년같은 해후년은	Last year went well.
꿈결잠시 보냈건만	But in this new year
신년새해 (新年)접어드니	you will go here and there and every-
어디아니 출입(出入)을 허랴	where.

멀 원자 (遠) 가까울 근(近)자 댕길 행(行)자 올 래자 (來)자 들 　입(入)자 출입왕래(出入往來) 할지라도 노중액살 (路中厄煞) 제쳐주시고	Whether far or near, wherever you leave or enter, may you 　avoid misfortune and find
동(東)으로 가면 재수소망(財數所望) 서(西)로 가면 만고복덕 (萬古福德) 북(北)으로 가면 수명장수 (壽命長壽) 남(南)으로 가면 소원성취 (所願成就)	wealth and happy events in the east, incomparable good fortune in the west, long life in the north wishes granted in the south,
동서사방(東西四方) 흩어진 재물(財物) 무지개 발로 휘어다가 서기 발로 나꿔다가	treasures dispersed in all corners. Sweep them all in with lucky spirits.
오늘 여기오신분들 여러 분전에 전법 (傳法) 하니 일일에 만사 (萬事)가 소원(所願)만 성취(成就)로구려	Bestow them on those who came here 　today. Therefore in all that you do Your hopes will come to pass.
만복(萬福)이라 에헤에 사실지라도 늘여서 사대(四代)만 사십소사 사랑 에헤에 에헤에 어험이로다 보오오오 오호오 에헤에 ~~~	(refrain) Be blessed with good fortune. Live a long life. Sarang e-he-e e-he-e ŏhŏm iroda Bo-o-o-o o-ho-o e-he-e ~~~
복 (福)만 많구요 명(命)이 짧아도 못사느니 명 (命)만 길어도 복(福)이 없이는 못사느니	Good fortune is useless to a 　short life. A long life is unlivable without good 　fortune.
짧은 명(命)은 잇어주고 긴 명(命)은 사려 담아서 무쇠목숨에 돌끈 달아 百歲三壽를 누려살제	Stretch the short life and make it long. Bind up the long life so that it does not 　snap off. May you live up to three hundred years.
명(命)도 주고 복(福)도 줄제 명(命)일랑은 주시려면	The fates give long life and good fortune. So if you're giving life,

옛날옛적 삼천갑자(三千甲子) 동방삭(東方朔)의 기나긴 명(命)을 점지(點指)하시고	give a long life like Tong Pangsak from old China.
복(福)을 주시려거든 대국부자(大國富者) 왕개(王愷), 석숭(石嵩) 장자 김한태 복(福)을 점지(點指)하시고	And if you're giving fortune, give good fortune like Wanggae and Sŏksung from old China and Kim Hant'ae from old Korea.
단명(短命)하신 일문권속(一門權屬) 상하탁시(上下濁時)할지라도, 말끝에 재처먹고, 글 끝에 낚처먹고, 악한 인간 일 서러워 착한인간 맞아들고, 인간 오복만복(五福萬福)을 점지하니, 일일(日日)에 만사(萬事)가 소원(所願)만 성취(成就)로구려	Even if the family died young, Even the date of death is not correct, swallow spoken words, hold back written words. Sorrow for evil persons, welcome for good persons. These all foretell human fortune. Each and every thing is a hope come to pass.
만복(萬福)이라 에헤에 사실지라도 늘여서 사대(四代)만 사십소사 사랑 에헤에 에헤에 어험이로다 보오오오 오호오 에헤에 ~~~	(refrain) Be blessed with good fortune. Live a long life. *Sarang e-he-e e-he-e ŏhŏm iroda Bo-o-o-o o-ho-o e-he-e* ~~~
오늘 여기 오신분들 만복(萬福)을 받았거니와 만고액살(萬古厄煞) 제쳐줄제 삼재팔난(三災八難) 관재구설(官災口舌) 우환질병(憂患疾病) 잡귀잡신(雜鬼雜神) 일체액살(一切厄煞)을 휘몰아다가	All who came here today: May you be blessed. May you be rid of evil spirits. All the misfortunes, all the diseases all the worries, gather them up and we will have a sincere ritual with great care today. If a good wind blows, throw them all in the river.

금일정성(今日精誠) 고사(告祀) 대를 바쳐 좋은 순풍(順風) 불거들랑 월미도 앞 강에 소멸(消滅)을 합시다. 영창목에 행주나 복일지라도 어드레 풀이며 삼재(三災)풀이며 동가주아 의주(義州) 압록강(鴨綠江) 　에다 덩기덩 덩기덩 두둥실 떠내려 보냈습니다. 나아하 보오오 에에헤에 헤험이로다. 보오오오 오호오 에헤에 ~~~~~	And we will have a sincere ritual with great care today. If a good wind blows, throw them all in the river. (refrain) Whether this or that, there is disaster, three disasters that befall humans. Let's send all the fortune bobbing down the Yalu River. *Na-a-ha bo-o-o e-ehe-e hehŏm iroda Bo-o- o-o o-ho-o e-he-e* ~~

Translated by Dr. Byoung Sug Kim and Dr. Ji-Yeon Yuh, with additional Chinese language support by John Jonghyo Lee.

a To my knowledge, this is the first published translation of the pinari text into English. It is based on a text that was performed in 2009 in Washington, DC, by SamulNori Hanullim. The performance was held at the Smithsonian National Museum on Korean American Day (January 13) and celebrated US-Korea relations and the recent presidential inauguration of Barack Obama. This ambitious translation project was envisioned by Dr. Kim Byoung Sug (associate professor of elementary education at Roosevelt University; director of Global P'ungmul Institute) in collaboration with Dr. Ji-Yeon Yuh (associate professor in Asian American history at Northwestern University) and musician So Ra Kim. I am deeply indebted to Drs. Kim and Yuh for granting me permission to include their skillfully rendered translation in this manuscript. It is their hope, as well as mine, that this first academic translation of the pinari will inspire future iterations and future studies.

b It should be noted that the translators strove to make the translation comprehensible to English readers. In certain cases, idiomatic expressions were chosen over literal ones. It is beyond the scope of this book to provide detailed explanations of the many historical, religious, or cultural terms in this text. Given the complexity and the richness of the pinari, an annotated translation of the pinari would be a welcome resource for scholars and samul nori enthusiasts alike.

c Many efforts were made by the translators to interpret this line that appears in the Ch'ukwŏn tŏkdam. Since the Chinese characters for the cognates (원사속경) were not retrievable, the translators were faced with the decision to forgo translation of this particular line. Based on his careful examination of the text, John Jonghyo Lee offers a possible interpretation for the missing Chinese characters: 원사속경 (源事速經) 공양각서 (供養覺書). This would translate into "As you wish, write short phrases in the notes of offering."

d This is a refrain that appears four times in this text. While the majority of SamulNori's "Pinari" is sung by one singer, the refrain is sung by the group of musicians who accompany the singer on samul nori instruments. The refrain is composed mostly of nonlexical vocables and it is performed in a musical style similar to a Buddhist chant known as *yŏmbul*.

APPENDIX 2

SamulNori

"Tradition Meets the Present"

English program notes for SamulNori's standard ninety-minute performances, written by SamulNori's first managing director, Suzanna Samstag

*Binari (Prayer Song)**

A sweeping prayer song that used to signal the beginning of a stay at a village. *Binari* can now be heard at events such as the opening of a new business or building, or at a performance such as tonight's. The shaman sings the extensive prayer, which touches on many aspects important to Korean beliefs. It recounts the tale of creation and it calls upon the various spirits that reside in the village and homes, eventually asking for a blessing upon the people, the players and the ground they inhabit.

Placed on the altar is an abundance of food offerings to the gods and to ancestors, and a pig's head. Audience members are invited to approach the altar, bringing with them their prayers. They may also light an incense stick, pour rice wine and bow. It is customary to place an offering of money on the altar. The head of the pig signifies wealth, health and abundance; and, if an offering of money is placed in the mouth of the pig, it is believed that the prayers brought to the altar will be answered generously.

Samdo Sul Changgo Karak (Changgo Rhythms from Three Provinces)

All four men are seated with *changgo* (hourglass drum) and play an arrangement consisting of the most representative *changgo karak* (rhythm patterns) of three Korean provinces.

Originally, one player would fasten the *changgo* to his body and perform a showy solo piece, flaunting his unique style of dance and technique. SamulNori created this new arrangement to be played while seated, shifting the focus from showmanship to musicality. This piece consists of five movements, showcasing five different *karak*, beginning with the technically demanding "Tasurim," and finishing off with the climactic "Hwimori."

Samdo Nongak Karak (Nongak Rhythms from Three Provinces)

Samdo Nongak Karak also is an arrangement of different rhythms from the three provinces. Some of the *karak* that appeared in *Samdo Sul Changgo Karak* also appear here, now interpreted by the four different instruments. During festivals, performers would traditionally have played these instruments while dancing, but SamulNori has broadened the scope of the many *karaks* that appear by playing seated and developing the musical possibilities of this arrangement.

The music's intimacy with the land and agrarian culture is evident in the verses the performers exclaim before the climactic portion of this piece:

Look to the sky and gather stars.	Moon, moon, bright moon
Look to the ground and till the earth.	As bright as day;
This year was bountiful	In the darkness,
Next year let it also be so.	Your light gives us illumination.

Intermission

Pan Kut

You will see in this dance portion of the program, that the drummers must also be dancers. The dance features the *sangmo* (a ribboned hat) and the *bubpo* (a feathered hat) which the performers will make move and spin with the energy of their dancing bodies. This particular *Pankut* is a modern rendition of the large group dances of the farming festivals made suitable for four men on a stage.

Because farmers were traditionally recruited as soldiers when a war broke out, there was a great exchange of ideas between the military musical tradition and the village dances. Most of the choreography is based on military exercises, and the hats the performers wear resemble ancient helmets. It has also been said that the *sangmo* originally had shards of glass and metal attached to the ribbon and were used as weapons during battle.

With feet treading the earth, ribbons flying upward, and rhythms sounding through the air, the players attempt to consummate the union of Heaven, Earth and Humankind.

The banner, the spiritual member of the troupe, with its stake driven into the ground, and its feathers reaching for the sky, embodies the desire for cosmic harmony.

Tradition Meets the Present

From ancient days up until the outbreak of the Korean War, wandering entertainers called *Namsadang* roamed across Korea visiting villages and cities. Upon announcing their arrival at the main gate of a village, they would make their way to the central courtyard and occupy it for the next few days and nights, performing satirical mask dramas, puppet plays, acrobatic acts and shamanistic rites. After bidding the evil spirits to leave and good ghosts to come, the performers would invite all the villagers to gather, watch their acts and revel with them all night. These gatherings were an integral and important part of affirming life for the people of these isolated Korean villages for a countless number of centuries. The music that accompanied these gatherings can be described generally as *PoongmulNori*, "the playing of folk instruments."

At the time of the Korean War, Koreans were becoming more familiar with the city and its Western oriented culture, losing touch with rural life and its rhythms. *Namsadang* and their music were quickly relegated to mythology and obsolescence. True to this new Western influence, an elevated proscenium stage equipped with microphones, lights and hi-tech equipment now stands where a stretch of grass used to be. SamulNori was formed in 1978 by descendants of these *Namsadang*, confronted by the changes in performance presentation, upheavals in Korean society and the quiet disappearance of their valuable musical heritage.

"We were shamans who played for the villagers' needs and well being, and since the villagers have changed we too must change," notes Kim Duk Soo, master drummer and one of the founding members of SamulNori.

The stage setting may now be twentieth century, but the instruments remain the same: *K'kwaenggwari*, *Ching*, *Changgo*, and *Buk*. The name SamulNori, literally meaning "To play four things," refers to these four instruments, each associated with an element in nature. *K'kwaenggwari*, the small gong, represents lightning; the *Ching*, the large gong, represents wind, the *Changgo*, the hourglass drum, represents rain, and the *Buk*, the barrel drum, represents clouds.

When learning the music, it is necessary to understand the rudiments and the rich philosophy that cultivated the music. The theory of *yin* and *yang* (in Korean *um* and *yang*), prevalent throughout the music, is illustrated, among innumerable other examples, in the balance of the two metal instruments and the two leather ones. Most importantly, the four players must become one through *Ho-Hup*, the meditative technique that tames the mind, body, and spirit through breath control.

Although the music and presentation have been reinvented, their foundation remains unchanged and SamulNori intends to faithfully recreate for you the spirit of those massive village gatherings. In a few moments they will herald their arrival with the sounds of the drums and cry out:

Open the doors! Open the doors!
The Guardians of the Five Directions, Open your doors!
When all of humankind enters, they shall bring with them endless joy!

We invite all of you to enter and be a part of the festivities.

* Same as *pinari*. The program's romanization of Korean terms has been retained.

NOTES

Introduction

1. During the 2000s, South Korean films, television dramas, and popular music categorized as "K-pop" became immensely popular throughout East and Southeast Asia. Dubbed the "Korean Wave" (also known as "Hallyu," in Korean), this phenomenon took many by surprise, including South Koreans themselves. The Kim Dae Jung administration (1998–2003) observed the overseas fascination with films and television serials and began to invest heavily in the cultural industry—a prime example of a national "soft power" strategy at work. Although the outward spread of samul nori is much more modest in comparison to the popularization and spread of K-pop, I view the story of samul nori as a precursor to Hallyu.

2. A quick survey of just one of these genres—hip-hop—gives a sense of the range of analytical approaches: Knight 1991; Keyes 1996, 2002; Krims 2000; Mitchell 2001; Durand 2002; Maxwell 2003; Fenn 2004; Watkins 2005; Condry 2006; Manabe 2006; Osumare 2007; Keeler 2009; Ntarangwi 2009; Sharma 2010; Terkourafi 2010; Williams 2010; Künzler 2011a, 2011b; Saucier 2011; Charry 2012; Schweig 2013; Helbig 2014; Appert 2016.

3. See also Veit Erlmann's chapter on "Communities of Style" in *Music, Modernity, and the Global Music Imagination* (1999, 246–67) for a discussion of the iterative musical figures in African and African American musical performance.

4. I thank my new colleague Tim Taylor for pushing me to think more carefully and critically about samul nori's actual circulation and its "circulatability"—or in other words, its *ability* to circulate. I see the latter as closely connected to the concept of samul nori's affordances of its rhythmic form.

5. Ethnomusicologist Bonnie Wade utilized the concept of affordance (building on Gibson's theory) in her ethnographic study of Japanese composers and their relationship to Japanese society and culture (2014). Wade's list of five components of affordance is useful here: (1) an environment, in this example, a door; (2) a quality of that environment (affordance), as in this example, the door having a handle or some other mechanism that

allows it to be opened; (3) an individual; (4) an action to be performed by the individual; (5) the requisite capability on the part of the individual (12).

6. There is an expansive literature on form in other disciplines such as literature and philosophy that I do not address here. For those interested in venturing afield to medieval studies, I direct readers to Seeta Chaganti's illuminating theorization of medieval poetic form (2018, 64–96) to get a sense of the longer intellectual trajectories that inform contemporary formalist studies.

ONE Space and the Big Bang

1. See Delissen 2001, 254.

2. This description comes from an undated promotional pamphlet, *SamulNori Hanullim* (artistic director Kim Duk Soo), with Lee Sun Chul [Yi Sŏnchŏl] listed as the managing director. It is likely that the pamphlet was printed for distribution in 1994.

3. The Live House Nanjang studio was officially opened on November 16, 1990, in Sinch'on (in northern Seoul) (SamulNori Hanullim t'ansaeng samsip chunyŏn kinyŏm saŏphoe 2009, 82). The studio served as an open space where budding samul nori enthusiasts could freely come and go, to take lessons from the SamulNori quartet members or to generally hang out. It was at the Sinch'on studio (often shortened as "Sinch'on Nanjang") where SamulNori (and SamulNori Hanullim) began to develop their first pedagogical textbooks and notation.

4. Despite these discrepancies, SamulNori Hanullim chooses to refer to the "founding members" of the quartet as Kim Duk Soo, Kim Yong-bae, Lee Kwang Soo [Yi Kwangsu], and Choi Jong Sil. See chapter 2 of Joo Jay-youn [Chu Chaeyŏn], "Samul nori ŭi yŏksajŏk" (2010), for a discussion and critique of the errors that often appear in scholarly and journalistic descriptions of SamulNori's early history and membership.

5. For a brief discussion of other professional samul nori groups such as Durae Pae and Dulsori see Howard 2015, 95–102, and Hesselink 2012, 129.

6. An alternate spelling is Kim Swoo Geun. Kim's most famous projects included the Konggan [Space] Group Building (1977), the Masan Catholic Church (1979), and the Olympic Stadium built for the 1988 Seoul Summer Olympics. Historian Alain Delissen referred to Kim as an "essential architect of modern South Korea" (2001, 246).

7. The Konggan Group Building also featured a stone pagoda in its outdoor courtyard.

8. *Konggan* magazine—now called *Space*—remains in circulation and is one of the leading publications of architecture, culture, art, and design from South Korea. See Space, www.vmspace.com.

9. For more information on Kim's role as an activist, impresario, and "cultural historian" see Delissen's "The Aesthetic Pasts of *Space*" (2001).

10. Kang's brother, Kang Chunil (1944–2015), was a well-known art composer who

fused elements of Korean folk music with Western classical music. He composed specific works for samul nori. His most frequently performed composition is *Madang*—a concerto for samul nori quartet and Western orchestra.

11. For a summary of the types of events programmed at Space Theater from 1977 to 1989 see appendix 1 in "Encounters with *Samulnori*" (Lee, Katherine In-Young 2012b).

12. Unique to Korea, p'ansori is a form of storytelling through song. The genre is performed by a solo singer and accompanied by a barrel drum (puk) player. For an in-depth study of p'ansori see Chan E. Park's *Voices from the Straw Mat* (2003). Kayagŭm refers to a twelve-string zither that is played solo or as part of a chamber ensemble.

13. In his master's thesis, Kang Jae Hoon [Kang Ch'aehun] includes a section of the interview with Kim Sugŭn quoted in the *Choson Ilbo*, March 8, 1976. See Kang Jae Hoon 2008, 31.

14. Prior to this, there had been concerts at Konggan Sarang under the series title "Evening of Traditional Arts." See appendix 1 in "Encounters with *Samulnori*" (Lee, Katherine In-Young 2012b).

15. Members of the Minsogakhoe Sinawi were graduates of the Seoul Arts School. See Ch'oe T'aehyŏn, "Minsogakhoe sinawi" (1991) for a summary of the group's history (Korean only) and Hesselink 2012, 51–56.

16. Although the word "improvisation" may be slightly misleading on the first reading, I employ this term to reflect the spirit of experimentation that accompanied the first performance of the quartet's arrangement of rhythms drawn from p'ungmul.

17. Nathan Hesselink describes this set of rhythms as a "condensed version of the nationally designated *namsadang* troupe repertoire" (Hesselink 2012, 56). As this description leads to a much longer and complicated discussion on SamulNori's connections to namsadang and p'ungmul, I will return to this point later in chapter 2.

18. Although Yi played the puk (barrel drum) at the February 1978 performance, Yi specialized in the *p'iri* (small double reed instrument) and the *taegŭm* (transverse bamboo flute).

19. Following his tenure at the Space Theater, Kang went on to found Studio METAA (Metabolic Evolution through Arts and Architecture) in 1989. Similar in some ways to Kim Sugŭn's Konggan Group, METAA has functioned as a multifaceted organization that presents and promotes a variety of performing arts. It has also offered strategic consulting services for developing "culture spaces" (*munhwa konggan*) within urban settings. Despite the passing of Kang in 2014, METAA continues. See www.metaa.net.

20. Nongak (literally, "farming music") can also be used to refer to p'ungmul ("objects of the wind"). Although the term nongak has been problematized and contested by scholars and practitioners alike, some musicians and groups still use nongak to describe their musical tradition (e.g., Imsil P'ilbong Nongak of the North Chŏlla region). For a brief summary of this debate see Hesselink 2006, 15–16.

21. This is a point that Nathan Hesselink dwells on in his scholarly work on SamulNori, positing an expansionist view of what is construed as "tradition." For a development of this line of thinking see Hesselink 2004 and 2012.

22. In contrast, Choi Jong Sil gives credit to Ch'oe T'aehyŏn (and not Sim Usŏng) for having first proposed the idea of performing in a seated position. See Choi Jong Sil 2009, 144.

23. Sim's name also appears as "Shim Woo-sung" in some English-language publications.

24. More will be said of the namsadang later in this chapter.

25. Kim Munhak (Kim Duk Soo's father) was a specialist of the *sogo* handheld-drum dance. He was formerly a member of the Sim Sŏnok namsadang troupe.

26. More information on the quartet's April 1978 performances appears in chapter 2.

27. To further complicate the matter, the term *samul* is also commonly used to refer to four percussion instruments found at Buddhist temples throughout Korea: *mokŏ* (wooden fish), *pŏpko* (large barrel drum), *pŏmjong* (large bell), and *unp'an* (cloud-shaped gong). The instruments are used in Buddhist ceremonies and are performed daily to symbolize the liberation of all sentient beings and the spreading of the dharma. The word *nori* has many semantic meanings in the Korean language. Aside from "play," it can also mean "entertainment" or "game." Since the SamulNori quartet preferred to render *nori* as "play," I have opted for that translation.

28. I am grateful to Ro Jaemyeong [No Chaemyŏng] for providing access to this document and for allowing me to conduct research at the Korean Classical Music Record Museum in Yangp'yŏng.

29. See chapter 3 for a brief summary of the significant socioeconomic changes that occurred in modern (South) Korean history.

30. Emphasis is my own.

31. Sim's study of the namsadang *(Namsadangp'ae yŏn'gu)* includes photographs of the members of the 1970s Seoul-based namsadang troupe ([1974] 1994). Kim Yong-bae and Lee Kwang Soo are pictured.

32. In an interview, Lee Kwang Soo confirmed that he first joined the SamulNori quartet as a member in 1980, making his formal debut on September 29, 1980 (Lee Kwang Soo interview, February 20, 2009). See Lee Kwang Soo 2009, 125–26. This corrects some reports that mistakenly claim that Lee joined the quartet one (or even two) years earlier.

33. Nathan Hesselink has provided important English translations of key passages from Sim Usŏng's definitive work on the namsadang (Hesselink 2012, 17–37). Korean readers may also consult Sim's manuscript (Sim Usŏng [1974] 1994).

34. For historical background on the namsadang see Howard 2015, 26; and Hesselink 2012, 17–37.

35. A special book of photography, released in commemoration of SamulNori's tenth anniversary, includes a poetic essay by Kim Rihae [Kim Rihye] (dancer and wife to Kim Duk Soo) that was translated into Japanese and English (SamulNori 1988). The English translation—rendered by former manager Suzanna Samstag—is especially evocative. The essay describes the "children of wandering minstrels" who follow in their father's footsteps, only to traverse greater distances and lands. The namsadang connection was also emphasized in shorter promotional materials that were used during SamulNori's overseas tours.

36. Ch'a Kijun and Hwang Kŭmman were Lee Kwang Soo's first teachers of the pinari (Kim Suyong 2005, 37).

37. In Korea, pagodas (*t'ap*) are linked with Buddhism and can be found at Buddhist temples. Similar in religious function to South Asian stupas, pagodas are tall towers with multiple-tiered eaves. Pagodas typically enshrine Buddhist relics and are therefore considered sacred sites.

38. Emphasis is my own.

39. Ethnomusicologist Donna Lee Kwon discusses the complex conceptual frame of the *p'an*—as it relates to *p'an kut*—in her doctoral dissertation (2005). For its relevance, I include a section here: "*P'an-gut* [*p'an kut*] . . . denotes a kind of *p'ungmul* that is formatted to be performed in a *p'an*, a large open space designated for entertainment and participation. Showcasing the rhythms and choreography of the style and the skills of the performers, *p'an-gut* is by far the most common format of *p'ungmul* that is performed today. . . . Though *p'an-gut* is often performed on its own, it can also be performed as the culminating event of a larger ritual or fundraising event" (68).

40. The *mul soji* ritual involves presenting an offering to the spirits, along with the ritual burning of paper. Lee admitted that he had trouble stacking the fruit offerings atop the bowl of rice in the ritual, which would have been viewed as a somewhat inauspicious sign (Lee Kwang Soo interview, February 20, 2009).

41. See endnote 35, this chapter.

42. For a complete SamulNori / samul nori discography see Hesselink 2012, 152–55.

TWO *The Dynamics of Rhythmic Form*

1. I include the *Oxford English Dictionary*'s entry for "dynamic" to give readers a sense of the common meanings of the term. (See https://en.oxforddictionaries.com/definition/dynamic.)

ADJECTIVE

1 (of a process or system) characterized by constant change, activity, or progress. '*a dynamic economy*'

1.1 *Physics* Relating to forces producing motion. Often contrasted with static

1.2 *Linguistics* (of a verb) expressing an action, activity, event, or process. Contrasted with stative

1.3 Denoting or relating to web pages that update frequently or are generated according to an individual's search terms.

'the dynamic content of these sites keeps their audience informed and up to date'

2 (of a person) positive in attitude and full of energy and new ideas.

'a dynamic young advertising executive'

3 Relating to the volume of sound produced by an instrument, voice, or recording.

4 *Electronics* (of a memory device) needed to be refreshed by the periodic application of a voltage.

NOUN

1 A force that stimulates change or progress within a system or process.

'evaluation is part of the basic dynamic of the project'

2 *Music* another term for dynamics (sense 3)

2. See also Lee, Katherine In-Young 2015.

3. In the 1990s, SamulNori Hanullim partnered with an instrument craft shop in Yangp'yŏng (in Kyŏnggi Province) to support the manufacture and production of samul nori instruments in response to the growing interest in samul nori. The company—now known as Hanullim Korean Music Instrument Company—specializes in the production and international export of samul nori instruments, as well as other Korean music instruments. For more information see the website for Hanullim Music, www.hanullim music.com.

4. Different local terms can be used to describe the category of "rhythmic patterns." The Korean term *karak* (meaning "strand" or "finger") is often used interchangeably with the word *changdan*. A Sino-Korean cognate, changdan (literally, "long, short") is typically translated into English as "rhythmic cycle." Nathan Hesselink has reviewed some of the scholarly preferences in terminology and usage. See Hesselink 2006, 158. In this manuscript, I employ the term karak since it is more commonly used by SamulNori and SamulNori Hanullim in speech and in written materials.

5. For more analysis on "groove" in Korean p'ungmul music and dance see Kwon, Donna Lee 2015.

6. Nathan Hesselink translates *chaegusŏng* in slightly different ways: "reorganizing" or "recomposing" (Hesselink 2012, 57).

7. As labeled on the map, Kyŏngsangbuk-do [Gyeongsangbuk-do] is also known as North Kyŏngsang Province, and Kyŏngsangnam-do [Gyeongsangnam-do] is South Kyŏngsang Province.

8. See chapter 1, endnote 20.

9. See chapter 1, 19.

10. In an interview conducted in March 2009, Choi Jong Sil clarified that the style of p'ungmul that was transmitted to him by his father was originally classified as Songp'o nongak. According to Choi, this was distinct from the style of p'ungmul practiced in Samch'ŏnp'o. When the Cultural Property for Nongak sibich'a was designated in 1966, Songp'o nongak became subsumed into what is now called Chinju Samch'ŏnp'o nongak.

11. In South Korea, Intangible Cultural Heritage (ICH) was formerly called Important Intangible Cultural Properties. For more information on the ICH system see the dissertations by CedarBough Tam Saeji (2012) and Roald Maliangkay (1999).

12. I refer to this research and musical experimentation as the SamulNori project in chapter 1.

13. I kindly thank Nathan Hesselink for sharing the 1979 recording with me.

14. In other recordings, *pyŏlgŏri talgŏri* is shortened to *pyŏldalgŏri* and performed only once.

15. Ethnomusicologist Keith Howard notes these discrepancies in timing in *Creating Korean Music* (2006, 43).

16. Soojin Kim's doctoral dissertation (2011) offers insight into the transmission of p'ungmul from South Korea to the United States. Whereas p'ungmul was traditionally learned by rote without notation, the learning of p'ungmul in the Korean diaspora is reliant on the use of notation and audio/visual recordings. Audio recordings made or acquired in Korea are dubbed and shared among members of diasporic p'ungmul (and samul nori) groups.

17. See Overseas Koreans Foundation 1999.

18. In an effort to employ SamulNori Hanullim's own notation in this chapter, I have modified the box notation only slightly for clarity. My use of this particular notational system is deliberate; it is my hope that the notation in this chapter will be accessible to not only music specialists but also to samul nori enthusiasts.

19. For information on how Im Dong-chang linked rhythm and SamulNori pedagogical techniques to geomantic principles and the cosmos see Hesselink 2012, 83–101.

20. This movement is an important point to consider. Although seated samul nori pieces such as "Yŏngnam nongak" do not feature dance and large-scale choreographies, performers are nevertheless moving and breathing in time with particular rhythmic cycles.

21. SamulNori Hanullim's notation book indicates that the p'ungmul choreography for *yŏngsan tadŭran* is a single circular shape.

22. Nathan Hesselink includes a translation of Kim Inu's essay "P'ungmulgut and Communal Spirit" in his *P'ungmul* text (2006, 100–118) and in an article published in *Asian Music* (Hesselink 1999/2000).

THREE *Dynamic Korea and Samul Nori*

1. The video lecture series was also sponsored by the Korean National University of Arts (now known as K Arts) and features former members of the SamulNori Hanullim ensemble: Park An-ji [Pak Anji]; Kim Han-bok [Kim Hanbok]; Shin Chan-sun [Sin Ch'ansŏn]; Jang Hyun-jin [Chang Hyŏnjin]; and Lee Dong-ju [Yi Tongju]. Videotape 1 begins with a forty-five-minute lecture on samul nori, followed by a lecture and performance of the "basic seated performance" (*anjŭnban*). Videotape 2 features the "basic standing performance" (*sŏnban*). The series aims "to provide a systematic teaching device for overseas Koreans in learning their cultural roots" (Overseas Koreans Foundation 1999).

2. Emphasis is my own.

3. FIFA stands for the Fédération Internationale de Football Association. An international competition for men's football (also known as soccer in the United States) is held every four years.

4. Emphasis is my own.

5. A list of the sponsors appears on the front page of the Hanjeon Artspool Center program booklet, *Kim Duk Soo's Dynamic Korea*. See figure 3.1.

6. See chapter 1, endnote 12, for a brief description of p'ansori.

7. Many venues devoted to traditional Korean music feature "sampler" programs. The National Gugak Center (Kungnip Kugakwŏn) offers a regular Saturday afternoon variety concert. A typical program may include dance, folk songs, and chamber ensemble music and conclude with a samul nori composition. For more information on the programming at venues such as the Chŏngdong Theater (Chŏngdong Kŭkchang) and the National Gugak Center see Jin-Woo Kim's PhD dissertation, "Twentieth-Century Discourses on Korean Music in Korea" (2002).

8. The opening ceremony for the 2002 World Cup featured a number that announcers dubbed "Digital Samul." The segment began with a white-clad "digital messenger," who had been hoisted by cables, descending from the sky to a high-level platform. The distinctive strains of the *t'aep'yŏngso* (double reed shawm) could be heard clearly on the soundtrack. Upon descent, he began to play a futuristic-looking changgo, which was placed near the other three instruments (ching, puk, and kkwaenggwari). Below him on the pitch, performers danced in formations, wearing bizarre costumes that included a television monitor as a head. According to the announcers, the concept underlying the number was the fusion between digital technology and traditional Korea, symbolized by the samul nori instruments. A search on YouTube or a South Korean video streaming service such as Naver.com or Daum.net will provide access to excerpts of the opening ceremony.

9. Kim Duk Soo's "A-he-hŏ" was included on the Red Devil 2002 Official Album. "Red Devil" is short for South Korea's Red Devils National Football Team Supporters Club.

10. See Min-jung Son (2012). Son writes of the rock versions of "O p'ilsŭng K'oria"

("O victory, Korea") by the Yun Tohyŏn Band and Crying Nut that became patriotic anthems and a "crucial component for stimulating and cementing unity" during the 2002 World Cup. I see the Yun Tohyŏn Band's version of "O p'ilsŭng K'oria," in particular, as a kind of stadium rock song that became modified into a rhythmic chant. The refrain of "O—p'ilsŭng K'oria, (XX), O—p'ilsŭng K'oria, (XX), O—p'ilsŭng K'oria, (XX), O, olé, olé" was broadcast into the sports arenas during matches. Fans sang along and performed the requisite hand claps (signified by "X") in between the phrases. The interactive rhythms within the chant were often punctuated by the sounds of drums in the stands.

11. The Red Devils National Football Team Supporters Club is South Korea's largest football fan club. During the World Cup, the Red Devils rose to prominence as the lead cheerleaders for the South Korean team. The red T-shirts, inscribed with the message of "Be the Reds," were worn not only by the Red Devils but also by the majority of South Korean fans. For more information about the background of the fan club see the website Pulgŭn angma (Red Devil), www.reddevil.or.kr.

12. Rachael Miyung Joo has written about the significant impact that mass media had on cultivating images of Koreanness and national unity during the 2002 World Cup (2006, 2010). The SK Telecom commercial "Sŭp'idŭ 011 CF—Ŭngwŏn kuho Taehan min'guk p'yŏn (2002)" (Cheer catchphrase—Republic of Korea edition) can be viewed at http://www.youtube.com/watch?v=5pC2jGCa8_8.

13. Emphasis is my own.

14. Since retiring from SamulNori Hanullim, Kim Dong-won has pursued a career as a musician, specializing in Korean percussion and voice. He is affiliated with the Silk Road Ensemble.

15. Ethnomusicologist Martin Stokes has pointed out to me that the rhythm employed in the "Taehan Min'guk" chant is identical to a chant used by fans of Manchester United. Despite this fact, the rhythm was zealously adopted (without question and perhaps without knowledge of its foreign origin) as South Korea's most nationalistic chant during the 2002 FIFA World Cup.

16. When I worked as the overseas coordinator for SamulNori Hanullim in Seoul, I received a personal copy of the VHS videocassette from Kim Duk Soo.

17. For a different perspective on the 2002 World Cup and the promotion of a distinct, regional identity within a unified national culture see Yun, Kyoim 2006, 10.

18. A black-and-white silent documentary, *Im Lande der Morgenstille* (In the land of morning calm, 1925), by Father Norbert Weber of the German Benedictine order provides visual footage of daily life in early twentieth-century Korea. The film was intended to show Weber's religious community in Germany a glimpse of Korean culture and the Benedictine order's missionary activities in Korea. In 1986, a VHS tape of the film was republished by the Benedictine Audiovisual Center in Seoul. The title of the documentary was translated into Korean as *Choyonghan ach'im ŭi nara* (Quiet morning country).

While Weber's "Morgenstille" is a clear reference to Morning Calm, the Korean usage of the term "quiet" signals an interesting sonic linkage to the moniker.

19. Margaret Walker Dilling's *Stories inside Stories*, published posthumously in 2007, chronicles the undertaking of the elaborate musical production for the 1988 Seoul Olympics. The slogan associated with the Seoul Olympics was "Harmony and Progress."

20. Rabindranath Tagore's concise poem inspired Korean nationalist sentiment during the Japanese Colonial Period (1910–1945) and endeared South Koreans to the Indian poet. The 150th anniversary of Tagore's birth was marked by the unveiling of a statue of him in downtown Seoul in 2011. See *Korea Times* 2011.

21. Emphasis is my own.

22. Korean Culture and Information Service, "Dynamic Korea—Listen" (2006). Many of the Dynamic Korea promotional videos are still archived on the Korea.net website.

23. "Hi Seoul" was adopted by the Seoul City government in 2002. It was later modified to "Hi Seoul, Soul of Asia" in 2007.

24. The National Theater of Korea promoted "national brand performances" (*kukka p'ŭrandŭ kongyŏn*) for each of its four resident companies, beginning in the mid-2000s. Andrew Killick presents the following description from a 2006 program guide: "These National Brand Performances are programs of representative Korean works worthy to be presented to the world with the Republic of Korea as their brand-name. The aim is to produce works that, while based on Korean tradition, embrace contemporary aesthetics and unique individuality, and can be shared by Korea and the world together" (Killick 2010, 144–45).

25. See Taet'ongnyŏng kirokkwan (Presidential archives) 2009, "Kukka p'ŭraendŭ wiwŏnhoe" (Presidential council on nation branding).

26. See Marayag 2010, 45–47; Schmuck 2011, 105. It should be noted that Ŏ's Presidential Council on Nation Branding announced a ten-point action plan in 2009 to develop South Korea's image and reputation. These included plans (1) to promote *taekwŏndo*, (2) to dispatch three thousand volunteers abroad every year, (3) to adopt a "Korean Wave" program, (4) to introduce the Global Korea Scholarship, (5) to adopt "Campus Asia" programs, (6) to increase external aid, (7) to develop state-of-the-art technologies, (8) to nurture culture and tourism industries, (9) to treat foreigners and multicultural families better, and (10) to help Koreans become "global citizens."

FOUR *Global Encounters with Samul Nori*

1. The term "SamulNorian" has been used to describe a devoted fan of SamulNori. Although I have been unable to verify the precise genesis of "SamulNorian," many press materials on SamulNori (and subsequent newspaper articles) note that the term was included in the *Encylopaedia Britannica*.

2. See Kim, Soojin 2011, 151–84.

3. There is a growing body of scholarly work investigating the learning and practice of p'ungmul by overseas Koreans in the United States. S. Sonya Gwak's ethnography of a Philadelphia-based p'ungmul group uncovers the ways in which a group of Koreans in America engage in cultural practices such as p'ungmul performance as a means to cultivate a sense of ethnic identity (Gwak, S. Sonya 2008). Donna Lee Kwon's article, "Roots and Routes of *P'ungmul* in the United States," provides a concise overview of p'ungmul groups (particularly collegiate and cultural activist groups) that formed in the United States beginning in the 1980s. (See also Kim, Mi-yon 1993.) Similarly, Youngmin Yu and Soojin Kim in their dissertations also consider the performance of p'ungmul by Korean Americans in Los Angeles (Yu and Kim) and New York (Kim), zeroing in on the many cultural negotiations that take place in the quest to reflect a hybridized Korean American identity (Yu, Youngmin 2007; Kim, Soojin 2011). The late Margaret Walker Dilling conducted interviews with Korean American p'ungmul groups—in particular, the Korean Youth Cultural Council (KYCC) in Oakland, California. Many of Dilling's interviews and field notes are housed in the Margaret Walker Dilling collection at the Jean Gray Hargrove Music Library at the University of California, Berkeley. While it may seem that global p'ungmul and samul nori are mutually exclusive categories, their histories are actually closely intertwined.

4. I borrow from an oft-cited headline that appears in SamulNori's press kit. See Anderson 1985.

5. On January 9, 2009, in Seoul, I moderated a panel titled "Encounters with Samul-Nori" at the International SamulNori Symposium. In a public interview format, I directed questions to Suzanna Samstag, Kim Rihae (Kim Duk Soo's wife), and Kim Dong-won. The contents of the interviews and discussion were transcribed by Yeo Sang-bum [Yŏ Sangbŏm] and incorporated into a 2009 publication funded in part by the Ministry of Culture, Sports, and Tourism. See SamulNori Hanullim t'ansaeng samsip chunyŏn kinyŏm saŏphoe [SamulNori's Thirtieth Anniversary Committee] 2009, 211.

6. See appendix 2 for an example of Samstag's prose.

7. The group's web page (now defunct) has since migrated to their Facebook page: https://www.facebook.com/groups/Shinparam/ (accessed July 3, 2016).

8. As with many samul nori and p'ungmul groups based in Korea and in other countries, the group's name takes on significance and is often imbued with several semantic meanings that operate across different linguistic domains. The name "Shinparam" is derived from the Sino-Korean cognate *sin* (신, 神, spirit) and the Korean term *param* (바람, wind). Param is a play on the p'ung of p'ungmul, which is the Sino-Korean translation for "wind." In combination, the two terms foster a connection to traditional Korean drumming forms and construct evocative imagery that aligns with both ancient and local Korean conceptualizations of nature's kinship with the spiritual world (Sarah Lee, personal communication, July 8, 2010).

9. See endnote 7.

10. For more information on the *Korean Quarterly* see http://www.koreanquarterly.org/About.html.

11. The performance at Saint John's University marked the kickoff of SamulNori Hanullim's 2004 U.S. tour. I worked closely in 2003 with SamulNori Hanullim's managing director Joo Jay-youn and Rob Robbins (formerly of Herbert Barrett Management) to plan and see through the logistics of the monthlong 2004 U.S. tour.

12. The Korean Institute of Minnesota received the set of instruments and costumes through a grant administered by the Overseas Koreans Foundation (OKF), an affiliate of the Ministry of Foreign Affairs and Trade. For several years the OKF earmarked funds for a special "samul nori instrument" grant program for interested samul nori groups and Korean cultural organizations outside Korea. The grants were designed to support the global transmission of Korean music.

13. Although my tenure as overseas coordinator for SamulNori Hanullim / Nanjang Cultures had officially ended by late 2004, I still occasionally assisted in various events. In this case I was asked by Joo Jay-youn (SamulNori Hanullim's managing director) to recommend a samul nori team from the United States to participate in the 2005 festival. Because of my connections with the Korean adoptee community, I had become acquainted with Stephen Wunrow; in 2003, I was asked to write an article on SamulNori for the *Korean Quarterly*, commemorating the twenty-fifth anniversary of SamulNori's founding. The following year I helped arrange a visit for Wunrow and *Korean Quarterly* reporter Kyong Halverson at the Puyŏ SamulNori School. In the meantime I became aware of the Shinparam group and thought that it would be a good opportunity for the group to participate in the SamulNori festival, even despite their fledgling status.

14. Sangho Kim mentioned that these samul nori performances by the South Korean army's *munhwa sŏnchŏndae* (abbreviated as *"mun-sŏn-tae"*) were broadcast on loudspeakers at strategic locations along the Demilitarized Zone that separates North from South Korea. The loud and boisterous performances of Korean percussion could easily be heard on the North Korean side. According to Kim, the broadcasts were part of a strategic military operation akin to psychological warfare. Other Korean males that I have spoken with (who had some kind of training in kugak) have discussed their participation in these cultural propaganda units. The militaristic musical units were designed to demonstrate (1) a sense of unified, collective energy; (2) an atmosphere of excitement and fun that could only be had south of the DMZ; and (3) South Korea's cultural superiority over North Korea.

15. Former Shinparam members Lia Bengtson, Nik Nadeau, and Shirley Sailors have all spent time in Korea, studying either samul nori or p'ungmul.

16. The personal website of Suzanne Nketia includes a description of Swissamul: http://www.suzanne-nketia.ch/swissamul.html (accessed July 3, 2017).

17. I draw here from Kay Kaufman Shelemay's article on musical communities. She-

lemay posits that attention to processes of "descent, dissent, and affinity both elucidates music's generative role in shaping new collectivities and unsettles the notion of music as a static sonic marker of social groupings" (Shelemay 2011, 390). She puts forth a new typology for the study of musical collectivities—communities of descent, dissent, and affinity. A musical community of affinity emerges from individual preferences—affinities—for a musical genre or tradition, "quickly followed by a desire for social proximity or association with others equally enamored" (2011, 373).

18. Nketia's first husband (now deceased) was a musician and dancer from Ghana.

19. TakeTiNa is a trademarked, pedagogical method that "creates rhythm consciousness through the interaction of feet, hands, and voice" (Flatischler 1992, 145). Since the 1970s Flatischler has led workshops in Europe, the Americas, and Australia on the TakeTiNa method. He incorporates a variety of different percussion styles and genres into his workshops, including variations on Korean rhythmic patterns, typically played on the changgo drum. For further information see Flatischler's website, http://www.taketina.com (accessed November 2, 2016).

20. The Red Sun jazz group was born out of a mutually meaningful encounter between SamulNori and Austrian saxophonist Wolfgang Puschnig in 1987, at the Megadrums Festival organized by Reinhard Flatischler. For a concise summary of the jazz group's formation and long-term collaboration with SamulNori see Hesselink 2012, 110–11. It is important to point out that Red Sun has had a fluid membership over time and in different locations. Therefore different musicians have appeared as part of the Red Sun ensemble in performances and recordings issued on European and Korean labels. When I worked for SamulNori Hanullim in 2003, Red Sun was invited to perform for SamulNori's twenty-fifth anniversary concerts at Ho-am Art Hall in Seoul. This was when I first met Wolfgang Puschnig, jazz vocalist Linda Sharrock (Puschnig's former partner and musical collaborator), bassist Jamaaladeen Tacuma, and guitarist Rick Iannacone. In August 2010, during a follow-up research trip to Korea, I had the pleasure of meeting Red Sun once again—this time with a slightly different configuration of Puschnig, Tacuma, and an Armenian jazz pianist named Karen Asatrian. Despite all the changes over the years, Puschnig and Tacuma have remained fixtures in the group.

21. Huber is a puppeteer and was invited to participate in the weeklong International Puppet Festival in Korea in 1991 (Rubin 1998, 271).

22. Im Dong-chang was a frequent visitor at the Nanjang Studio in Sinch'on. Im had a burgeoning interest in (and good ear for) traditional Korean music and became quite skilled at learning the rhythms that the SamulNori quartet played in their compositions. As discussed in chapter 2, Im was largely responsible for transcribing the samul nori rhythms into notational form. Nketia noted that Lee Kwang Soo was the first to show her how to use the *sangmo* (a hat with a long white streamer that is activated through body movements).

23. This is documented on a loose-leaf insert—"1990 SamulNori International and Domestic Performances"—that was attached to SamulNori's ten-year commemorative publication (SamulNori 1988).

24. Martha Vickery also profiled Suzanna Nketia and Swissamul in her *Korean Quarterly* publication. See Vickery 2005–6a, 76–77.

25. The Samul GwangDae team was one of the first groups to apprentice under the SamulNori quartet in the early 1990s. Park An-ji [Pak Anji], Shin Chan-sun [Sin Ch'ansŏn], Jang Hyun-jin [Chang Hyŏnjin], and Kim Han-bok [Kim Hanbok] were all graduates of the same high school in Kŭmsan and moved to Seoul upon graduation. The GwangDae team performed extensively with Kim Duk Soo as part of the SamulNori Hanullim organization from 1993 to 2007.

26. The prayer song that Lange heard performed by Park An-ji is the pinari. The pinari will be discussed in chapter 5.

27. Parts of the concert can be viewed on YouTube. See "05 Gyonggi Dodang Gut—Traditional—Kim Dong-Won and Swissamul," http://www.youtube.com/watch?v=jU02Y1uBSR0 (accessed July 18, 2010).

28. A full update on Lange's experiences in Korea at K-Arts and the National Gugak Center is beyond the scope of this work. I focus instead on the initial encounters with SamulNori / samul nori in this chapter.

29. See endnote 17.

30. In 2003 the broadcasting of the Korean melodrama *Winter Sonata* (known as "Fuyu no sonata" in Japanese) on Japan's NHK television led to popularity of unprecedented proportions. The drama's male lead, Bae Yong-joon [Pae Yongjun], became a regional superstar and an object of affection for a demographic of infatuated middle-aged women in Japan. Bae was even bestowed with the high honorific title of "Yon Sama" by his adoring fans and the Japanese media. The unexpected hit in Japan (which impacted the Korean economy through a surge in Hallyu tourism and Hallyu-related spending) was a catalyst in the aggressive exporting of Korean dramas and films during the mid-2000s. The Hallyu "market" originally broadcast dramas and movies in East and Southeast Asia but later expanded to the Middle East and South America.

31. *All about Eve* (Munhwa Broadcasting Corporation, 2000), starring Chang Tonggŏn, was one of the first Korean dramas to be broadcast in Mexico with Spanish subtitles in the early 2000s (see Kim Chŏngsŏp 2005). Kwŏn Sang'u became well known after his appearances on the SBS (Seoul Broadcasting System) melodrama series *Stairway to Heaven* (2003–4).

32. See also Asian Fanatics Forum, 2007, http://asianfanatics.net/forum/topic/372908-mexico-hallyu-korean-wave-already-on-the-rise/.

33. I visited the CCC in Mexico City in November 2009 but was unable to meet the

samul nori group composed of ethnic Koreans. I did, however, meet with Ch'oe Namyun, the teacher for the Canto del Cielo group.

34. The Zona Rosa district in Mexico City is home to a small but distinct "Koreatown." Many Korean restaurants and businesses are located on Florencia Street.

35. Like other group names, Canto del Cielo or its Korean translation "Hanul Sori" invokes concepts that SamulNori has emphasized in its pedagogy. See Hesselink 2004.

36. Extracurricular activities and organizations at Japanese universities are often called *sa-kuru*, which is a Japanized pronunciation of the English loan word "circle." In Korea the same concept applies, with the word *tongari* designating a college group.

37. The term/name of *sinawi* has appeared previously in chapter 1; SamulNori cofounders Kim Duk Soo and Kim Yong-bae were members of the Minsogakhoe Sinawi group (Folk music society "Sinawi") that performed at the Space Theater in Seoul.

38. Literally, "elder/junior," *sŏn(bae)-hubae* refers to types of relationships that are defined hierarchically by age and usually cultivated between older and younger classmates during college years. In Korea these strong relationships typically last well beyond college. Elder students are accorded respect by their juniors, while younger classmates benefit from mentorship and wisdom from their more senior classmates.

39. See the Shinawi blog, http://shinawi.blog64.fc2.com/blog-entry-1.html (accessed August 14, 2010).

FIVE *Transnational Samul Nori and the Politics of Place*

1. Kim Duk Soo's remarks on the significance of the 2008 World SamulNori Festival appeared in the festival's program. Emphasis is my own. See Kim Duk Soo 2008, 4.

2. Kim Yong-bae (one of the original members of the SamulNori quartet) died by suicide in 1986.

3. Nam also became the changgo player for the in-house samul nori quartet of the National Gugak Center (then, National Center for Korean Traditional Performing Arts) in 1986.

4. The term *hanmadang* has many semantic meanings. In this usage, it refers to a gathering or festival. The SamulNori Kyŏrugi Hanmadang did not take place in 1990, 1996, 1998, or 2009. In 2009 the South Korean government canceled the festival/competition and a number of other performing arts festivals because of concerns about a potential swine flu outbreak in the country.

5. For a list of the SamulNori Kyŏrugi events see the website for the 2011 World SamulNori Festival, http://www.samulfestival.co.kr/festival/festival_02_04.asp.

6. During my tenure as the overseas coordinator for SamulNori Hanullim, I worked closely with the international teams at the 2003 SamulNori Kyŏrugi Hanmadang, held in

Yangp'yŏng. One of my main duties was to facilitate communication between the festival planning committee and the international participants regarding meals, rehearsals, and other event logistics.

7. SamulNori's presentation of the mun kut (a ritual performed at a door or gate) at the beginning of their standard performance is inspired by older traditions within p'ungmul and itinerant performance culture. More will be said of the mun kut in this chapter.

8. The judges are usually established kugak (traditional Korean music) performers or teachers. In 2008 some of the judges included Im Pyŏnggo, director of the SamulNori Hanullim Puyŏ Educational Institute; Yu Chihwa, a Chŏngŭp nongak practitioner and a "holder" of the Chŏngŭp nongak designated cultural asset; Kim Kwangbok, former member of the Minsogakhoe Sinawi group and a p'iri (small double reed instrument) player; and Suzanna Samstag, former managing director of SamulNori.

9. An Suksŏn is one of the most famous contemporary p'ansori artists. She has previously collaborated with SamulNori and the jazz ensemble Red Sun, in addition to serving on the advisory board for the SamulNori Hanullim organization.

10. The Kyŏrugi did not take place in 1990, 1996, 1998, and 2009.

11. The South Korean government has an official Korean language romanization system that is used in lieu of the McCune-Reischauer for signs and publications. For the sake of consistency, I will include the McCune-Reischauer rendering in brackets.

12. Ariane Mnouchkine, director of Théâtre du Soleil, first saw Kim Duk Soo's SamulNori Hanullim group perform at the Festival d'Avignon in 1998. Taken aback by what she heard, Mnouchkine approached Kim Duk Soo directly about the possibility of arranging percussion lessons for her theatrical troupe. Mnouchkine and Kim negotiated to have Han Jae Suk [Han Chaesŏk] travel to Paris to serve as an instructor to the actors for six months. The intensive training sessions then became the musical basis for Mnouchkine's production *Tambours sur la digue* (Drummers on the dike), based on a play by Hélène Cixous (Tan 2012, 57–88). The experience then led several actors such as Vincent Mangado, Dominique Jambert, and Matthieu Rauchvarger to continue their studies of Korean percussion as members of a French samul nori group. Mangado, Jambert, and Rauchvarger later traveled to South Korea to participate in the 2008 World SamulNori Festival.

13. SamulNori Hanullim uses "overseas" to refer to samul nori teams that are non-Korean. This is contrasted with the term *kungnae*, which is understood as "Korean."

14. A brief translation of some of the terms in this section: a *hanbok* is a traditional two-piece garment from Korea; a *cheongsam* (ch'i-p'ao) is a one-piece style of dress from China; a *pup'o* is a hat made of feathers typically worn by the kkwaenggwari player during a *p'an kut* performance in SamulNori's regular program; a *sangmo* is a hat with a long white streamer worn by samul nori performers in the *p'an kut*. *Ilch'ae* is a "one stroke" rhythm; *hwimori* is the name of a duple rhythmic pattern; *hohŭp*, or breath, is an integrated and

embodied breathing technique and philosophy employed by SamulNori in their pedagogy; *ch'wit'a* is military processional music; *kosa* is a ritual offering ceremony; "Mun Yŏpsio!" means "Open the gates!"

15. Kim refers here to the financial crisis of 2007–8, which began with the collapse of large U.S. investment banks and financial institutions and led to widespread global panic and an economic recession. By October 2008 (the month when the World SamulNori Festival was held), the South Korean economy was already severely impacted by the crisis.

16. See appendix 2 for a description of "Pinari" in SamulNori Hanullim's program notes. Appendix 1 includes a translation of a sample pinari text into English.

17. Kim Suyong's master's thesis, "Namsadangp'ae pinari pigyo yŏn'gu," features a comparative analysis of four representative pinari texts performed by namsadang musicians: Ha Ryong-nam (1900–1980); Yang Toil (1908–1980); Yi Suyŏng (b. 1940); and Lee Kwang Soo (b. 1952).

18. For a collection of pinari texts (transcribed into Korean only) see Kim Hŏnsŏn 1995, 259–401. Lee Kwang Soo's "Sori kut 'Pinari'" CD on Synnara records also includes the texts for his rendition of various pinari texts.

19. In Lee's rendition there is dramatic emphasis and prolongation on the first word, sky, followed by a rapid delivery of text that lies between speech and song.

20. Translation by author. The reader should note that this translation differs slightly from the one featured in appendix 1. Many Sino-Korean characters can yield more than one interpretation. Thus the translation of such a text must involve careful consideration of historical, cultural, and geographical contexts.

21. See appendix 1 for an English translation of a version of the pinari text.

22. I transcribe from my field video footage of the opening concert at the World SamulNori Festival.

23. The term "Zainichi" refers to non-Japanese residents who live in Japan. Zainichi Koreans—most of whom first entered Japan during Japan's occupation of Korea (1910–1945)—are considered permanent residents of Japan, yet often do not hold Japanese citizenship. The Kŏn'guk school is an ethnic school for Zainichi Koreans in Osaka. It caters its pedagogy toward the fervent transmission of Korean language and culture.

24. And along those same lines, the Russian team—composed mainly of fourth-generation ethnic Koreans residing on Sakhalin Island—selected one of the two native Russian members to deliver the solo in Russian.

Epilogue

1. Within five months of its debut, the video recorded over one billion views on YouTube. "Gangnam Style" was the most downloaded video on YouTube for over four years (2012–2017).

2. Many samul nori groups are connected on social media platforms such as Facebook and YouTube. Users often share resources and keep in touch on such websites.

3. And the opening "Gangnam Style" example of this chapter proves that the rhythmic form of the song (and video) trumped a proficiency in the Korean language and knowledge of the satirical lyrics.

4. In *Analytical Studies in World Music* (2006), editor Michael Tenzer provides a useful description of "periodicity"—"a term from mathematics and physics referring to regular recurrence of waveforms, functions, or phenomena (orbits)." He continues: "In music, periodicity has long signified repetition or restatement, literal or transformed, of all kinds—of beats, rhythms, motives, melodies, structures, timbres: virtually any musical elements can create a sense of stability through return or constancy, and such stability will always be in dynamic dialog with change" (22).

BIBLIOGRAPHY

Adorno, Theodor W. (1941) 2002. "On Popular Music [With the assistance of George Simpson]" In *Essays on Music: Theodor W. Adorno*, selected, with introduction, commentary, and notes by Richard Leppert, 437–69. Berkeley: University of California Press.

Agawu, Kofi V. 1995a. *African Rhythm: A Northern Ewe Perspective*. New York: Cambridge University Press.

———. 1995b. "The Invention of 'African Rhythm.'" *Journal of the American Musicological Society* 48 (3): 380–95.

———. 2003. *Representing African Music: Postcolonial Notes, Queries, Positions*. New York: Routledge.

Alvarez, Luis. 2008. "Reggae Rhythms in Dignity's Diaspora: Globalization, Indigenous Identity, and the Circulation of Cultural Struggle." *Popular Music and Society* 31 (5): 575–97.

Anderson, Jack. 1985. "From Korea, Drums and Dancers." *New York Times*, February 1.

Anholt, Simon. 1998. "Nation-Brands of the Twenty-First Century." *Journal of Brand Management* 5 (6): 395–406.

———. 2003. *Brand New Justice: The Upside of Global Branding*. Oxford: Butterworth-Heinemann.

———. 2011. "Beyond the Nation Brand: The Role of Image and Identity in International Relations." *Exchange: The Journal of Public Diplomacy* 2 (1): 1–7. http://surface.syr.edu/exchange/vol2/iss1/1/.

Aoyama, Yuko. 2007. "The Role of Consumption and Globalization in a Cultural Industry: The Case of Flamenco." *Geoforum* 38 (1): 103–13.

Appert, Catherine. 2016. "On Hybridity in African Popular Music: The Case of Senegalese Hip Hop." *Ethnomusicology* 60 (2): 279–99.

Arirang TV. 2009. "The Beauty of Korean Style—*Samul Nori*." Broadcast on September 30, 2009. Seoul.

Aronczyk, Melissa. 2013. *Branding the Nation: The Global Business of National Identity*. New York: Oxford University Press.

Bañagale, Ryan Raul. 2014. *Arranging Gershwin: "Rhapsody in Blue" and the Creation of an American Icon*. New York: Oxford University Press.

Bender, Shawn. 2012. *Taiko Boom: Japanese Drumming in Place and Motion*. Berkeley: University of California Press.

Benedictine Audiovisual Center. 1986. *Choyonghan ach'im ŭi nara* [Quiet morning country] (Redistributed video of *Im Lande der Morgenstille* [In the land of morning calm], 1925). VHS. Seoul.

Berry, Wallace. (1966) 1986. *Form in Music*. 2nd ed. Englewood Cliffs, NJ: Prentice-Hall.

Bigenho, Michelle. 2012. *Intimate Distance: Andean Music in Japan*. Durham, NC: Duke University Press.

Bonds, Mark Evan. 2010. "The Spatial Representation of Musical Form." *Journal of Musicology* 27 (3): 265–303.

Breen, Michael. 2008. "Seoul's Frustration with National Branding Initiatives." *Korea Times*, October 28. http://www.koreatimes.co.kr/www/news/issues/2014/10/260_33453.html.

Brookhart, Edward. 1964. "Musical Form: Dynamic vs. Static." *Music Educators Journal* 51 (1): 91–93, 146–47.

Bussell, Jennifer L. 1997. "A Life of Sound: Korean Farming Music and Its Journey to Modernity." BA thesis, University of Chicago.

Caplin, William E. 1998. *Classical Form: A Theory of Formal Functions for the Instrumental Music of Haydn, Mozart, and Beethoven*. New York: Oxford University Press.

Chaganti, Seeta. 2018. *Strange Footing: Poetic Form and Dance in the Late Middle Ages*. Chicago: University of Chicago Press.

Charry, Eric, ed. 2012. *Hip Hop Africa: New African Music in a Globalizing World*. Bloomington: Indiana University Press.

Chernoff, John Miller. 1981. *African Rhythm and African Sensibility: Aesthetics and Social Action in African Musical Idioms*. Chicago: University of Chicago Press.

Ch'oe T'aehyŏn. 1991. "'Minsogakhoe sinawi ŭi hoego-wa chŏnmang" [A retrospective and prospective look at the Sinawi Folk Music Society]. *Hanguk umaksa hakpo* 7:27–47.

Choi Jong Sil [Ch'oe Chongsil]. 2009. "Ch'oe Chongsil ŭi mal hanŭn samul nori" [Choi Jong Sil speaks on samul nori]. In *Commemoration of SamulNori's Thirtieth Anniversary*, edited by SamulNori Hanullim t'ansaeng samsip chunyŏn kinyŏm saŏphoe [SamulNori's Thirtieth Anniversary Committee], 140–55. Seoul: Ministry of Culture, Sports, and Tourism [and Nanjang Cultures].

Chosun ilbo. 2006. "Capital to Promote Itself as 'Soul of Asia.'" November 13. http://english.chosun.com/site/data/html_dir/2006/11/13/2006111361019.html.

Chung, Ah-young. 2006. "Kim Duk-soo Reinvents Tradition: Man Who Came before Hallyu Talks about Sustaining Hallyu." *Korea Times*, October 26.

Condry, Ian. 2006. *Hip-Hop Japan: Rap and the Paths of Cultural Globalization.* Durham, NC: Duke University Press.

Cooper, Grosvenor W., and Leonard B. Meyer. 1960. *The Rhythmic Structure of Music.* Chicago: University of Chicago Press.

Delissen, Alain. 2001. "The Aesthetic Pasts of *Space* (1960–1990)." *Korean Studies* 25 (2): 243–60.

Dilling, Margaret Walker. 2007. *Stories inside Stories: Music in the Making of the Korean Olympic Ceremonies.* Berkeley: Institute of East Asian Studies, University of California.

Do, Je-he. 2010. "Changing Slogans Confusing, Costly." *Korea Times*, February 8. http://www.koreatimes.co.kr/www/news/nation/2010/02/116_60489.html.

Dueck, Byron. 2013. "Rhythm and Role Recruitment in Manitoban Aboriginal Music." In *Experience and Meaning in Music Performance*, edited by Martin Clayton, Byron Dueck, and Laura Leante, 135–60. New York: Oxford University Press.

Durand, Alain Philippe, ed. 2002. *Black, Blanc, Beur: Rap Music and Hip-Hop Culture in the Francophone World.* Lanham, MD: Scarecrow.

Eckert, Carter J., Ki-Baik Lee, Young Ick Lew, Michael Robinson, and Edward W. Wagner. 1990. *Korea Old and New: A History.* Seoul: Ilchokak.

Ellingson, Ter. 1992. "Notation." In *Ethnomusicology: An Introduction*, edited by Helen Myers, 153–64. New York: W. W. Norton.

Erlmann, Veit. 1996. "The Aesthetics of the Global Imagination: Reflections on World Music in the 1990s." *Public Culture* 8 (3): 467–87.

———. 1999. *Music, Modernity, and the Global Imagination: South Africa and the West.* New York: Oxford University Press.

Feld, Steven. 1988. "Notes on World Beat." *Public Culture Bulletin* 1 (1): 31–37.

———. 1994. "From Schizophonia to Schismogenesis: Notes on the Discourses of World Music and World Beat." In *Music Grooves: Essays and Dialogues*, edited by Charles Keil and Steven Feld, 265–71. Chicago: University of Chicago Press.

———. 2000. "A Sweet Lullaby for World Music." *Public Culture* 12 (1): 145–72.

Fenn, John. 2004. "Rap and Ragga Musical Cultures, Lifestyles, and Performances in Malawi." PhD diss., Indiana University.

Flatischler, Reinhard. 1992. *The Forgotten Power of Rhythm.* Mendocino, CA: LifeRhythm.

Garofalo, Reebee. 1993. "Whose World, What Beat: The Transnational Music Industry, Identity, and Cultural Imperialism." *World of Music* 35 (2): 16–32.

Gibson, James J. 1977. "The Theory of Affordances." In *Perceiving, Acting, and Knowing: Toward an Ecological Psychology*, edited by Robert Shaw and John Bransford, 67–82. Hillsdale, NJ: Lawrence Erlbaum.

———. 1979. *The Ecological Approach to Visual Perception.* Boston: Houghton Mifflin.

Gordon, Beate Sirota. 1997. *The Only Woman in the Room: A Memoir.* Tokyo: Kodansha International.

Griffis, William Elliot. 1882. *Corea, the Hermit Nation*. New York: Scribner.

Guerrero, Jesús. 2011. "La ola 'Hallyu' llega con festival coreano" [The Hallyu wave comes with a Korean festival]. *Milenio*, February 23, p. 36.

Guilbault, Jocelyne. 1993. *Zouk: World Music in the West Indies*. Chicago: University of Chicago Press.

———. 1997. "Interpreting World Music: A Challenge in Theory and Practice." *Popular Music* 16 (1): 31–44.

———. 2005. "Audible Entanglements: Nation and Diasporas in Trinidad's Calypso Music Scene." *Small Axe* 9 (1): 40–63.

———. 2006. "On Redefining the 'Local' through World Music." In *Ethnomusicology: A Contemporary Reader*, edited by Jennifer Post, 137–46. New York: Routledge.

Gwak, S. Sonya. 2008. *Be(com)ing Korean in the United States: Exploring Ethnic Identity Formation through Cultural Practices*. Amherst, NY: Cambria.

Han, Myung-hee [Han Myŏnghŭi]. 1993. "Samulnori: Providing a Musical Release." *Koreana* 7 (4): 34–35.

Han'guk Hyangt'osa Yŏn'gu Chŏn'guk Hyŏbŭihoe. 1994. *Han'guk ŭi nongak. Honam p'yŏn* [Korean *nongak*. Honam region]. Seoul: Susŏwŏn.

Han'guk ŭi hon: Kim Tŏksu SamulNori [The soul of Korea: Kim Duk Soo SamulNori]. 2005. 3 DVDs. Seoul: Dawoori Entertainment.

Hanjeon Artspool Center [Hanjŏn ach'ŭp'ul sent'ŏ]. 2002. *Kim Duk Soo's Dynamic Korea*. Program brochure. Seoul.

Harris, Richard. 2004. *Faces of Korea: The Foreign Experience in the Land of the Morning Calm*. Seoul: Hollym.

Hasty, Christopher. 1997. *Meter as Rhythm*. New York: Oxford University Press.

Helbig, Adriana N. 2014. *Hip Hop Ukraine: Music, Race, and African Migration*. Bloomington: Indiana University Press.

Hesselink, Nathan. 1998. "A Tale of Two Drummers: Percussion Band Music in North Chŏlla Province." PhD diss., University of London.

———. 1999/2000. "Kim Inu's 'P'ungmulgut and Communal Spirit': Edited and Translated with an Introduction and Commentary." *Asian Music* 31 (1): 1–34.

———. 2001. "On the Road with 'Och'ae Chilgut': Stages in the Development of Korean Percussion Band Music and Dance." In *Contemporary Directions: Korean Folk Music Engaging the Twentieth Century and Beyond*, edited by Nathan Hesselink, 54–75. Berkeley: Institute of East Asian Studies, University of California.

———. 2004. "*Samul Nori* as Traditional: Preservation and Innovation in a South Korean Contemporary Percussion Genre." *Ethnomusicology* 48 (3): 405–39.

———. 2006. *P'ungmul: South Korean Drumming and Dance*. Chicago: University of Chicago Press.

———. 2011. "Rhythm and Folk Drumming (*P'ungmul*) as the Musical Embodiment of

Communal Consciousness in South Korean Village Society." In *Analytical and Cross-Cultural Studies in World Music*, edited by Michael Tenzer and John Roeder, 3–87. New York: Oxford University Press.

———. 2012. *SamulNori: Contemporary Korean Drumming and the Rebirth of Itinerant Performance Culture.* Chicago: University of Chicago Press.

Hong, Euny. 2014. *The Birth of Korean Cool: How One Nation Is Conquering the World through Pop Culture.* New York: Picador.

Hong Sŏngsik. 2002. "'Samul nori'-ro Han'guk ŭl allyŏra" [Getting to know Korea through samul nori], May 31. Ohmynews.com. http://www.ohmynews.com/NWS_Web/View/at_pg.aspx?CNTN_CD=A0000077040.

Howard, Keith. 1989. *Bands, Songs, and Shamanistic Rituals: Folk Music in Korean Society.* Seoul: Royal Asiatic Society.

———. 1991/92. "Why Do It That Way? Rhythmic Models and Motifs in Korean Percussion Bands." *Asian Music* 23 (1): 1–59.

———. 2006. *Creating Korean Music: Tradition, Innovation and the Discourse of Identity.* Perspectives on Korean Music, vol. 2. Aldershot, UK: Ashgate.

———. 2015. *SamulNori: Korean Percussion for a Contemporary World.* Aldershot, UK: Ashgate.

Hŭngsadan [Young Korean Academy]. 1978. "Ham Sŏk-hŏn Sŏnsaengnim Ch'ilsipch'ilhoe saengsin ch'ukkamoim" [An invitation to the seventy-seventh birthday celebration for teacher Ham Sŏk-hŏn]. Seoul.

Hutchinson, Sydney, ed. 2014. *Salsa World: A Global Dance in Local Contexts.* Philadelphia: Temple University Press.

Hwang Byung-ki [Hwang Pyŏnggi]. 1977. "Characteristics of Korean Music." *Konggan* 12 (5): 62–65.

———. 2001. "Philosophy and Aesthetics of Korean Music." In *The Garland Encyclopedia of World Music.* Vol. 7, *East Asia: China, Japan, and Korea*, edited by Robert C. Provine, Yosihiko Tokumaru, and J. Lawrence Witzleben, 813–16. New York: Routledge.

Jeon, Won Kyung. 2013. "The 'Korean Wave' and Television Drama Exports, 1995–2005." PhD diss., University of Glasgow.

Joo Jay-youn [Chu Chaeyŏn]. 2010. "Samulnori ŭi yŏksajŏk chŏn'gae-wa munhwa sanŏpchŏk sŏnggwa" [Achievements of cultural-commercial aspects of samul nori through an analysis of its history]. MA thesis, Korea University.

Joo, Rachael Miyung. 2006. "Consuming Visions: The Crowds of the Korean World Cup." *Journal of Korean Studies* 11 (1): 41–67.

———. 2010. *Transnational Sport: Gender, Media, and Global Korea.* Durham, NC: Duke University Press.

Kang Jae Hoon [Kang Ch'aehun]. 2008. "Kihoek kongyŏnjang ŭi sarye rosŏ 'Konggan

Sarang' kŭkchang yŏn'gu" [Theater study on the "Space Theater"—focusing on the example of presenting theater]. Master's thesis, Sŏnggonghoe University.

Kang Joon-hyuk [Kang Chunhyŏk]. 2006. "Samulnori kongyŏn yangsik ŭi yŏksa." In *"SamulNori": 30 Years of Performing Arts* (symposium proceedings). Puyŏ: SamulNori Hanullim.

Keeler, Ward. 2009. "What's Burmese about Burmese Rap? Why Some Expressive Forms Go Global." *American Ethnologist* 36 (1): 2–19.

Keyes, Cheryl. 1996. "At the Crossroads: Rap Music and Its African Nexus." *Ethnomusicology* 40 (2): 223–48.

———. 2002. *Rap Music and Street Consciousness*. Urbana: University of Illinois Press.

Killick, Andrew P. 2010. *In Search of Korean Traditional Opera*. Honolulu: University of Hawai'i Press, 2010.

Kim Chŏngsŏp. 2005. "Mexico chŏlmŭnidŭl Hallyu-wa yŏrae chung" [Mexican youths crazed for Hallyu]. *Kyunghyang Shinmun*, July 28.

Kim Duk Soo [Kim Tŏksu]. 2007. *Gŭllobŏl kwangdae Kim Tŏksu sinmyŏng ŭro sesang ŭl tudŭrida*. [Global *kwangdae* Kim Duk Soo drums around the world with spirit]. P'aju, Kyŏnggi-do: Kimyŏngsa.

———. 2008. "Greeting Messages from the Artistic Director and Festival Chairman." In World SamulNori Festival program. Seoul: SamulNori Hanullim.

Kim Hŏnsŏn. 1988. *Samul nori-ran muŏshinga* [What is samul nori?]. Seoul: Kwiinsa.

———. (1991) 1994. *P'ungmulgut-esŏ samul nori-kkaji* [From *P'ungmulgut* to samul nori]. Seoul: Kwiinsa.

———. 1995. *Kim Hŏnsŏn ŭi samulnori iyagi* [Kim Hŏnsŏn's account of the SamulNori (story)]. Seoul: P'ulpit.

———. 1998. *Kim Yongbae ŭi salm-kwa yesul: Kŭ widaehan samul nori ŭi sŏsashi* [The life and art of Kim Yongbae: An epic of that grand SamulNori]. Seoul: P'ulbit.

Kim, Jin-Woo. 2002. "Twentieth-Century Discourses on Korean Music in Korea." PhD diss., University of Michigan.

Kim, Mi-yon. 1993. "Musical Organizations in an Ethnic Student Group: The Korean Church Choir and the Samulnori Pae." In *Community of Music: An Ethnographic Seminar in Champaign-Urbana*, edited by Tamara E. Livingston et al., 84–92. Champaign, IL: Elephant and Cat.

Kim, Sarah. 2012. "Swiss Woman Marches to Beat of Own Drum." *Korea Joongang Daily*, February 7. http://koreajoongangdaily.joins.com/news/article/Article.aspx?aid=2948029.

Kim, Soojin. 2011. "Diasporic P'ungmul in the United States: A Journey between Korea and the United States." PhD diss., Ohio State University.

Kim Suyong. 2005. "Namsadangp'ae pinari pigyo yŏn'gu" [A comparative study of *pinari* by various *namsadang* groups]. MA thesis, Yongin taehakkyo (Yongin University).

Kim Yang-gon. 1967. "Farmer's Music and Dance." *Korea Journal* 7 (10): 4–9, 29.

Knight, Roderic C. 1991. "Music out of Africa: Mande Jaliya in Paris." *World of Music* 33 (1): 52–69.

Koetting, James. "Analysis and Notation of West African Drum Ensemble Music." *Selected Reports in Ethnomusicology* 1 (3): 116–46.

Konggan. 1976. Untitled. *Konggan* 11 (1): 103.

———. 1989. Untitled. *Konggan* 24 (10): 266.

Korea.net: Gateway to Korea. 2002. "2002 FIFA World Cup Korea/Japan." http://www.korea.net/AboutKorea/Sports/2002-FIFA-World-Cup-Korea-Japan.

Korean Conservatorium of Performing Arts, SamulNori Academy of Music—Kim Duk Soo, Lee Kwang Soo, Kang Min Seok, with Im Dong-Ch'ang [Im Tongch'ang]. 1990. *SamulNori: Changgo ŭi kibon* [SamulNori: Changgo fundamentals]. Seoul: Samho ch'ulp'ansa.

———. 1992. *Korean Traditional Percussion: Samulnori Rhythm Workbook I; Basic Changgo*. Translated by Suzanna M. Samstag. Seoul: Sam-Ho Music.

———. 1993. *SamulNori Korean Traditional Percussion SamulNori Rhythm Workbook 2: Samdo sul changgo karak*. Transcriptions by Im Dong Ch'ang and English text by Suzanna M. Samstag. Seoul: Sam-Ho Music.

———. 1995. *Kim Tŏksu p'ae samul nori-ga yŏnju hanŭn samdo sŏlchanggo karak, yŏnju p'yŏn* [SamulNori: Korean traditional percussion SamulNori rhythm workbook 3, "Samdo sul changgo karak"]. Seoul: Sam-Ho Music.

Korean Culture and Information Service (KOCIS). 2006. "Dynamic Korea—Listen." Korea.net: Gateway to Korea. http://www.korea.net/Resources/Multimedia/Video/view?articleId=1349.

Korean Overseas Information Service. 2007. *Dynamic Korea: Origin and Concept*. Seoul: Korean Overseas Information Service.

Korea Times. 2011. "The 150th Birth Anniversary of Poet Tagore." May 6.

Krims, Adam. 2000. *Rap Music and the Poetics of Identity*. Cambridge: Cambridge University Press.

Ku, Hee-seo [Ku Hŭisŏ]. 1994. "SamulNori: Taking Korean Rhythms to the World." *Koreana* 8 (3): 24–27.

Ku Hŭisŏ. 1983. "Korean Spirit, Korean Rhythm." *Konggan* 18 (3): 98–99.

Kukka pŏmnyŏng chŏngbo sent'ŏ [National (legal) statute information center]. 2005. "Kukka imiji wiwŏnhoe kyuchŏng" [Institution of the national image committee], February 12. http://law.go.kr/lsInfoP.do?lsiSeq=66814#0000.

Künzler, Daniel. 2011a. "Rapping against the Lack of Change: Rap Music in Mali and Burkina Faso." In *Native Tongues: The African Hip-Hop Reader*, edited by P. Khalil Saucier, 23–49. Trenton, NJ: Africa World Press.

———. 2011b. "South African Rap Music, Counter Discourses, Identity, and Commodification beyond the Prophets of Da City." *Journal of Southern African Studies* 37 (1): 27–43.

Kwon, Donna Lee [Kwon Hyeryŏn]. 2001. "Miguk-esŏ ŭi p'ungmul: Kŭ ppuri wa yŏjŏng" ["The Roots and Routes of *P'ungmul* in the United States"], translated into Korean by Kim Hyŏn-chŏng. *U'mak-kwa munhwa* [Music and culture] 5 (2001): 39–65.

———. 2005. "Music, Movement, and Space: A Study of the *Madang* and *P'an* in Korean Expressive Folk Culture." PhD diss., University of California, Berkeley.

———. 2015. "'Becoming One': Embodying Korean *P'ungmul* Percussion Band Music and Dance through Site-Specific Intermodal Transmission." *Ethnomusicology* 59 (1): 31–60.

Kwŏn Hŭidŏk. 1981. *Nongak, Sŏnye kut, Akki nori* [*Nongak, Sŏnye kut*, instrumental play]. Seoul: Huban'gi ch'ulp'ansa.

———. 1995. *Nongak kyobon* [Nongak manual]. Seoul: Seilsa.

Kwon, Mee-yoo. 2016. "'Creative Korea' Is New National Slogan." *Korea Times*, July 4. http://www.koreatimes.co.kr/www/news/culture/2016/08/135_208575.html.

Latour, Bruno. 2005. *Reassembling the Social: An Introduction to Actor-Network Theory*. New York: Oxford University Press.

Laušević, Mirjana. 2007. *Balkan Fascination: Creating an Alternative Music Culture in America*. New York: Oxford University Press.

Lee, Benjamin, and Edward LiPuma. 2002. "Cultures of Circulation: The Imaginations of Modernity." *Public Culture* 14 (1): 191–213.

———. 2004. *Financial Derivatives and the Globalization of Risk*. Durham, NC: Duke University Press.

Lee, Katherine In-Young. 2004. "An Expatriate's Life in Korea: A Profile of Suzanna Samstag Oh." *Korean Quarterly* 8 (3): 37.

———. 2008. "Making New Music from Old: Reflections on SamulNori (1978–2008)." *Korean Quarterly* 11 (3): 74.

———. 2012a. "The Drumming of Dissent during South Korea's Democratization Movement." *Ethnomusicology* 56 (2): 179–205.

———. 2012b. "Encounters with *Samulnori*: The Cultural Politics of South Korea's Dynamic Percussion Genre." PhD diss., Harvard University.

———. 2015. "Dynamic Korea: Amplifying Sonic Registers in a Nation Branding Campaign." *Journal of Korean Studies* 50 (1): 113–48.

———. 2017. "Ethnography of the Transnational." In *Out of Bounds: Ethnography, History, Music*, edited by Ingrid T. Monson, Carol J. Oja, and Richard K. Wolf, 45–57. Cambridge, MA: Harvard University Press.

Lee Kwang Soo [Yi Kwangsu]. 2009. "Yi Kwangsu ŭi mal hanŭn samul nori" [Yi Kwangsu speaks on samul nori]. In *Commemoration of SamulNori's Thirtieth Anniversary*, edited by SamulNori Hanullim t'ansaeng samsip chunyŏn kinyŏm saŏphoe [SamulNori's

Thirtieth Anniversary Committee], 119–39. Seoul: Ministry of Culture, Sports, and Tourism [and Nanjang Cultures].

Lee Yong-shik. 2006. *Minsok, munhwa, kŭrigo ŭmak* [Folk, culture, and music]. P'aju, Kyŏnggi-do: Chimmundang.

Levine, Caroline. 2015. *Forms: Whole, Rhythm, Hierarchy, Network*. Princeton, NJ: Princeton University Press.

Litle, Joshua Atesh. 2010. *The Furious Force of Rhymes*. Washington, DC: Smithsonian Networks. DVD.

London, Justin. (2004) 2012. *Hearing in Time: Psychological Aspects of Musical Meter*. 2nd ed. New York: Oxford University Press.

Lowell, Percival. 1886. *Chosön, the Land of the Morning Calm: A Sketch of Korea*. Boston: Ticknor.

Lunsqui, Alexandre. 2009. "Rhythm and Globalization: Aesthetics, Culture, and Creativity in Contemporary Classical Music." PhD diss., Columbia University.

Mailman, Joshua B. 2010. "Temporal Dynamic Form in Music: Atonal, Tonal, and Other." PhD diss., University of Rochester.

Maliangkay, Roald Heber. 1999. "Handling the Intangible: The Protection of Folk Song Traditions in Korea." PhD diss., School of Oriental and African Studies, University of London.

Manabe, Noriko. 2006. "Globalization and Japanese Creativity: Adaptations of Japanese Language to Rap." *Ethnomusicology* 50 (1): 1–36.

Marayag, Heherson Fugaban. 2010. "Soft Power and Nation Branding: A Case of Korea's National Branding Strategy." Master's thesis, Seoul National University.

Margulis, Elizabeth Hellmuth. 2013. *On Repeat: How Music Plays the Mind*. New York: Oxford University Press.

Matsue, Jennifer Milioto. 2016. "Drumming to One's Own Beat: Japanese Taiko and the Challenge to Genre." *Ethnomusicology* 60 (1): 22–52.

Maxwell, Ian. 2003. *Phat Beats, Dope Rhymes: Hip Hop Down Under Comin' Upper*. Middletown, CT: Wesleyan University Press.

Meintjes, Louise. 1990. "Paul Simon's Graceland, South Africa, and the Mediation of Musical Meaning." *Ethnomusicology* 34:37–73.

Mitchell, Tony, ed. 2001. *Global Noise: Rap and Hip-Hop outside the USA*. Middletown, CT: Wesleyan University Press.

Monson, Ingrid. 1999. "Riffs, Repetition, and Theories of Globalization." *Ethnomusicology* 43 (1): 31–65.

Needham, Rodney. 1967. "Percussion and Transition." *Royal Anthropological Institute of Great Britain and Ireland* 2 (4): 606–14.

Norman, Donald A. 1988. *The Psychology of Everyday Things*. New York: Basic Books.

———. 2013. *The Design of Everyday Things*. Rev. and expanded ed. New York: Basic Books.

Novak, David. 2013. *Japanoise: Music at the Edge of Circulation*. Durham, NC: Duke University Press.

Ntarangwi, Mwenda. 2009. *East African Hip Hop: Youth Culture and Globalization*. Urbana: University of Illinois Press.

Osumare, Halifu. 2007. *The Africanist Aesthetic in Global Hip-Hop: Power Moves*. New York: Palgrave Macmillan.

Overseas Koreans Foundation and the Korean National University of the Arts. 1999. *A Samulnori Class with Kim Duk Soo: Learning Korean Culture Series; Parts 1 and 2*. 2 videocassettes (VHS). Seoul.

Pak Ch'ŏnghun. 2009. "Kukka sŭllogŏn 'tainaemik K'oria' pakkwŏya" [We must change the national slogan "Dynamic Korea"]. July 16. dongA.com. http://news.donga.com/3//20090716/8756232/1?dis_box=30.

Pak Hŏnbong and Yi Tuhyŏn. 1964. *Kkoktugaksi norŭm* [*Namsadang* puppetry]. Muhyŏng munhwajae chosa pogosŏ 1 [Intangible cultural asset report of investigation no. 1]. Seoul: Munhwajae kwalliguk.

Pareles, Jon. 1983. "4 Percussionists from Korea." *New York Times*, November 23.

Park, Chan E. 2003. *Voices from the Straw Mat: Toward an Ethnography of Korean Story Singing*. Honolulu: University of Hawai'i Press.

Park, Shingil. 2000. "Negotiating Identities in a Performance Genre: The Case of *P'ungmul* and *Samulnori* in Contemporary Seoul." PhD diss., University of Pittsburgh.

Patel, Aniruddh D. 2008. *Music, Language, and the Brain*. New York: Oxford University Press.

Pilzer, Joshua. 2011. "Baseball Support Songs, Participatory Sound Culture, and Korean Modernity." Paper presented at the "Sound and Music in Mass Performance" Symposium at the Jackman Humanities Institute, University of Toronto, April 29–30. http://www.humanities.utoronto.ca/event_details/id=372.

Pongch'ŏn norimadang. 1994. *Minsok kyoyuk charyojip* [A collection of resources for folk arts (instruction)]. Seoul: Uri kyoyuk.

Provine, Robert C. 1975. *Chŏnbuk nongak changgo changdan* [Drum rhythms in Korean farmers' music]. Seoul: Shinjin munhwasa.

———. 1985. "Drumming in Korean Farmer's Music: A Process of Gradual Evolution." In *Music and Context: Essays for John M. Ward*, edited by Anne Dhu Shapiro, 441–52. Cambridge, MA: Harvard University Press.

Rose, Tricia. 1994. *Black Noise: Rap Music and Black Culture in Contemporary Africa*. Middletown, CT: Wesleyan University Press.

Rubin, Don. 1998. *World Encyclopedia of Contemporary Theatre*. Vol. 5, *Asia/Pacific*. London: Routledge.

Saeji, CedarBough Tam. 2012. "Transmission and Performance: Memory, Heritage, and Authenticity in Korean Mask Dance Dramas." PhD diss., University of California, Los Angeles.

Samstag, Suzanna. 2008a. "What Time Teaches: SamulNori Performance Showcased Skill and Power but Lacked Feeling." *Korean Quarterly* 11 (3): 75.

———. 2008b. "Why Are Foreign Audiences Thrilled by SamulNori?" In *The 2008 World SamulNori Festival* (program), 8. Seoul: SamulNori Hanullim.

Samul-Nori. 1984. *The Legendary Recording by Original Members in 1983*. Nonesuch. 7559-72093-2.

SamulNori. 1988a. *SamulNori/10 Years*. Seoul: Art Space.

———. 1988b. *SamulNori*. Photographs by Ichiro Shimizu, translations by Suzanna M. Samstag, Kim Ri-hae [Kim Rihye], and Kwak Hye-song [Kwak Hyesŏng]. Seoul: Art Space.

———. 2007. *Samulnori vs. Suntory Hall*. VHS. Tokyo: Sony.

SamulNori Hanullim. 2002. *Samul ŭngwŏn: Wŏldŭkŏp ŭngwŏn ŭl wihan chŏnt'ong ridŭm hwallyong p'ŭrogŭraem* [Samul nori chants: Program for utilizing traditional rhythms for the World Cup cheers]. Videocassette (VHS). Seoul.

———. 2004. *Yŏngnam nongak: Samul nori anjŭnban ui kich'o-1*. ["Yŏngnam nongak": Fundamentals (1) of seated samul nori.] Puyŏ: SamulNori Hanullim Puyŏ Kyoyukwŏn.

———. 2007. *2007 Segye samul nori kyŏrugi hanmadang: Kyŏlgwa pogosŏ* [2007 World SamulNori Kyŏrugi Hanmadang results report].

———. 2008. *2008 Puyŏ segye samul nori taech'ukche: kyŏlgwa pogosŏ* [2008 World SamulNori Festival: Results report]. Seoul.

SamulNori Hanullim t'ansaeng samsip chunyŏn kinyŏm saŏphoe [SamulNori's Thirtieth Anniversary Committee]. 2009. "SamulNori: SamulNori t'ansaeng samsip chunyŏn kinyŏm" [SamulNori: Commemoration of SamulNori's thirtieth anniversary]. Seoul: Ministry of Culture, Sports, and Tourism [and Nanjang Cultures].

Sandomir, Richard. 2002. "Baseball; Creating Noise, and an Uproar." *New York Times*, October 16. http://www.nytimes.com/2002/10/16/sports/baseball-creating-noise-and-an-uproar.html.

Saucier, P. Khalil, ed. 2011. *Native Tongues: The African Hip-Hop Reader*. Trenton, NJ: Africa World Press.

Savigliano, Marta E. 1995. *Tango and the Political Economy of Passion*. Boulder, CO: Westview.

Schmuck, Alena. 2011. "Nation Branding in South Korea: A Modern Continuation of a Developmental State?" In *Korea Yearbook, Korea 2011: Politics, Economy, Society*, edited by Rüdiger Frank, James E. Hoare, Patrick Köllner, and Susan Pares, 91–117. Boston: Brill.

Schweig, Meredith Lynne. 2013. "The Song Readers: Rap Music and the Politics of Storytelling in Taiwan." PhD diss., Harvard University.

Segal, Lewis. 1985. "Asian Music/Dance Series Begins: Samul-Nori Folk Troupe in Little Tokyo; Korean Shamanistic Priests Heed a Different Drummer—Blending Energy, Technical Mastery and Spirituality at the Japan America Theatre." *Los Angeles Times*, January 19.

Seok, Huajeong. 2013. "Race, Imperialism, and Reconstructing Selves: Late Nineteenth-Century Korea in European Travel Literature." In *Race and Racism in Modern East Asia: Western and Eastern Constructions*, edited by Rotem Kowner and Walter Demel, 261–79. Boston: Brill.

Sharma, Nitasha Tamar. 2010. *Hip Hop Desis: South Asian Americans, Blackness, and a Global Race Consciousness*. Durham, NC: Duke University Press.

Shelemay, Kay Kaufman. 2011. "Musical Communities: Rethinking the Collective in Music." *Journal of the American Musicological Society* 64 (2): 349–90.

Shin Yong-ha [Sin Yongha]. 1985a. "Social History of Ture Community and *Nongak* Music Pt. 1." *Korea Journal* 25 (3): 4–17.

———. 1985b. "Social History of Ture Community and *Nongak* Music Pt. 2." *Korea Journal* 25 (4): 4–18.

Silverman, Carol. 2012. *Romani Routes: Cultural Politics and Balkan Music in Diaspora*. New York: Oxford University Press.

Sim Usŏng. 1968. *Namsadang: Muhyŏng munhwajae chosa pogosŏ 40* [*Namsadang*: Intangible cultural asset investigative report no. 40]. Seoul: Munhwajae kwallikguk.

———. 1971. "Disappearing Heritage." *Konggan* 6 (7): 27–32.

———. (1974) 1994. *Namsadangp'ae yŏn'gu* [Research on *namsadang* troupes]. Seoul: Tosŏ ch'ulp'an tongmunsŏn.

———. 1975. "What Have We Done, and What Has to Be Done?" *Konggan* 10 (5): 42–47.

———. 1980. "What Is Gut [*kut*] (and What Has Been Studied over [*sic*] It)?" *Konggan* 15 (2): 80–84.

———. 2008. "SamulNori Manmanse!" [SamulNori hurrah!]. In *The Thirtieth Anniversary of SamulNori* (program), 16. Seoul: SamulNori Hanullim.

SK Telecom. 2002. "Sŭp'idŭ 011 CF—Ungwŏn kuho Taehan Min'guk p'yŏn" [Cheer catchphrase—Republic of Korea edition]. Television commercial. http://www.youtube.com/watch?v=5pC2jGCa8_8.

Son, Min-jung. 2012. "An Odyssey for Korean Rock: From Subversive to Patriotic." *Asian Music* 43 (2): 47–70.

Spiller, Henry. 2015. *Javaphilia: American Love Affairs with Javanese Music and Dance*. Honolulu: University of Hawai'i Press.

Stokes, Martin. 2004. "Music and the Global Order." *Annual Review of Anthropology* 33:47–72.

Taet'ongnyŏng kirokkwan [Presidential archives]. 2009. "Kukka pŭraendŭ wiwŏnhoe"

[Presidential council on nation branding]. http://17koreabrand.pa.go.kr/gokr/en/cms/selectKbrdCmsPageTbl.do?cd=0116& m1=1&m2=1.

Tan, Marcus Cheng Chye. 2012. *Acoustic Interculturalism: Listening to Performance*. New York: Palgrave Macmillan.

Taylor, Timothy D. 1997. *Global Pop: World Music, World Markets*. New York: Routledge.

———. 2012. *The Sounds of Capitalism: Advertising, Music, and the Conquest of Culture*. Chicago: University of Chicago Press.

Tenzer, Michael, ed. 2006. *Analytical Studies in World Music*. New York: Oxford University Press.

Tenzer, Michael, and John Roeder, eds. 2011. *Analytical and Cross-Cultural Studies in World Music*. New York: Oxford University Press.

Terkourafi, Marina, ed. 2010. *The Languages of Global Hip Hop*. New York: Continuum.

Toussaint, Godfried T. 2013. *The Geometry of Musical Rhythm: What Makes a "Good" Rhythm Good?* Boca Raton, FL: Chapman and Hall / CRC.

Vickery, Martha. 2005/6a. "Beat of Their Own Drummers: Foreign Groups Interpret Samulnori through Their Own Cultures." *Korean Quarterly* 9 (2): 76–78.

———. "2005/6b. Pulse of the Earth: Local Drummers Find a Network at Korean Samulnori Festival." *Korean Quarterly* 9 (2): 57, 74–76.

Wade, Bonnie C. 2014. *Composing Japanese Musical Modernity*. Chicago: University of Chicago Press.

Wallach, Jeremy, Harris M. Berger, and Paul D. Greene, eds. 2011. *Metal Rules the Global: Heavy Metal around the World*. Durham, NC: Duke University Press.

Watkins, S. Craig. 2005. *Hip Hop Matters: Politics, Pop Culture, and the Struggle for the Soul of a Movement*. Boston: Beacon.

White, Bob W., ed. 2012. *Music and Globalization: Critical Encounters*. Bloomington: Indiana University Press.

Whithall, Arnold. 2001. "Form." Grove Music Online. http://www.oxfordmusiconline.com:80/subscriber/article/grove/music/09981.

Williams, Angela. 2010. "'We Ain't Terrorists, but We Droppin' Bombs': Language Use and Localization in Egyptian Hip Hop." In *The Languages of Global Hip Hop*, edited by Marina Terkourafi, 67–95. New York: Continuum.

Wolf, Richard K. "Embodiment and Ambivalence: Emotion in South Asian Muharram Drumming." *Yearbook for Traditional Music* 32:81–116.

Wong, Deborah. 2004. *Speak It Louder: Asian Americans Making Music*. New York: Routledge.

Yano, Christine Reiko. 2013. *Pink Globalization: Hello Kitty's Trek across the Pacific*. Durham, NC: Duke University Press.

Yi Pohyŏng and Chu Kanghyŏn. 1989. *Nodong kwa kut: Irhanŭn saramdŭl ŭi salm kwa *segyegwan* [Labor and ritual: The life and worldview of working people]. Seoul: Hangminsa.

Yu, Youngmin. 2007. "Musical Performance of Korean Identities in North Korea, South Korea, Japan, and the United States." PhD diss., University of California, Los Angeles.

Yun, Kyoim. 2006. "The 2002 World Cup and a Local Festival in Cheju: Global Dreams and the Commodification of Shamanism." *Journal of Korean Studies* 11 (1): 7–39.

INDEX / GLOSSARY

Page numbers in italics indicate illustrations.

Abe, Mayumi, *102*, 103, 104
acceleration, 35, 56, *59*
Adorno, Theodor, 136
affordance, 4–5, 151n5
African (Ewe) drumming, 94, 135–36
African American musics, 4
African diaspora, 4
All about Eve (Korean TV melodrama), 164n31
amateur enthusiasts, 7, 9, 12, 35, 46; arrangement of rhythmic patterns for, 135; *pinari* 비나리 as least performed genre, 122–23
Anholt, Simon, 74–75, 78
anjŭnban 앉은반 (samul nori performed from a seated position), 46, 48
An Suksŏn 안숙선, 113, 166n9
architecture, 14, 15, 23
"Arirang" "아리랑" (Korean folk song), 71, 72, 118–19
Arirang TV, 90, 106, 134
Arndt, Jennifer Yang Hee, *88*, 90
Aronczyk, Melissa, 75
art music, Western, 6
Asatrian, Karen, 163n20
Asia Society (New York), 30, 31, 43, 44, 80, 86

Bae Yong-joon [Pae Yongjun 배용준], 164n30
Bañagale, Ryan, 42

Basel, Switzerland, 1, 92, 94, 96, 97, 111
Baumann, Nathalie, 93, *93*, 96
Beauty of Korean Style—Samul Nori, The (Arirang TV documentary, 2009), 134
Belgium, 8, 111
Bengtson, Lia, *88*, 162n15
Berlin, SamulNori workshops in, 95, 96
Bermúdez Ortíz, Martha, *98*, 100
Berry, Wallace, 6
bhangra, 3
Bigenho, Michelle, 3
Bonds, Mark Evan, 6
Branding the Nation: The Global Business of National Identity (Aronczyk, 2013), 75
Brookhart, Edward, 6
Buddhism, 25, 26, 77, 120, 122; Chŏngnim Temple 정림사(지) (Puyŏ 부여), 114–15, *116*, 119, 120, 130; "International Pinari" ceremony and, 115; Kŭmsan Temple 금산사 (Kimje 김제), 97; pagodas (*t'ap* 탑/塔), 25, 155n37; percussion instruments in temples, 154n27; *yŏmbul* 염불 (Buddhist chant/prayer), 123

call-and-response, 4, 55, 57, 58
Campos Pérez, Mariana, *98*, 100
Canto del Cielo (Song of Heaven), 10, 97–101, 111, 164–65n35; group portrait at Samul-Nori festival, *98*; "International Pinari"

ceremony and, 125, 127, *128*; renamed SamulNori Mexico, 97, 101
Caplin, William E., 6
Cario Martínez, Bárbara, *98*, 100, 101
Cecil Theater [Sesil Kŭkchang 세실극장] (Seoul), 28, 84
Centro Cultural Coreano en México (CCC), 98–99, 100–101, 165n33
ch'ae 채 (percussion sticks or mallets), 34
chaebŏl 재벌 (corporate conglomerates), 75
chaech'angjo 재창조 (re-create), 36
chaegusŏng 재구성 (reconfigure/restructure), 36, 156n6
chajinmori 자진모리 (12/8 rhythmic cycle), 121, 123
changdan 장단/長短 (rhythmic cycle; "long, short"), 156n4
changgo 장고 (hourglass drum), 12, 30, 34, 58, 85, 147, 163n19; *kil kunak* 길군악 pattern and, 48; in *pan kil kunak* 반길군악, 51; *pyŏldagŏri* 별달거리 (*pyŏlgŏri talgŏri* 별거리 달거리) and, 54–55; rain represented by, 149; rhythmic patterns and, 35, 84; Swissamul and, 93; in World Cup opening ceremony, 158n8; *yŏngsan tadŭraegi* 영산 다드래기 pattern and, 54
Ch'anggyŏng Palace 창경궁, 112
ch'angjak (*ŭmak*) 창작/創作 (음악/音樂) (newly created or composed music), 112
Chang Tonggŏn Fanclub, 98
chants: Buddhist *yŏmbul* 염불 chant, 123; *pinari* 비나리 and, 24; of *pyŏlgŏri talgŏri* 별거리 달거리 (*pyŏldalgŏri* 별거리 달거리), 42–43, 54–56, *59*; *ŭngwŏn'ga* 응원가 ("support") songs), 71; for World Cup (2002), 71–74, *74*
cheongsam (ch'i-p'ao), 119, 166–67n14
China, 64, 111, 119, 145, 166–67n14
chinbŏp 진법/陣法 (ground formation/s), 47, 51
ching 징 (large gong), 34, 35, 50; wind represented by, 149; in World Cup opening ceremony, 158n8; in "Yŏngnam nongak" "영남농악," 58
Chinju Samch'ŏnp'o nongak 진주삼천포농악 (nongak from Chinju and Samch'ŏnpo), 36, 38, 42, 50, 60; "Kyŏngsang nongak" "경상농악" (samul nori arrangement; nongak rhythms from the Kyŏngsang provinces) compared with, 40–41, *40*; twelve sections of, 38–40, *40*; "Yŏngnam nongak" "영남농악" (samul nori arrangement) rhythmic patterns and, 46. See also *kil kunak* 길군악
Ch'oe Ch'an-kyun 최찬균, 122, 125, 129, *130*
Ch'oe Chongsŏk 최종석, 19, 36, 39, 43
Ch'oe Namyun 최남윤, *98*, 99, 100–101, 164–65n33
Ch'oe T'aehyŏn 최태현, 16, 17, 19, 36, 153n15, 154n22
Choi Jong Sil [Ch'oe Chongshil 최종실], 13, 19, 39, 94, *110*, 152n4, 154n22; competitive spirit of, 48, 84; entry into quartet, 36; in "original" quartet, 17, 31, 109; portrait, *20*; on *p'ungmul* 풍물 styles, 157n10; Swissamul and, 95
Chongdong Theater [Chŏngdong Kŭkchang 정동극장], 69, 158n7
Ch'ŏngsa Ch'orong 청사초롱 (Amagasaki, Japan), 111
chŏnsu 전수/傳受 (transmission), 91
Chosŏn 조선 (Yi dynasty/period) (1392–1910), 24, 26; *pinari* 비나리 and, 122–23, 125, 139; Western view of Korea during, 62–65
Chosŏn, the Land of the Morning Calm (Lowell, 1886), 62–63
chowang kut 조왕굿 (ritual for kitchen god), 26
Ch'usŏk 추석 autumn harvest festival, 42, 54
circulation, of music, 4, 151n4
classical music, Western, 15, 32, 153n10
Confucianism, 25, 76
Cooper, Grosvenor, 44
Corea: The Hermit Nation (Griffis, 1882), 63–65
costumes, 89, 95, 119–20, 166–67n14; at

"International Pinari" ceremony, 127, *128*, 129; *pup'o* 부포 (feathered hats), 120, 148, 166–67n14
counterpoint, tonal, 35
"Creative Korea" nation brand, 78
cultural activists, 13, 15
cultural industry, South Korean, 66, 151n1
Cultural Property for Nongak sibich'a 농악 12차 문화재, 157n10

dance, 8, 69, 100, 136, 157n20; *puch'ae ch'um* 부채춤 (Korean fan dance), 99; traditional Korean dance, 15; West African, 94
Delissen, Alain, 11, 14, 21, 22
Denmark, 7
design theory, 4, 5
diaspora formation, 3
Dilling, Margaret Walker, 160n19, 161n3
"Disappearing Heritage" (Sim Usŏng, 1971), 23
Dulsori 들소리, 12
Durae Pae SamulNori 두레패 사물놀이, 12
"dynamic," meanings of, 32–33, 155–56n1
"Dynamic Korea" brand, 9, 33, 62; brochure detailing overview of, 66–68, *68*, 76–77; dark side of, 78–79; Korean word (*yŏkdongjŏgin* 역동적인), 72; nation-branding strategy, 74–78; origin of, 66; promotional videos, 77, 160n22; samul nori and, 68–74
dynamics, in music, 32
dynamism, of samul nori, 33, 92, 108; dynamic forms in circulation, 135–37; dynamic rhythmic form, 59–60, 62; multifaceted, 44, 135; non-Koreans' first impressions of, 82, 106; South Korea's identity and, 67, 72, 73, 76, 77

Ecological Approach to Visual Perception, The (Gibson, 1979), 5
Eichmann, Hildegard, 93, *93*, 96
Emminger, Gudrun, 93
English language, 23, 86, 87; "Dynamic Korea" slogans in, 66; Samstag's program notes in, 147–50; subtitles in Korean-language videos, 46

ethnography, 7–8, 9, 136; ethnographic interviews, 13; folk musicians and, 18; formal analysis paired with, 34
ethnomusicologists, 3, 12, 136–37, 151n5, 155n39
Europe, 9, 27, 61, 80, 94
Expats SamulNori Team, 97

Feld, Steven, 81
FIFA World Cup (South Korea and Japan, 2002), 66, 67, 76, 159n12; football supporters and, 71, 79, 159n11; opening ceremony, 158n8; samul nori chants for, 68–74, *74*, 159n15
financial crisis, global (2007–8), 167n15
Flatischler, Reinhard, 94, 163n19
folk music, Korean, 16, 23, 153n10
form, musical, 2, 4–7; defined, 6; dynamic, 9, 59–60; of "Gangnam Style," 133; national cultural boundaries crossed by, 3; rhythmic form as type of, 44; transnational mobility of, 136
formal analysis, 6–7, 34, 59
Forms (Levine), 4
France, 8, 111, 166n12
French language, 125
"Friends of SamulNori" Saturday concert, 112

gamelan, 1, 3
"Gangnam Style" "강남스타일" (Psy, 2012), 132–34, 167n1, 168n3
geomancy, 122
German language, 125, 134
Germany, 111
Gibson, James J., 4–5, 151n5
globalization, 1, 2, 3–4, 10, 61; *segyehwa* 세계화 policy, 67; on small-scale and personal level, 107, 161n3
gongs, 34
Gordon, Beate, 30–31
Goryeo period [Koryŏ 고려 period] (918–1392 CE), 115
Goto, Yuki, 101, *102*, 103, 104
"grace note" figures, 48

Index **185**

Griffis, William Elliot, 63–65
"groove," 4, 34, 35, 136
Guilbault, Jocelyne, 4

haegŭm 해금 (two-string fiddle), 17
Hallyu 한류/韓流 ("Korean Wave"), 2, 9, 62, 135, 151n1; early period of, 66; influx of capital into, 134; TV melodramas, 98, 164nn30–31
Han Jae Suk 한재석 [Han Chaesŏk], 166n12
hanji 한지/漢紙 (traditional handmade paper; Korean paper), 27
Han Myung-hee 한명희 [Han Myŏnghŭi], 30
Han Taep'ung 한 대풍 (Osaka, Japan), 111, 125
Hanullim Korean Music Instrument Company, 156n3
Han Yŏng'ae 한영애, 113
harmony, Western, 44
Herbert Barrett Management, 87, 162n11
"Hermit Kingdom" (old nickname for Korea), 63–65, 68, 76
Hernández Vélez, Maria del Carmen Donají, 98, 100
Hesselink, Nathan, 12, 26, 153n17, 154n21, 154n33; "Honam nongak karak" "호남농악가락" (samul nori arrangement; nongak rhythms from the Honam/Chŏlla region) analyzed by, 41; on samul nori notation, 49–50
hip-hop, 1, 3, 136, 151n2
hohŭp 호흡 (breath or breathing), 52–53, 54, 94, 110, 119, 149
Hommura, Ryo, 87
"Honam udo karak" "호남우도가락" (samul nori arrangement; rhythmic patterns from the western Chŏlla region), 24, 34
"Honam udo kut" "호남우도굿" (samul nori arrangement; rhythms from the western Chŏlla region), 41
"Hongdae Style" "홍대스타일" (parody of "Gangnam Style"), 132
Hong Yunki 홍윤기, 129
Howard, Keith, 2

Huber, Michael, 95, 163n21
Hwang Byung-ki [Hwang Pyŏnggi 황병기], 60
hybridization, 3, 161n3

Iannacone, Rick, 163n20
ilch'ae 일채 (one-stroke rhythmic pattern), 118
IlGwaNori drumming group (Chicago), 90
Im Dong-chang [Im Tongch'ang 임동창], 49, 95, 163n22
IMF financial crisis (1997), 66, 75
Im Lande der Morgenstille [In the land of morning calm] (Weber, 1925), 159n18
Im Pang'ul 임방울, 15
imperialism, Western, 3
innovation, 7, 18, 31, 41
Intangible Cultural Heritage (ICH), 157n11
International SamulNori Symposium (2009), 109
isolationism, image of, 64–67, 75

Jambert, Dominique, 166n12
Jang Hyun-jin [Chang Hyŏnjin 장현진], 164n25, 158n1
Japan, 10, 27, 83; fascination with Andean music, 3; FIFA World Cup (2002) in, 66; *gyaku yunyu* ("reverse importation") phenomenon, 62; imperialist conquest of Korea, 64–65; popularity of Korean TV melodramas in, 164n30; samul nori groups in, 111; SamulNori quartet's international debut in, 29; SamulNori tours in, 80, 87; Shinawi group, 101–5, *102*; world music circuit and, 8; Zainichi Koreans in, 102, 103, 118, 125, 167n23
Japanese language, 125
Joo, Rachel Miyung, 71, 159n12
Joo Jay-youn [Chu Chaeyŏn 주재연], 114, 118, 162n11

Kang Chunhyŏk 강준혁 [also written as Kang Joon-hyuk], 15, 42; on first performance of "Uttari p'ungmul" "웃다리풍물," 17–18;

METAA founded by, 153n19; Minsogakhoe Sinawi 민속악회시나위 and, 19; SamulNori project and, 21; on seated performance position, 28

Kang Chunil 강준일, 152–53n10

Kang Min-seok 강민석, 94, 95, 109

karak 가락 ("rhythmic patterns"), 41, 44, 156n4; arranged into standardized "compositions," 134, 135; hwimori 휘모리 (duple meter), 99, 100, 120, 148; memorization of, 35; progression of, 58; repetition in cycles, 38; "Sŏl changgo karak" "설장고가락," 84. See also kil kunak 길군악; pyŏldalgŏri 별달거리

kayagŭm 가야금 (twelve-string zither), 16, 153n12

KBS TV, 90

kil kunak 길군악 ("road military music"; samul nori and p'ungmul rhythmic pattern), 39, 54, 58, 59; comparison of "Kyŏngsang nongak" "경상농악" and "Yŏngnam nongak" "영남농악," 45; comparison of p'ungmul 풍물 and samul nori 사물놀이, 40; notation for, 47–49, 49; p'ungmul choreography for, 47–48, 47

Killick, Andrew, 160n24

kilnori 길놀이 ("street play"), 113

Kim, Paul Namhoon, 90

Kim, Sangho (Sam), 88, 88, 91, 92

Kim, Soojin, 157n16, 161n2, 161n3

Kim Dae Jung [Kim Taejung 김대중], 66, 67, 75, 151n1

Kim Dong-won [Kim Tongwŏn 김동원], 53, 72, 159n14, 161n5; Shinparam 신바람 and, 92; Swissamul and, 93, 94, 95, 96, 97

Kim Duk Soo [Kim Tŏksu 김덕수], 7, 8, 16, 39, 110, 116, 130; competitive spirit of, 48, 84; "Dynamic Korea" brand and, 68–74; Folk Music Society "Sinawi" and, 165n37; as founding member of SamulNori Hanullim 사물놀이 한울림, 44, 149, 152n4; on globalization of samul nori, 108; on hohŭp 호흡, 54; instructional videos for beginners, 46–47; instructional videos for beginners in, 50–51; on karak 가락 (rhythmic patterns), 57; namsadang 남사당 family background, 24, 149, 155n35; in "original" quartet, 17, 31, 109; on performing in seated position, 18; portrait, 20; on preservationist impulse in South Korea, 21–22; on role of Samstag, 86; SamulNori Hanullim founded by, 12; Swissamul and, 94, 95; World SamulNori Festival and, 113, 117–21, 126, 127

Kim Han-bok [Kim Hanbok 김한복], 164n25

Kim Hŏnsŏn 김헌선, 124

Kim Kyŏng-nan 김경란, 102

Kim Mukyŏng 김무경, 19

Kim Munhak 김문학, 18, 154n25

Kim Myŏngsu 김명수, 20

Kim Rihae [Kim Rihye 김리혜], 155n35, 161n5

Kim Sohŭi 김소희, 15

Kim Sugŭn 김수근 [also written as Kim Swoo Geun], 14–16, 31, 111, 152n6

Kim Suyong 김수영, 124

Kim Yong-bae [Kim Yongbae 김용배], 12, 16, 94, 152n4; competitive spirit of, 48, 84; death of, 165n2; Folk Music Society "Sinawi" and, 165n37; namsadang 남사당 and, 24; in "original" quartet, 17, 31, 165n2; portrait, 20

Kim Young Sam [Kim Yŏngsam 김영삼], 67

kkwaenggwari 꽹과리 (small gong), 19, 27, 34, 35, 39, 43, 58, 125; kil kunak 길군악 pattern and, 47, 48; lightning represented by, 149; in pan kil kunak 반길군악, 51; pyŏldalgŏri 별달거리 (pyŏlgŏri talgŏri 별거리 달거리) and, 54–55; in ssangjinp'uri 쌍진풀이 section, 57; Swissamul and, 93; in World Cup opening ceremony, 158n8; yŏngsan tadŭraegi 영산 다드래기 pattern and, 54

Kodo Drummers, 68

Kŏllipp'ae p'ungmul 걸립패 풍물 (1980 SamulNori arrangement; fund-raising group; itinerant p'ungmul troupe), 23–27, 25

Konggan Group 공간그룹, 14, 18
Konggan Group Building 공간그룹건물 (Kim Sugŭn, 1977), 25, 26, 152nn6-7
Konggan magazine 공간잡지, 14, 22–23, 29, 152n8
Konggan Project 공간 프로젝트, 9, 22–23, 31
Korea, Japanese colonial period (1910–1945), 24, 65, 160n20, 167n23
Korea, North, 65–66, 78, 92, 162n14
Korea, South, 10, 29, 131, 134–35; democratization movement, 78; FIFA World Cup (2002) in, 66, 67; formation of, 65–66; government promotion of music, 13, 38, 61–62; "Hub of Asia" slogan, 67; as key player in global economic market, 126, 130; media outlets, 90, 97; military, 91–92, 162n14; as modernizing nation, 14, 21–22, 31; nation-branding campaign, 9, 33, 62, 72, 74–78; provinces and regions of, 36, 37, 156n7; sonic landscape of, 11. *See also* "Dynamic Korea" brand; Seoul; Summer Olympics (Seoul, 1988)
"Korea, Sparkling" slogan, 78
Korea, unified in premodern era. *See* Chosŏn 조선
Korea Herald, 90
Koreana (English-language publication), 30
Korean adoptees, 87, 126
Korean Americans, 87, 89, 161n3
Korean Classical Music Record Museum, 19
Korean diaspora, 1, 157n16
Korean Institute of Minnesota (KIM), 89, 162n12
Korean language, 23, 39, 84; in football (soccer) chants, 71; instructional videos for beginners in, 46–47; in Japan, 167n23; in Mexico, 98, 99; parodies of "Gangnam Style" and, 133, 168n3; *pinari* 비나리 and, 123; romanization systems for, 150n, 166n11; Sino-Korean characters, 62, 123, 139–46, 167n20
Korean music, traditional, 8, 11, 101; flexibility in performance, 56; preservation of, 23; "sampler" programs, 158n7

Korean National University of Arts, 44
Korean Overseas Information Service, 66, 68, 76
Korean Quarterly newspaper, 87, 89, 90, 91, 92
"Korean Spirit, Korean Rhythm" (Ku Hŭisŏ 구희서, 1983), 29
Korean Traditional Percussion workbook (SamuNori), 52–53
Korean War (1950–1953), 24, 65–66, 67, 75, 149
Korea Tourism Organization (KTO), 77–78
K-pop, 2, 9, 62, 135, 151n1
kugak 국악/國樂 (traditional Korean music; "national music"), 11, 15, 162n14, 166n8
Ku Hŭisŏ 구희서 [also written as Ku Hee-seo], 29
kut pan 굿판 (*kut* ritual gathering), 29
Kwon, Donna Lee, 155n39, 161n3
Kwŏn Sang'u Mexican Fanclub, 98
Kwŏn T'aesŏn 권태선, 20
Kyŏnggi todanggut 경기도당굿 (shamanic tutelary ritual from the Kyŏnggi region), 93–94
"Kyŏngsang nongak" "경상농악" (samul nori arrangement; nongak rhythms from the Kyŏngsang provinces) 36, 50; Chinju Samch'ŏnp'o nongak 진주삼천포농악 compared with, 40–41, *40*; formal structure, 42, 43, *45*; renamed as "Yŏngnam nongak" "영남농악," 43; twelve sections of, 39, *40*

"Land of the Morning Calm" (old nickname for Korea), 62–63, 64, 68, 76–77
Lange, Hendrikje, 93, *93*, 94, 96, 97, 105
"Learning Korean Culture Series" (1999), 44–45
Lee, Benjamin, 4
Lee, Sarah, 87–88, *88*, 89–90, 91
Lee Chŏng-u [Yi Chŏng-u 이정우], 99, 100
Lee Kwang Soo [Yi Kwangsu 이광수], 26, 94, *110*, 152n4; competitive spirit of, 84; *namsadang* 남사당 family background, 24,

25; in "original" quartet, 17, 31, 109, 154n32; *pinari* 비나리 performed by, 122, 123; portrait, 20; Swissamul and, 95, 163n22; on U.S. tour (1983), 43
Lee Myung-bak [Yi Myŏngbak 이명박], 78
Levine, Caroline, 4, 5, 136
LG corporation brand, 75, 151n1
Lilac (Harbin, China), 111
LiPuma, Edward, 4
localization, 3
London, Justin, 136
Loose Roots (drumming group at U. of Chicago), 89
Los Angeles, 1, 29, 161n3
Lowell, Percival, 62–63, 64, 65
Lunar New Year, 90, 97

Madang 마당 (Kang Chunil), 153n10
madang 마당 (village common; large open courtyard or field), 22
maegu kut 매구굿 (local name for p'ungmul; village ritual), 38
maeji 맺이 (conclusion; concluding section in Yŏngnam nongak), 59
Mailman, Joshua, 59
Mangado, Vincent, 166n12
Margulis, Elizabeth Hellmuth, 136
Marugg, Bettina, 93, *93*, 96, 97
Marxism, 3
Masan Catholic Church 마산천주교회 (Kim Sugŭn, 1979), 152n6
media technologies, diffusion of, 1, 3
METAA (Metabolic Evolution through Arts and Architecture), 153n19
meter, musical, 60, 136–37
Mexico, 8, 83, 97–101, 118
Mexico City, 1, 10; Zócalo (main square), 127; Zona Rosa district, 99, 100, 165n34
Meyer, Leonard, 44
military music tradition, 38, 47, 70, 148; *ch'wit'a* 취타/吹打, 118, 119; *munhwa sŏnchŏndae* 문화 선전대 (cultural propaganda units), 91–92, 162n14

Mindan 민단 (Korean Residents Union in Japan), 29
Minsogakhoe Sinawi 민속악회시나위 (Folk Music Society "Sinawi"), 10, 16, 153n15, 165n37, 166n8; named by Sim Usŏng 심우성, 18–19; program (March 1, 1979), 38; SamulNori project and, 21; SamulNori quartet and, 23
Minsokkŭkhoe Namsadang 민속극회남사당 (Folk Theater Association Namsadang 남사당), 18
Mnouchkine, Ariane, 166n12
mokŏ 목어/木魚 (wooden fish instrument), 77, 154n27, 160n22
Monson, Ingrid, 3–4
mŏri pak 머리 박/拍 (first beat of rhythmic pattern), 54
Mujigae (Rainbow) group from Belgium, 111
mul soji 물소지/物燒紙 (ritual burning of paper/objects), 26, 27, 155n40
munhwa konggan 문화공간 (culture spaces), 153n19
munhwa sŏnchŏndae 문화선전대 (cultural propaganda units), 91–92, 162n14
mun kut 문굿/門굿 (ritual performed at a gate), 26, 27, 113, 166n7; *pinari* 비나리 and, 121
musicology, Western, 6
Musik-Academie Basel (Switzerland), 93, 94, 96, 97
musok 무속/巫俗 (shamanic tradition; shamanism), 94

Nadeau, Nik, 126–27, 162n15
naego, talgo, maetgo, pulgo 내고, 달고, 맺고, 풀고 (produce, stir up, fasten, unbind) aesthetic, 56, 60
Nam Kimun 남기문, 109, *110*, 165n3
namsadang 남사당 (itinerant troupes of male performers), 18, 24, 25, 153n17, 154n25, 154n31; history of, 149; *kilnori* 길놀이 ("street play") and, 113
Namsadang troupe 남사당패, 109

Nanjang Studio 난장스튜디오 (Seoul), 95, 163n22
napal 나발 (bugle-like instrument), 38, 118
National Gugak Center [Kungnip Kugagwŏn 국립국악원], 69, 97, 100, 112, 165n3
National Image Committee [Kukka Imiji Wiwŏnhoe 국가이미지위원회], 76
National Theater of Korea, 160n24
N'Dour, Youssou, 82
neoliberalism, 1, 67, 135
Nketia, Suzanne, 92–97, *93*, 105–6, 162n16, 163n18, 164n22
Noguchi, Yuko, *102*, 103
No Hongch'ŏl 노홍철, 133
nongak 농악/農樂 ("farming music"), 17, 29, 36, 153n20. See also *p'ungmul* 풍물
Norman, Donald, 4, 5
notation, musical, 2, 9, 43, *54*; beginning students and, 46; *pan kil kunak* 반길군악 pattern, 50–51, *51*; *pyŏldalgŏri* 별달거리, *55*, *56*; *ssangjinp'uri* 쌍진풀이, *58*; "wallpaper" in Centro Cultural Coreano en México, *99*; *yŏngsan tadŭraegi* 영산 다드래기 pattern, 53–54, *53*, *54*
Novak, David, 62

Olsen, Peggy, *88*
"O p'ilsŭng K'oria" "오 필승 코리아" (O, victory Korea) chant, 73
oral histories, 13
Osaka, Japan, 1
Overseas Koreans Foundation (OKF) 해외동포재단, 44, 46, 134; grant to Shinparam, 89, 162n12; as Ministry of Foreign Affairs wing, 61
Oxford Dictionary of Music, 6
Ŏ Yundae 어윤대, 78, 160n26

Paekche 백제 [also written as Baekje] kingdom (sixth century), 114, 115
Pak Ch'ŏrhyŏn 박철현, 77
Pak Kwihŭi 박귀희, 16
pan kil kunak 반길군악 pattern, 51–52, 58,

59; notation for, 50–51, *51*; *p'ungmul* 풍물 choreography for, 52
p'an kut 판굿 (exuberant p'ungmul drumming and dance; concluding section of a standard SamulNori program), 26, *28*, 41, 155n39; American critical reception of, 80; "Dynamic Korea" brand and, 70; *pup'o* 부포 hat worn during, 166–67n14; Samstag's program note for, 148–49
p'ansori 판소리 (storytelling through song), 15, 16, 57, 153n12; *Sugungga* 수궁가 epic, 69; An Suksŏn and, 113, 166n9
Paraguay, 100
Pareles, Jon, 80
Paris, 2, 132, 166n12
Park An-ji [Pak Anji 박안지], 25, 123, 164n25
Park Chung Hee [Pak Chŏnghŭi 박정희], 66
percussion music, 2, 8, 17, 26, 29, 99, 133; first encounters with, 81, 82, 85; Korea as nation of percussion, 69–70; sensory experience of, 80; as "traditional" music, 22. See also *nongak* 농악; *p'ungmul* 풍물; *samul nori* 사물놀이
Percussive Arts Society International Convention (PASIC), 29, 30
periodicity, musical, 136, 168n4
P'ilbong *nongak* 필봉농악/筆峰農樂 (nongak from Imsil P'ilbong), 93, 153n20
Pilzer, Joshua, 73
"Pinari" 비나리 (SamulNori arrangement), 109, 121–23, 146fnd
pinari 비나리 [also written as *binari*] (narrative prayer song), 24, 25, 27, 109, 113; Ch'ukwŏn tŏkdam 축원덕담 (Blessing) section, 123, 139, 142–46; English translation of text, 139–46; "International Pinari" ceremony, 10, 115, 120; performance of, 121–24; politics of place in "International Pinari," 124–31, *128*, *130*; Samstag's program note for, 147; as text-based form eluding cultural portability, 136
p'iri 피리 (small double reed instrument), 153n18

polyphony, Western, 35
polytimbral texture, 35
pŏmjong 범종/梵鐘 (large bell), 154n27
pŏpko 법고/法鼓 (large barrel drum), 154n27
postcolonial theory, 3
preservation, 18, 21, 41, 63
Presidential Council on Nation Branding [Kukka Pŭraendŭ Wiwŏnhoe 국가브랜드위원회], 78, 160n26
Psy (Pak Chaesang 박재상), 132–33
puch'ae ch'um 부채춤 (Korean fan dance), 99
puk 북 [also written as *buk*] (barrel drum), 34, 35, 153n18; clouds represented by, 149; in *pan kil kunak* 반길군악, 51; in World Cup opening ceremony, 158n8
p'ungmul 풍물/風物 (rural band percussion music and dance), 8, 9, 31, 112; core set of instruments, 19, 34; dance integrated with music, 60; five regional styles of, 36, 38; "improvisation" based on, 16–17, 153n16; *kilnori* 길놀이 ("street play") and, 113; Kŏllipp'ae p'ungmul 걸립패 풍물, 23–27, 25; in Korean military, 38; *p'ungmul nori* 풍물놀이, 88, 149; practiced by overseas Koreans in United States, 161n3; regional styles of, 157n10; repository of regional rhythms, 134; transmitted to United States, 157n16; in the United States, 87–88; urban audiences and, 22; used interchangeably with *nongak* 농악, 36. See also Chinju Samch'ŏnp'o nongak진주삼천포농악; *nongak* 농악; *p'an kut* 판굿
p'ungmul 풍물 choreography: for *kil kunak* 길군악, 47; for *pan kil kunak* 반길군악, 52; for *pyŏldalgŏri* 별달거리, 57; for *ssangjinp'uri* 쌍진풀이/雙陣, 57, 58
"Pungnyu kut" [P'ungnyu kut 풍류굿] (samul nori rhythms; "p'ungnyu ritual"), 92
pup'o 부포 (feathered hats worn by *samul nori* musicians), 120, 148, 166–67n14
Pusan Nongak 부산농악, 91
Puschnig, Wolfgang, 163n20
Puyŏ SamulNori School. See SamulNori Hanullim Puyŏ Educational Institute
Pyŏldalgŏri 별달거리 (rhythmic chant in Yŏngnam nongak): (*pyŏlgŏri talgŏri* 별거리달거리), 40, 42, 46, 59, 157n14; audience response to, 57; chanted portion in German, 134; in "Kyŏngsang nongak" "경상농악," 39, 40; musical notation for, 54–56, 55, 56; performed at "International Pinari" ceremony, 129; *p'ungmul* 풍물 choreography for, 57; in Russian transliteration, 128

Ramírez Lealde, Ariadna, 98, 100, 101
Rauchvarger, Matthieu, 166n12
Red Devil Corea National Football Team and fan club, 71, 72, 79, 158n9, 159n11
Red Sun jazz group, 94, 163n20
reggae, 3
repetition, 5, 35, 59, 168n4; of *kil kunak* 길군악 pattern, 47; riffs and, 4
rhythmic form, 2, 9, 136, 151n4; affordances of, 5; critical to globalization of samul nori, 72; defined, 44; dynamic, 33, 41, 59–60; in global circulation, 7, 10; Western harmony and, 44; of "Yŏngnam nongak" "영남농악," 33, 41, 44, 46–58, 59
rhythmic patterns. See *karak* 가락
Rhythmic Structure of Music, The (Cooper and Meyer, 1960), 44
"riffs," 3–4, 136
Ro, Kyung Un [No Kyŏngŭn 노경은], 90
Robbins, Rob, 162n11
Rodríguez Muñoz, Wendy, 98, 98, 99–100, 105
Roeder, John, 136
Roh Moo Hyun [No Muhyŏn 노무현], 76
Ro Jaemyeong [No Chaemyŏng 노재명], 19
rubato, 56
Russia, 111, 119–20
Russian language, 125, 167n24

Sailors, Shirley, 88, 90, 162n15
Sakhalin Korean Culture Center (Sakhalin Island, Russia), 111, 125, 167n24

Index **191**

samba, 136
"Samch'ŏnp'o 12-ch'a 36-karak" "삼천포 12차 36가락" (12 sections of 36 rhythms from Samch'ŏnp'o), 24
"Samdo nongak karak" "삼도농악가락" (nongak rhythms from three provinces), 70, 92, 108, 148
"Samdo sul changgo karak" "삼도설장고가락" [also written as Samdo sŏl changgo karak] (changgo rhythms from three provinces), 30, 147–48
Samgak Mountain 삼각산, 122–23
Samstag, Suzanna, 10, 28, 30, 105, 155n35, 161n5; description of *pinari* 비나리, 121; as pivotal figure in global spread of samul nori, 83–87; program notes in English by, 147–50; as SamulNori's first agent and manager, 86, 95, 147; at World SamulNori Festival, *84*, 87
Samsung corporation brand, 66, 75
Samul GwangDae 사물광대, 123, 164n25. *See also* SamulNori Hanullim (사물놀이 한울림)
Samul GwangDae 사물광대 (Samul Kwangdae), 12, 96
samul 사물 instruments, 19, 22, 70, 154n27, 156n3
samul nori 사물놀이/四物놀이 (neo-traditional Korean percussion genre; "four things play"): beginning students of, 46; circulation of, 4, 9, 151n4; defined, 1; emergence in process of adaptation and revision, 134; ethnography of, 7–8; first documented reference on a program, *20*; as first successful South Korean musical export, 9; global encounters with, 80–83, 105–7; globalization of, 1–2, 12, 61, 108, 130, 136; as precursor to Hallyu, 2, 151n1; rhythmic form and mobility of, 33; as sonic symbol of South Korea, 62, 134–35; in the United States, 87–92
"SamulNorians" (devoted fans of SamulNori), 81, 120, 133, 162n1
SamulNori Class with Kim Duk Soo, A (Overseas Koreans Foundation, 1999), 46, 50–51, 53–54, 61, 158n1
SamulNori Hanullim 사물놀이 한울림, 7, 8, 44, 55; beginnings of, 11; Canto del Cielo and, 99; FIFA World Cup (2002) and, 68–74, *74*, 79; founding members ("founding fathers"), 13, 109, *110*, 152n4; global encounters with, 81; notation booklets of, 9, 34, 47, 82, 92, 103, 157n18; pedagogical mission, 34, 108, 133–34; performances in the United States, 89, 162n11; significance of name, 12; workshops sponsored by, 105, 129; World SamulNori Festival organized by, 10. *See also* Samul GwangDae
SamulNori Hanullim Puyŏ Educational Institute [SamulNori Hanullim Puyŏ Kyoyugwŏn 사물놀이 한울림 부여교육원], 81, 93, 96, 97, 114; Shinawi founders at, 102; World SamulNori Festival and, 111, 115
Samulnori Mexico. *See* Canto del Cielo (Song of Heaven)
SamulNori project, 13, 21–23, 34, 109, 134
SamulNori quartet, 2, 8, 28–31, 135; condensed format for p'ungmul, 22; disbanding of (1993), 11, 12; early reception of, 8–9, 12; group portrait at Space Theater, *20*; international tours of, 61; Kŏllipp'ae p'ungmul program, 23–27, *25*; managing directors of, 10; musical arrangements, 42–46; "original" quartet, 12–13, 17, 109; origins in Space Theater milieu, 14–17; *p'an kut* 판굿 performance, 28; *pyŏldalgŏri* 별달거리 performance, 55, 56; recordings, 9, 31; Red Sun jazz group and, 94; state endorsement of, 61–62
Samul-Nori: The Legendary Recording by Original Members (1983), 31
Samul over the Rainbow (Paris), 111, 125
Sánchez Zaragoza, Viridiana, 98, *98*, 99, 100–101, 127
sangmo 상모/象毛 (tasseled hats), 25, 38, 53, 118, 148, 163n22

Santillán Moreno, Aidée, *98*, 100, 101
Segal, Lewis, 80
Sejong Center for the Performing Arts [Sejong munhwa hoegwan 세종문화회관], 28–29, 109–10
Senari (Berlin), 111
Seok, Huajeong, 63
Seoul, 1, 85, 139; Cecil Theater [Sesil Kŭkchang], 28, 84; Gangnam [Kangnam 강남] district, 132; as global hub city, 67; Hanjeon Artspool Center, 68; Hanyang as predecessor of, 122, 125; Ho-am Art Hall, 163n20; Nanjang Studio, 95, 163n22; Olympic Stadium, 95, 111, 152n6; Sejong Center [Sejong munhwa Hoegwan 세종문화회관], 28–29, 109–10; UNESCO hall, 29. *See also* Space Theater [Konggan Sarang] (Seoul); Summer Olympics (Seoul, 1988)
Seoul Arts High School, 18, 19
Seoul Drum Festival, 96
shamans/shamanism, 15, 25, 26, 27, 121; *namsadang* 남사당 and, 149; *pinari* 비나리 and, 147
sharing, networks of, 82
Sharrock, Linda, 162–63n17
Shelemay, Kay Kaufman, 163n17
Shimizu, Ichiro, 27
Shinawi シナウィ/시나위 (*samul nori* group from Japan), 101–5, *102*, 111
Shin Chan-sun [Sin Ch'ansŏn 신찬선], 164n25
Shinparam 신바람 (USA), 10, 87–92, 105, 111, 162n15; group portrait, *88*; "International Pinari" ceremony and, 125, 126–27; significance of name, 88, 161n8
"Sibi-ch'a samsip-yuk karak" "십이차 삼십육가락" (12 sections, 36 rhythmic patterns), 36
Sim Sŏnok 심선옥, 154n25
Sim Usŏng 심우성 [also written as Shim Woo-sung], 18, *20*, 154n22; essays for *Konggan* magazine, 23; as folklorist and advocate, 18–19, 21; *namsadang* 남사당 and, 24, 154n31; SamulNori project and, 21
Sinawi 시나위. *See* Minsogakhoe Sinawi (Folk Music Society "Sinawi")
Sinch'on Live House Nanjang Studio 신촌난장 스튜디오, 12, 152n3
social media, 168n2, 168n4
"soft power," 151n1
sogo 소고/小鼓 (handheld drum), 154n25
"Sŏl changgo karak" "설장고가락" [also written as Sŏlchanggo karak] (samul nori arrangement of rhythms performed on changgo), 34, 84, 92, 93, 95, 100
sŏnban 선반 (samul nori performed while standing/dancing), 46
sŏngju kut 성주굿 (house god ritual), 26
Songp'o nongak 송포농악 (nongak from Songp'o), 157n10
Space Theater [Konggan Sarang 공간사랑] (Seoul), 8, 9, 28, 42, 109; cultural activists and, 13; culture of innovation, 31; Evening of Traditional Music, 15, 16–17; "experimental stage" (black box theater), 15, 27; mission of, 11; origins of SamulNori quartet in milieu of, 14–17; SamulNori project and, 21, 34; sign for, *14*; Sogŭkchang 소극장 (small theater), 14, *16*
Spanish language, 99, 125
ssangjinp'uri 쌍진풀이/雙陣 (samul nori rhythms; p'ungmul ground formation) section, 57–58, *57*, *58*, *59*
Stairway to Heaven (Korean TV melodrama), 164n31
Stokes, Martin, 3
Sugungga 수궁가/水宮歌 (Tale of the underwater palace) epic, 69
Summer Olympics (Seoul, 1988), 9, 95, 111; "Harmony and Progress" slogan, 76, 160n19; Olympic Stadium, 95, 111, 152n6; SamulNori quartet and, 61
SwiKo trio, 96
Swissamul, 92–97, *93*, 111, 125, 134
Switzerland, 10, 83, 92–97, 111

Tacuma, Jamaaladeen, 163n20
tadŭraegi 다드래기 rhythmic pattern, 51–52, 53–54, 58, *59*
t'aegŭk 태극 (visual design of yin-yang), 51
taegŭm 대금/大笒 (transverse bamboo flute), 153n18
"Taehan Min'guk 대한민국" chant, at World Cup, 71, 72, 159n15
Taejŏn Expo '93 대전 엑스포, 9, 61
t'aep'yŏngso 태평소/太平簫 (double reed shawm), 121, 158n8
Tagore, Rabindranath, 76–77, 160n20
taiko 太鼓 (Japanese drum; Japanese drumming), 1, 3, 68, 136
TakeTiNa Rhythm Process, 94, 96, 163n19
t'alch'um 탈춤 (Korean masked dance drama), 85
Tambours sur la digue [Drummers on the dike] (Mnouchkine), 166n12
tangsan kut 당산굿 (shamanistic ritual; village shrine ritual), 26
Taoism, 51
Taylor, Timothy, 4, 81, 151n4
tch'ada 짜다 (to form or organize), 36
technology, digital, 70, 75, 158n8
television serials, Korean, 151n1
tempo, 9, 55, 60
Tenzer, Michael, 136, 168n4
Théâtre du Soleil, 166n12
Tŏksu Palace 덕수궁, 112
twip'uri 뒤풀이 (post-performance segment; "after-party"), 70

Uchida, Kyosuke, *102*, 103
umul kut 우물굿 (ritual played at village well), 26
ŭngwŏn'ga 응원가 ("support" songs), 71
ŭngwŏn maktae p'ungsŏn 응원막대풍선 (rhythmic noisemakers), 71
United States, 8, 9, 27, 83; overseas Koreans in, 161n3; SamulNori Hanullim tours in, 89, 162n11; SamulNori quartet regular tours in, 61, 80; SamulNori quartet's first time in (1982), 29, 86; Shinparam group, 87–92, *88*, 111; tour sponsored by Asia Society, 43, 44
unp'an 운판/雲版 (cloud-shaped gong), 154n27
"Uttari p'ungmul" "웃다리풍물" (1978 SamulNori arrangement; p'ungmul rhythms from the Uttari region), 16–18, 24, 34; in Canto del Cielo repertory, 100; SamulNori arrangement, 135; in Shinparam repertory, 92; in Swissamul repertory, 93
Uttari region (Kyŏnggi and Chungch'ŏng provinces), 36

Vangelis, 68
Vickery, Martha, 88–89, *88*, 90, 92
"viral" videos, 133
volume, 9, *59*, 60

Wade, Bonnie, 151n5
Weber, Norbert, 159n18
Westernization, 1
Western music, 3, 6, 49; classical, 15, 32, 153n10; rubato, 56; temporal dynamic form in, 59
"What Have We Done, and What Has to Be Done?" (Sim Usŏng, 1975), 23
"What is Gut [*kut*] (and What Has Been Studied over [*sic*] It)?" 23
White, Bob, 81
Winter Sonata 겨울연가 (Korean TV melodrama), 164n30
wŏn-pang-kak 원방각/圓方角 (metric visual indicator; circle, square, triangle), 49–50, *49*, 54
world beat, 3
world music, 2, 3, 8, 136
World SamulNori Festival and Competition [SamulNori Kyŏrugi Hanmadang 사물놀이 겨루기 한마당] (Puyŏ, South Korea 부여, 한국), 8, 10, 83, 87, 125; arrival in Puyŏ, 114–15; background to, 111–14; Canto del Cielo at, *98*, 100–101; map of festival grounds, *116*; opening ceremony, 115, 117–20; *pinari* performance at, 121–31, *128*, *130*; SamulNori thirtieth anniversary

(2008) and, 110–11; Shinawi at, *102*, 103, 105, 111; Shinparam at, 90–92, 111; Swissamul at, 93, *93*, 95, 96, 97, 111; years not held, 165n4

Wunrow, Emma, 90

Wunrow, Han Yong, *88*, 90

Wunrow, Madeleine Soon Young, *88*, 90

Wunrow, Stephen, *88*, 89, 90, 106, 125

Yanaka, Kenichi, 101–4, *102*, 105

Yang, Eunhee, *88*

Yangp'yŏng athletic field 양평운동장, 112

Yeo Sang-bum [Yŏ Sangbŏm 여상범], 161n5

Yi Ch'ŏlchu 이철주, 19

Yi Chomsŏk 이점석, 25

Yi Chongdae 이종대, 16, 36

Yi Maebang 이매방, 16

yin-yang (um-yang) theory 음양이론, 51, 149

Yongmunsan 용문산, 112

Yŏngnam/Kyŏngsang region 영남/경상지역, 36

"Yŏngnam nongak" "영남농악" (samul nori arrangement; nongak rhythms from the Kyŏngsang provinces), 9, 10, 27, *59*, 134; in Canto del Cielo repertory, 100; formal structure, 43–45, *45*; introduction to, 33–36, 38–41; learned by groups outside Korea, 108; notation for, 48; performed at "International Pinari" ceremony, 129, 130, *130*; popularity among amateur groups, 41, 44; rhythmic form of, 33, 41, 44, 46–60, *59*; SamulNori arrangement, 135; in Shinparam repertory, 92; in Swissamul repertory, 93. *See also specific karak (rhythmic patterns) in yŏngsan tadŭraegi* 영산 다드래기 (samul nori rhythm; p'ungmul ground formation) pattern, 53–54, *54*, 58, *59*

YouTube, 132, 168n1, 169n2

yurang tanch'e 유랑단체/遊浪團體 (itinerant performing arts troupes), 18

zouk genre, 4, 136

MUSIC / CULTURE
A series from Wesleyan University Press
Edited by Deborah Wong, Sherrie Tucker, and Jeremy Wallach
Originating editors: George Lipsitz, Susan McClary, and Robert Walser

Marié Abe
Resonances of Chindon-ya: Sounding Space and Sociality in Contemporary Japan

Frances Aparicio
Listening to Salsa: Gender, Latin Popular Music, and Puerto Rican Cultures

Paul Austerlitz
Jazz Consciousness: Music, Race, and Humanity

Harris M. Berger
Metal, Rock, and Jazz: Perception and the Phenomenology of Musical Experience

Harris M. Berger
Stance: Ideas about Emotion, Style, and Meaning for the Study of Expressive Culture

Harris M. Berger and Giovanna P. Del Negro
Identity and Everyday Life: Essays in the Study of Folklore, Music, and Popular Culture

Franya J. Berkman
Monument Eternal: The Music of Alice Coltrane

Dick Blau, Angeliki Vellou Keil, and Charles Keil
Bright Balkan Morning: Romani Lives and the Power of Music in Greek Macedonia

Susan Boynton and Roe-Min Kok, editors
Musical Childhoods and the Cultures of Youth

James Buhler, Caryl Flinn, and David Neumeyer, editors
Music and Cinema

Thomas Burkhalter, Kay Dickinson, and Benjamin J. Harbert, editors
The Arab Avant-Garde: Music, Politics, Modernity

Patrick Burkart
Music and Cyberliberties

Julia Byl
Antiphonal Histories: Resonant Pasts in the Toba Batak Musical Present

Daniel Cavicchi
Listening and Longing: Music Lovers in the Age of Barnum

Susan D. Crafts, Daniel Cavicchi, Charles Keil, and the Music in Daily Life Project
My Music: Explorations of Music in Daily Life

Jim Cullen
Born in the USA: Bruce Springsteen and the American Tradition

Anne Danielsen
Presence and Pleasure: The Funk Grooves of James Brown and Parliament

Peter Doyle
Echo and Reverb: Fabricating Space in Popular Music Recording, 1900–1960

Ron Emoff
Recollecting from the Past: Musical Practice and Spirit Possession on the East Coast of Madagascar

Yayoi Uno Everett and Frederick Lau, editors
Locating East Asia in Western Art Music

Susan Fast and Kip Pegley, editors
Music, Politics, and Violence

Heidi Feldman
Black Rhythms of Peru: Reviving African Musical Heritage in the Black Pacific

Kai Fikentscher
"You Better Work!" Underground Dance Music in New York City

Ruth Finnegan
The Hidden Musicians: Music-Making in an English Town

Daniel Fischlin and Ajay Heble, editors
The Other Side of Nowhere: Jazz, Improvisation, and Communities in Dialogue

Wendy Fonarow
Empire of Dirt: The Aesthetics and Rituals of British "Indie" Music

Murray Forman
The 'Hood Comes First: Race, Space, and Place in Rap and Hip-Hop

Lisa Gilman
My Music, My War: The Listening Habits of U.S. Troops in Iraq and Afghanistan

Paul D. Greene and Thomas Porcello, editors
Wired for Sound: Engineering and Technologies in Sonic Cultures

Tomie Hahn
Sensational Knowledge: Embodying Culture through Japanese Dance

Edward Herbst
Voices in Bali: Energies and Perceptions in Vocal Music and Dance Theater

Deborah Kapchan
Traveling Spirit Masters: Moroccan Gnawa Trance and Music in the Global Marketplace

Deborah Kapchan, editor
Theorizing Sound Writing

Max Katz
Lineage of Loss: Counternarratives of North Indian Music

Raymond Knapp
Symphonic Metamorphoses: Subjectivity and Alienation in Mahler's Re-Cycled Songs

Laura Lohman
Umm Kulthūm: Artistic Agency and the Shaping of an Arab Legend, 1967–2007

Preston Love
A Thousand Honey Creeks Later: My Life in Music from Basie to Motown—and Beyond

René T. A. Lysloff and Leslie C. Gay Jr., editors
Music and Technoculture

Allan Marett
Songs, Dreamings, and Ghosts: The Wangga of North Australia

Ian Maxwell
Phat Beats, Dope Rhymes: Hip Hop Down Under Comin' Upper

Kristin A. McGee
Some Liked It Hot: Jazz Women in Film and Television, 1928–1959

Rebecca S. Miller
Carriacou String Band Serenade: Performing Identity in the Eastern Caribbean

Tony Mitchell, editor
Global Noise: Rap and Hip-Hop Outside the USA

Christopher Moore and Philip Purvis, editors
Music & Camp

Rachel Mundy
Animal Musicalities: Birds, Beasts, and Evolutionary Listening

Keith Negus
Popular Music in Theory: An Introduction

Johnny Otis
Upside Your Head!: Rhythm and Blues on Central Avenue

Kip Pegley
Coming to You Wherever You Are: MuchMusic, MTV, and Youth Identities

Jonathan Pieslak
Radicalism and Music: An Introduction to the Music Cultures of al-Qa'ida, Racist Skinheads, Christian-Affiliated Radicals, and Eco-Animal Rights Militants

Matthew Rahaim
Musicking Bodies: Gesture and Voice in Hindustani Music

John Richardson
Singing Archaeology: Philip Glass's Akhnaten

Tricia Rose
Black Noise: Rap Music and Black Culture in Contemporary America

David Rothenberg and Marta Ulvaeus, editors
The Book of Music and Nature: An Anthology of Sounds, Words, Thoughts

Nichole Rustin-Paschal
The Kind of Man I Am: Jazzmasculinity and the World of Charles Mingus Jr.

Marta Elena Savigliano
Angora Matta: Fatal Acts of North-South Translation

Joseph G. Schloss
Making Beats: The Art of Sample-Based Hip-Hop

Richard M. Shain
Roots in Reverse: Senegalese Afro-Cuban Music and Tropical Cosmopolitanism

Barry Shank
Dissonant Identities: The Rock 'n' Roll Scene in Austin, Texas

Jonathan Holt Shannon
Among the Jasmine Trees: Music and Modernity in Contemporary Syria

Daniel B. Sharp
Between Nostalgia and Apocalypse: Popular Music and the Staging of Brazil

Helena Simonett
Banda: Mexican Musical Life across Borders

Mark Slobin
Subcultural Sounds: Micromusics of the West

Mark Slobin, editor
Global Soundtracks: Worlds of Film Music

Christopher Small
The Christopher Small Reader

Christopher Small
Music of the Common Tongue: Survival and Celebration in African American Music

Christopher Small
Music, Society, Education

Christopher Small
Musicking: The Meanings of Performing and Listening

Regina M. Sweeney
Singing Our Way to Victory: French Cultural Politics and Music during the Great War

Colin Symes
Setting the Record Straight: A Material History of Classical Recording

Steven Taylor
False Prophet: Fieldnotes from the Punk Underground

Paul Théberge
Any Sound You Can Imagine: Making Music/Consuming Technology

Sarah Thornton
Club Cultures: Music, Media and Sub-cultural Capital

Michael E. Veal
Dub: Songscape and Shattered Songs in Jamaican Reggae

Michael E. Veal and E. Tammy Kim, editors
Punk Ethnography: Artists and Scholars Listen to Sublime Frequencies

Robert Walser
Running with the Devil: Power, Gender, and Madness in Heavy Metal Music

Dennis Waring
Manufacturing the Muse: Estey Organs and Consumer Culture in Victorian America

Lise A. Waxer
The City of Musical Memory: Salsa, Record Grooves, and Popular Culture in Cali, Colombia

Mina Yang
Planet Beethoven: Classical Music at the Turn of the Millennium

ABOUT THE AUTHOR

Katherine In-Young Lee is assistant professor of ethnomusicology at the University of California, Los Angeles. She received her PhD from Harvard in 2012. Her work has appeared in the *Journal of Korean Studies*, the *Journal of Korean Traditional Performing Arts*, and *Ethnomusicology*.